Person-centred
COMMUNICATION

theory and practice

Person-centred COMMUNICATION

theory and practice

2ND EDITION

HANKA GROBLER
RINIE SCHENCK
DRIES DU TOIT

OXFORD
UNIVERSITY PRESS

OXFORD
UNIVERSITY PRESS

Southern Africa

Oxford University Press Southern Africa (Pty) Ltd

Vasco Boulevard, Goodwood, Cape Town, Republic of South Africa
PO Box 12119, N1 City, 7463, Cape Town, Republic of South Africa

Oxford University Press Southern Africa (Pty) Ltd is a wholly-owned subsidiary of
Oxford University Press, Great Clarendon Street, Oxford OX2 6DP.

The Press, a department of the University of Oxford, furthers the Univeristy's objective of
excellence in research, scholarship, and education in publishing worldwide in

Oxford New York

Auckland Dar es Salaam Hong Kong Karachi
Kuala Lumpur Madrid Melbourne Mexico City Nairobi
New Delhi Shanghai Taipei Toronto

With offices in

Argentinia Austria Brazil Chile Czech Republic France Greece
Guatemala Hungary Italy Japan Poland Portugal Singapore South Korea
Switzerland Turkey Ukraine Vietnam

Oxford is a registered trademark of Oxford University Press
in the UK and in certain other countries

Published in South Africa
by Oxford University Press Southern Africa (Pty) Ltd, Cape Town

Personal-centred communication
ISBN 978 0 19 578 687 3

© Oxford University Press Southern Africa (Pty) Ltd 2003

First edition published 2001
Second edition published 2003
Eighth impression 2008

The moral rights of the author have been asserted
Database right Oxford University Press Southern Africa (Pty) Ltd (maker)

Commissioning editor: Richard Cooke
Editor: Emily Bowles
Designer: Christopher Davis
Cover design: Christopher Davis
Indexer: Mary Lennox

Set in 10 pt on 13 pt Galliard by RHT desktop publishing, Durbanville
Reproduction by RHT desktop publishing, Durbanville
Cover reproduction by The Image Bureau
Printed and bound by ABC Press, Cape Town
108363

Contents

Foreword to First Edition

The demand for human services is on the increase throughout the world. Third World countries in particular are confronted with the dilemma of how to balance expenditure on poor relief, psycho-social health care, and literacy programmes with projects that will contribute toward economic growth.

Vast sums of money are earmarked for all kinds of projects that have as their goal the development and empowerment of people. This is because investment in human potential is believed to be as critically important for economic growth as is the development of good infrastructure and political stability.

Millions of people throughout the world experience all kinds of stressful situations that threaten their mental health and have become the focus of the activities of a variety of helping professions. Despite differences in training and helping techniques, these professionals all strive toward assisting people to lead productive lives by developing personal power as characterized by self-esteem and interpersonal harmony.

Whereas helping professions have in the past been, and are still at present, often associated with 'spending money on people with problems without obtaining equivalent results', helping professionals can in fact contribute to the overall capacity-building of people. Instead of being an economic liability, helping professions can contribute toward economic growth and social stability by empowering people to develop new strategies for effective living.

Person-centred Communication by Du Toit, Grobler and Schenck offers helping professionals an understanding of the theory, practice, and value base that underlie a person-centred approach to helping people within a development model to attain effective living.

I am convinced that this book can make a meaningful contribution towards the theory and skills of serving people.

Prof. Wilfried van Delft
Department of Social Work
University of South Africa

Acknowledgements

The authors would like to thank their respective colleagues who were available to discuss and think about their and our ideas about this approach. It underlined the proposition that in interaction with others the self (in this case our professional selves) is formed. Our colleagues are not the only significant others in this regard, as our students, with their unique perspective and contributions, were valuable collaborators in our continuing journey of exploration of the person-centred approach. We would like to continue this journey in interaction with others, including you, the reader, and therefore we are thanking you in advance for your ideas and perspectives.

As the approach was initiated and originally documented by Carl Rogers, we owe him a great debt for providing us with the basic tenets of a theory which we have found helpful in understanding and working with people in a humane and respectful way.

We would also like to thank all the people involved in the actual preparation of this book, as well as and especially our families, who supported us in our quest and patiently put up with our meandering minds and, sometimes, physical absence from home.

We want to thank the supervisors and students of Unisa for their comments on the first edition. Implementation of these comments and suggestions makes the second edition even more student friendly.

Hanka Grobler
Rinie Schenck
Dries du Toit

Introduction

What is the person-centred approach?

The reader might well pose two questions when reading this book. First, the reader may ask what the authors mean by the person-centred approach. The best way to answer this question is in the words of Carl Rogers, who developed the approach. According to Rogers, the facilitator in the person-centred approach tries to understand how the client sees himself or herself. Rogers (1987: 40–41) explains:

> *Psychotherapy deals primarily with the organization and function-ing of the self. There are many elements of experience which the self cannot face, cannot clearly perceive, because to face them or admit them would be inconsistent with and threatening to the current organization of self ... In the therapeutic experience, to see one's own attitudes, confusions, ambivalences, feelings, and perceptions accurately expressed by another ... paves the way for acceptance into the self of all the experiences which are now more clearly perceived. Reorganization of the self and more integrated functioning of the self are thus furthered.*

A few salient themes emerge from this description:
- the self – what it is and how it is experienced by the person
- experiences that the self can face
- those experiences that the self *cannot* face and why
- what kind of experiences both above instances entail
- what the therapeutic relationship must provide to enable the person to reorganize the self

- what could happen if the self were reorganized, and
- what knowledge, values, and skills are required of the facilitator to be able to create the therapeutic relationship necessary for this reorganization of the self to take place.

The chapters of Section A will be grouped along these themes.

Why have the authors started with nineteen theoretical propositions?

The second question that can be asked is why the authors start with the theoretical propositions once formulated by Rogers. Authors following the person-centred approach usually tend to focus on the attitudes of the facilitator, the so-called core conditions of *empathy, congruence,* and unconditional *positive regard.* Although these core conditions will be discussed in more detail in Sections B, C, and D, they need further discussion here because they are so often the starting point of any discussion on this approach.

The core conditions set the authors thinking about how we regard people. In other words, when we observe a person, what do we perceive and think? What does the word 'person' mean, or encompass? This becomes even more relevant when the person we are observing is experiencing some kind of difficulty or problem. Is our vision filled with the issue at hand and our need to alleviate the pain the person is experiencing? If so, then we are observing and thinking not primarily about them, but about the difficulty (pain or problem) they are experiencing. The question is: who is the person behind or in this difficult situation? How do we think about people and what do we take into consideration when thinking about them? Do we see and think primarily about their feelings of pain and the situation in which they experience the pain? Do we see and think about their behaviour, and what do we make of this behaviour?

The core conditions also set the authors thinking about the attitude of the facilitator, and we wondered what 'positive regard' implies. Is this just a passive acceptance of any person as 'good', even though we do not really think they (or what they do) are good? How then does one stay 'congruent'? Or, as some people argue, is positive regard an acceptance of the person, but not the behaviour that we find 'not good'? This implies that we do not accept the whole person, as we exempt the behaviour from our acceptance.

But what does acceptance mean? The Oxford dictionary defines it as 'approval, belief, toleration' (Sykes 1982: 6). If one goes along with this view, then judgement is implied, even if it is a positive one. That is, if we agree with (or approve of) what the other person does, our own values come into play, and we decide what is good/positive and what not. On the other hand, acceptance could also mean taking the person and whatever he/she does as given, without judging it in any way. Whether or not the person's actions are positive or negative then depends on the person.

When the authors turned to Rogers' writings and interviews for some guidance in this regard, we saw that he looks at much more than people's feelings or behaviour. He often refers to the 'self', the values and needs of the people he works with. (See Section C, where short excerpts from some of his interviews are given.) This wider view, and why Rogers uses it, became clear from the theoretical ideas he formulated by way of nineteen propositions. For instance, the third proposition states that when taking a person-centred approach, one has to look at and understand the whole person. But what would or could some of the dimensions of a 'whole person' be? The other propositions give concrete examples of what these experiences might entail and can thus serve as a reminder or guide to what else can be explored and understood while one is involved with another human being. (For example, proposition 2 refers one to perceptions; proposition 5 to needs and behaviour;[1] proposition 6 to the emotions; proposition 8 to the self; proposition 9 to interaction with others, and proposition 10 to the values and valuing process.)

These propositions about being human and what possibly motivates people, on various levels of consciousness, provide tentative guidelines for facilitators in their efforts to *understand, think about,* and *make sense* of what we can observe of others, like what they say, do, and feel when we encounter them. Considering these ideas, even if you do not agree with them, could enable you to think more broadly about other people. For example, you could have an experience like: 'I never thought of people like this before'; or 'I never thought of it quite like this before'; or 'I do not think of people like this, but rather like ...', adding your own perspective to the matter under discussion. It is for these reasons that the authors decided to use Rogers' propositions as a starting point in this book.

However, remember that the propositions mentioned above are by no means all that there is to human beings. There are other dimensions we can

---

[1] Exploring needs and behaviour from a person-centred approach differs significantly from the behaviour modification approach to behaviour. We mention this to avoid any confusion and even a sense of disappointment on the part of the reader, who might expect a discussion of that particular approach.

think of, like the physical and spiritual experiences. *One must therefore bear in mind that people are not the propositions, but the propositions can help us explore and consider a spectrum of possible dimensions on which people can be understood.*

It is also important to keep in mind that the ideas (about the theory, values, and skills) discussed in this book, are ways of thinking, believing, and acting that the facilitator can develop. They are not prescriptions for our clients. In other words, we cannot expect the people we work with to know this theory or to believe in the values we as professional facilitators need to uphold, or to act in accordance with the skills we describe in later sections of this book. These ideas cannot be imposed on our clients, as the approach holds that they have the right and the ability to grow and develop in their own unique ways. No one can even force you, the reader, to agree with what is written here. These ideas are for you to explore, and to see whether you think they will be useful to you in your future interaction with people.

How can these propositions be used practically?

We then thought about what this kind of approach means to the people we encounter, if they are not aware of our attitudes. In this regard we were also guided by Rogers' proposition 1, that is, that people's experiential world is private and known only to them, *unless* shared with others in some way or another. Facilitators thus have to share their experiences (perceptions, thoughts, and attitude) with the people encountered. *How can this be done?*

The communication skills discussed later in this book are seen as a way (and by no means the only or correct way) for facilitators to demonstrate their understanding of the whole person, and their respect for that person.

However, facilitators may encounter people in a variety of settings, and the understanding and respect that needs to be demonstrated will differ in each setting. We have therefore divided the possible setting into three categories, that is, encountering and relating with one other person, *an individual*, encountering others in *groups*, and in *community* settings.

We believe that the thinking about and attitude towards people, and demonstration of these experiences, is basically the same in all three situations. However, there are some variations in the implications of what happens in these different situations, and that is why each formation is discussed separately. So, for example, we discuss proposition 1 in terms of an individual, then what it entails when people are in a group, and then in a community.

In order to share our own ideas and understanding of the theory (propositions), values, and skills (actions of the facilitator) with you as the reader, we have used several examples from our own and our colleagues' practice. We have also included various activities, to provide an opportunity for your involvement, and to enable you to see whether these ideas are helpful to you as a person and to stimulate you (both as readers and facilitators) to contemplate and question the issues discussed. We would appreciate any comment and illustrations of these, from you, to be sent to the address provided on p. 232 of the book.

Structure of the book

The book is divided into five sections.

Section A: Theory: Thinking about people

This section consists of six chapters that focus on Rogers' nineteen propositions. The propositions are not dealt with in their original order, but have been grouped thematically. The reader will also notice that each proposition deals with a specific aspect of a person's and facilitator's functioning. The original order of the propositions is listed below for easy reference:

- *Proposition 1: Human experiences at a conscious and unconscious level (Chapter 4)*
- *Proposition 2: Human perceptions (Chapter 4)*
- *Proposition 3: Wholeness/unity (Chapter 4)*
- *Proposition 4: Self-determination (Chapter 1)*
- *Proposition 5: Needs and behaviour (Chapter 4)*
- *Proposition 6: Emotions (Chapter 4)*
- *Proposition 7: Frames of reference (Chapter 5)*
- *Proposition 8: The self (Chapter 1)*
- *Proposition 9: How our perception of our significant others influences the development of the self (Chapter 1)*
- *Proposition 10: Values, own and adopted from other people (Chapter 4)*
- *Proposition 11: Conscious experiences (which fit with the self) and unconscious experiences (which do not fit with the self) (Chapter 2 and Chapter 3)*
- *Proposition 12: Self and behaviour (Chapter 2)*
- *Proposition 13: Behaviour and unconscious experiences (Chapter 3)*
- *Proposition 14: Psychological tension (Chapter 3)*
- *Proposition 15: Reconstruction of self (Chapter 6)*

- *Proposition 16: Defence of self (Chapter 3)*
- *Proposition 17: Conditions for facilitation (Chapter 5)*
- *Proposition 18: Acceptance of self and others (Chapter 6)*
- *Proposition 19: Developing your value system (Chapter 6)*

Section B: The facilitator's values

In the next four chapters, the values of respect, individualization, self-determination, and confidentiality are discussed.

Section C: Putting thinking and values into practice: Dealing with symbolized experiences

Attentiveness, listening, and empathy are discussed in the next three chapters.

Section D: Putting thinking and values into practice: Dealing with unsymbolized experiences

These two chapters deal with advanced empathy and immediacy.

Section E: Some special considerations

In the final three chapters, some special situations that might stretch the ingenuity of the facilitator to its utmost are discussed: cross-cultural communication, people in conflict, and the self of the facilitator.

We hope that you will enjoy reading and using the book and will find it helpful in your encounters with others.

Theory:
Thinking about people

Introduction

In this section we explore how the person-centred approach influences our thinking about people. The question to be answered is: What does this approach imply? What does thinking in this way imply?

It was with reluctance that Rogers formulated his theory or assumptions about people in the form of nineteen propositions. He was afraid that students of his work would take it as dogma, that is, as rules written in stone, rather than ideas to be explored, tested, and adapted from own experience. It is for this reason that we have taken the liberty of rearranging the propositions in terms of certain themes that have emerged from our own work with this theory. These themes have been arranged into six chapters, with various propositions, which we see as constituting these themes, clustered in each chapter. We also do not want the reader to take this as dogma, but rather to see these themes as guiding our thoughts and making us aware of our own thoughts and those of others.

CHAPTER 1

The development of the self

1.1 Introduction

As the self is such a cornerstone of this approach, we will begin our discussion of the theory with what the self is (proposition 8), how it develops (proposition 9), and how it maintains itself (proposition 4). As you will see, the self is derived from all the experiences we have. It entails our identity, the way in which we perceive ourselves. Specific attention will be paid to the role of other people we interact with and perceive as significant in our lives.

1.2 Proposition 8: The self

> *'A portion of the total perceptual field gradually becomes differentiated as the self.' (Rogers 1987: 497). On page 498 Rogers gives a more detailed description of the self as 'an organized, fluid, but consistent conceptual pattern of perceptions of characteristics and relationships of the 'I' or the 'me'.*

A section of the individual's total perceptual field is gradually differentiated to become the *self*.

1.2.1 Proposition 8 and the individual

The *self* means the person's conception (perception/experience) of who he or she is. The concept 'total' implies that the self emerges from all our experiences, or put differently, all our experiences are part of who we are. As our experiences are always changing (as we will see in proposition 1), the self is also changing. That is why it is described as a 'fluid' picture, not a static one. It is also important to note that this picture of ourselves is our own perception (you will learn more about perceptions in proposition 2) of our identity. We determine our perceptions, and who we are, as we move through life. The important issue of determining the self will be discussed further under proposition 4.

It is important to keep in mind that, although the self is changing, it is not an easy process. We need a sense of stability and continuity regarding ourselves, to avoid a total sense of confusion, of not knowing who we are, or whether we are coming or going. Imagine you were in an accident and woke up with amnesia (loss of memory). You would not remember who you are, what you like or dislike, what you do or believe in, what relationships you have, and which people are important to you. If someone were to tell you about yourself, you would have to look inside yourself to see whether what they were saying was anything like you think you are, should be, or want to be. You would have to find out for yourself, as it would be impossible just to believe blindly what another person says about who you are.

In the same way, we need to understand that their sense of identity is important to our clients, and we cannot tell them who to be or what to do or believe in. It has to come from them. They might not believe in their own potential to do so, but in such a situation, it is even more important for us to keep on believing in them, using our skills to understand who they are at present, and enabling them to find their own sense of self in a changing world of experiences.

Example 1.1

A teacher teaching an adult literacy class asked her students to write down the figures 1 to 10. One man inverted the figure 7, reproducing a mirror image. When the teacher pointed this out the following dialogue ensued:

T: (teacher): That is not the figure 7.
S: (student): When I'm standing up, who am I?
T: You are Mr Phatudi.
S: And when I'm sitting down, who am I?
T: You are Mr Phatudi.
S: And if I bend sideways to left or right, who am I?
T: You are Mr Phatudi.
S: So if I remain Mr Phatudi whether I am sitting, standing, or bending sideways, then that figure on the page remains the figure 7 whichever way I write it.

If you reflect on yourself over the years, with all the changes that have happened, is there a central core that you can identify as peculiarly you? Or are the people that you were at the ages of 18, 25, and 30 completely different people? Individuals always retain some part of themselves in the midst of day-to-day change (proposition 1).

1.2.2 Proposition 8 and the group

This proposition relates to the group members as well as the group. An identity is built up that both the individual and the group perceive as the *self*. This *self* must be respected by the group facilitator. The following example illustrates how to deal with the individual's self.

> **Example 1.2**
>
> An elderly couple were becoming isolated. A group facilitator decided to start a group for the elderly in their neighbourhood. During a visit to the couple, the elderly man mentioned that he did not want to belong to the group because he thought of himself as 'the one who helps the other elderly people with their problems'. His wife, however, was keen to join the group, but could not do so because of her husband's refusal. The group facilitator realized that both could benefit from membership of the group. After the first group meeting, she again visited the elderly couple and, using the old man's image of himself, asked him whether he would come along to help her because she did not always know how to handle elderly people. The man agreed, and the facilitator made a point of asking him for advice during the following few meetings. It was not until the fourth meeting that this man realized that the group could also be of value to him and decided to become a permanent group member. *He also became a very active and positive group member.*

Proposition 8 also helps the facilitator to guard against ignoring the group's self-determination. Should a facilitator, for example, undertake directive action and see the group negatively, while group members consider themselves to be good, the facilitator's directive action will be detrimental to the motivation and functioning of the members.

This proposition also warns the facilitator that in institutions where various group sessions are conducted, care should be taken not to allow the self of groups to lead to competition between the various groups. If this happens, the overall functioning of the institution can be affected. This places a great responsibility on the group facilitator to facilitate the group's development in such a way that it will also strengthen the overall functioning of the institution.

1.2.3 Proposition 8 and the community

The *self* is the community's idea (perception or experience) of itself. This self cannot always be explicitly expressed by the community but it can be expressed through the actions, values, rituals, taboos, prejudices, and preferences of the people in the community.

Example 1.3

Children in an isolated, remote, rural community in the Richtersveld (a semidesert area in South Africa) were found to be malnourished. This community was historically referred to as 'coloured'. Several concerned external organizations tried to relieve the malnourishment. A number of projects were launched, such as establishing vegetable gardens along the banks of a big river near the community, feeding schemes, and soup kitchens. Apart from these projects, there was no lack of work opportunities offering good wages because mining activities within the area could easily have accommodated the entire community in its workforce. Nevertheless, none of the projects was successful in combating malnourishment among the community's children.

Community leaders attributed the failure of the development projects to 'lack of cooperation' of the members of the community with each other. Kotze (1989) found various reasons for this 'lack of cooperation'. First, she noticed that although the community was always keen for projects to be launched, the label 'coloured' had a very negative connotation for them. In the northern Richtersveld, inhabitants distinguish between the Namas, Basters, and coloureds. In addition, the community still distinguish between the local inhabitants or natives (*boorlinge*) and the newcomers or outsiders (*inkommers*). *Boorlinge* are perceived as belonging to the local community; *inkommers* are not. Even if someone was born in the community, the mere fact that his or her parents were originally from some other part of the country makes that person an *inkommer*. In other words, the people did not perceive themselves as one community, but the institutions treated them as one. Another social worker who lived and worked in a similar community who was an outsider (*inkommer*) for the community discovered that the *boorlinge*, who can all speak Afrikaans and Nama, will only use Nama if they want to exclude the outsider from the conversation, until they trust the person.

It was clear that this community could not be regarded and treated as a single community because their *self* was not perceived as such. It was important to recognize and respect the different identities (Kotze 1989: 50–51). This hypothesis was confirmed by the perception of the social worker. She worked in a neighbouring community who were allocated money from the government's 'Poverty Alleviation Fund' to start a communal vegetable garden. The project never got off the ground. On investigation she discovered that the community was strongly motivated to get a borehole but not to establish a communal vegetable garden. They prefer to have their own individual gardens. They then trade with each other. It was part of their tradition and way of survival to trade with each other. A communal garden calls for a totally different economic system.

The facilitator

The facilitator also has a self. Think about your own values, traditions, actions, and preferences. Think about your own 'self'. How does it play a role in your interactions with people? How has it changed?

1.3 Proposition 9: The self and significant others

1.3.1 Proposition 9 and the individual

> *'As a result of interaction with the environment, and particularly as a result of evaluational interaction with others, the structure of the self is formed (an organized, fluid, but consistent conceptual pattern of perceptions of characteristics and relationships of the "I" or the "me") together with values attached to these concepts.' (Rogers 1987: 498) (For the sake of clarity and continuity, the description of the self as given before was repeated here as originally formulated by Rogers.)*

This tells us that one of the experiences that affect the self is our interaction both with the environment and particularly with other people who we see as important to us. It is a flexible yet organized picture of the attributes and relationships of the self, as well as the values attached to that picture.

No person lives in isolation. Everybody interacts with others, and our perceptions of these interactions become part of who we are (or see ourselves to be). So, for instance, one can hypothesize that a person usually experiences the self as a parent in relation to a child. In other words, a mother or father can perceive themselves as a parent in relation to their own (or adopted or foster) child. This means that the 'I' or identity is defined in relation to the child, as in 'I am ... the caretaker, protector, nurturer, educator, disciplinarian of this child', or any other perception a person might have about what it means to be a parent of a child. (However, this is not necessarily always the case, as someone might relate to a pet or a grandchild in a parental way, or see themselves as parents in that relationship. On the other hand, if a person did not want to become a parent, the self might not change into a parent self in the event of such a child.) The same hypothesis applies to the perceived self in any other interaction, for instance between a wife in relation to a husband (and vice versa), or an employer in relation to an employee.

What is of great significance here is that it is our perception of others, ourselves, and our relationships that is relevant here. As people are different, and have different perceptions (see more on this in propositions 1 and 2), each person's perception of themselves, other people, and their relationship, will differ. It is thus very important to listen to the person sharing their perception with you, to understand their experiences and perceptions.

As other people are such an important part of the development of the self, we often find that clients will come and see a facilitator to talk about someone else. As in the above illustrations, it could be a mother about a child, a wife about a husband and so on. We might be tempted to discuss the other person, or try to understand or even defend or explain the other person to our client. It requires a mental effort to keep in mind that we need to concentrate on how the speakers are being affected by their perception of the self, the other, and their relationship. This does *not* mean that we 'forbid' clients to speak about others, or subtly steer them away from it. Instead, we need to listen very carefully to them, and try to understand how they experience, or believe they are being affected by, the person they are talking about. (For example, when a mother speaks about her naughty child she may experience herself as being a failure.)

Remember, the theory guides our behaviour and thinking, not that of clients. It is what we do with what they tell us, that is important. Theory is supposed to enable us to think and act in a professional manner, and also, to enable us to deal with anything the clients talk about, in a professional way.

It is only in interaction with our clients that we become professional facilitators. (In interaction with our clients, our 'self' as facilitators, develops.) The way we see ourselves, our clients, and the relationship between us, is different from any other. We determine how we perceive these elements and what we do with our perceptions in the professional relationship.

Initially, your self as facilitator, and the values attached to this self also develop in interaction with your lecturers. Proposition 10 teaches us more about values and the self.

1.3.2 Proposition 9 and the group

In South Africa we are living in an interesting era. Terms such as 'rainbow nation', 'equal rights', and 'mixed association' are well known and often used in the media. These terms will also have an influence in our working with groups. This is because groups will become more heterogeneous according to race, culture, language, communication patterns, and gender. Groups will become more open to different values, ideas, traditions, taboos, and behaviour patterns. These factors will have an effect on the interaction process, climate, structure, and also on the development of the group members' self and the selves of the group.

Because of the variety of values, ideas, and traditions you may encounter in one group, it may take longer to develop the group and the group members' selves. Facilitators can, however, facilitate the development of the self of each member and the group if:

- they are flexible to the values, purpose, and climate of the group
- they empower the members to participate and to express themselves without fear
- they recognize and accept the values of all the members. This is only possible if a climate which is open, compromising, and accepting exists in the group
- they recognize and show appreciation to all members, and
- they allow the building of relationships, the development of communication, praising, and facilitation.

If facilitators facilitate the aforementioned factors they will observe how very formal, quiet members can become the front-runners in the group.

1.3.3 Proposition 9 and the community

The values, ideas, traditions, and taboos of each community have been shaped through the ages by their own experiences, in interaction with others and have been assimilated into the self of the community. The community is still in continual interaction with other communities (and the individuals and groups in the community with each other). Therefore, the community's perception of itself may change and evolve in interaction with each other and in interaction with people from other communities. The perception of the community may be created through the media, or by way of comparisons between themselves and other communities. For example, communities may be labelled as 'backward, deprived, and underdeveloped' or 'rich and snobbish'.

However, Africa must be one of the best examples of changed ideas and perceptions of the self. The perceptions that African countries have had about themselves have definitely changed since colonization and the introduction of new normative indicators. Measured against current Western standards, these communities are underdeveloped and framed as underdeveloped. Today, Egypt is classified by some as a Third World country, while a few centuries ago it was considered to be the cradle of civilization.

In this regard writers like Chambers (1983, 1994, 1997), Korten (1984) and Pradervand (1990) have taught the professionals to appreciate people and communities. If communities are perceived and treated differently, this in turn can change their own perceptions of themselves. Chambers (1983/ 1997) sees the members of the community as resourceful and skilful people from whom we as professionals should learn. We learn from them, listen to them, and appreciate their expertise. Rahman (1993: 25) explains that he visited a community in Zimbabwe that was always referred to as poor by outsiders. Rahman, in his encounter with the people, discovered a wealth of knowledge and resources and a wealth of human creativity. He shared that with the community.

'I was deeply moved thereafter as villagers came to me to thank me saying that they were not poor as I had helped to lift a burden from their backs.'

In proposition 17 Rogers confirmed the importance of a respectful relationship in which people we interact with can appreciate themselves. It is within this interaction and relationship that people can change and develop without their ideas about themselves being threatened.

Freire (1994: 75–85), and consequently the social constructionists, see change and liberation as occurring through 'renaming' the world via interaction with others and the environment. Through the process of conscientization (becoming aware), interaction, and dialogue with other people, people discover their own selves and world and can rename their selves and their world and re-relate to them. During this process people can change attitudes, behaviours, and relationships as their ideas about themselves change in a non-threatening environment that we create.

The facilitator

This proposition puts great emphasis on us as facilitators as we facilitate the change process. People interact with us. Our interaction with them may influence their ideas about themselves. We are also shaped by the people around us, including our clients. Our selves may also change and be affected.

1.4 Proposition 4: Self-determination

> *'The organism has one basic tendency and striving – to actualize, maintain, and enhance the experiencing organism.'*
> *(Rogers 1987: 487)*

A human being has one basic striving: to actualize, maintain, and develop the total self. This is an extremely important principle, but very difficult to operationalize, particularly when it comes to people in need.

1.4.1 Proposition 4 and the individual

It is important to keep in mind that this proposition refers to the *self* of the person, as he or she experiences it. This self or identity might not be what an outsider sees as 'good', but then it is not the facilitator's experience of what is good or necessary that is at stake, but what the client sees as relevant to himself or herself. This is further complicated by unsymbolized experiences, which are dealt with under propositions 11 and 13.

Example 1.4

The client is a woman, married for the past eighteen years. She has two children and has never been employed outside the home. She left her parental home to move in with her husband. She sees herself as a homemaker, whose main aim in life is to provide a warm, caring, healthy environment for her family (husband and children). To enhance this self, she has attended various culinary and interior decoration courses.

At present her children have left home to start careers of their own. They are asking her why she does not have a career, why she relies so much on their father for money, instead of earning her own. She feels that all her efforts to be a good wife and mother have not been appreciated, that what she has spent her life trying to achieve is no longer valued.

In interaction with her older children, the self she has maintained and striven to enhance for the past eighteen years is being questioned and now she does not know what to strive for anymore. Should she, for instance, as a good mother, do as the children would think best, that is, to start thinking about a possible career outside the house? If yes, then the very effort to be a good mother as she understands a good mother to be, will threaten her self as a homemaking mother and wife.

This kind of conflict can be very confusing and painful. Although facilitators may have different ideas about motherhood, about how to be a career person and a homemaker that work for them, this does not entitle them to impose their ideas on the client. She has to define her own self, what she is, what she is becoming, and how to maintain and enhance that particular self.

Activity

Answering the following questions for yourself may help you to understand this proposition more clearly:

1 Why are you reading this book?
2 Do your efforts to achieve whatever it is you are trying to achieve by reading this book complicate your life?
3 Do they create problems that you will need to overcome?
4 Do you accept these problems as the price to be paid for your striving for self-actualization, self-development? Could problems perhaps be regarded as part of your aspirations to become more of what you are, as a person? For instance, if you are a facilitator of some kind, are you striving to become a better facilitator, thus enhancing your 'facilitator' self?
5 Do you think that the poor also aspire to self-respect and the respect of others? Or are they only concerned about food and clothing? For instance, when people are poor, and believe that this is their lot in life, can they strive to be honest or clean 'poor' people?
6 If you should have an accident and be left handicapped, would you still aspire to happiness? What would happiness be to you in those circumstances? Can you think of things to which your parents or family might aspire? (Ask them.)
7 Do you feel good when you do things for people and they then thank you and tell you that they could never have managed without you? How would you feel if you were forever dependent on other people's favours?

1.4.2 Proposition 4 and the group

One of the objectives of working with groups is to enable group members to grow or develop in terms of their self-actualization. In other words, group work should enable group members to feel good about their role fulfilment and about themselves. (See Corey 1990, Douglas 1976, and Schwartz and Zalba 1971.)

The process of group work furthermore assumes that group members can grow and develop when they are enabled to do so. Group members are enabled when the group facilitator does nothing more than facilitate their actions. This means that the group members themselves should decide on the objectives for the group, as well as the programme whereby the objectives will be realized. Allowing them to decide already shows respect for the self-actualizing of the group members. Group members, however, will only participate in the process of deciding for themselves in a safe and trusting climate. A safe climate can be defined as a climate in which the group and facilitator listen to one another without judgement and also observe and respect one another's needs. The professional ability of facilitators in the person-centred approach is therefore assessed according to their ability to link the needs presented by each individual group member during a specific session with those of the other members, as well as the goals for that specific session.

Example 1.5

When the facilitator arrived at the third group session with a group of teenage boys, all the group members were standing outside the venue. During the previous sessions, they had always waited for her in the group-work room. Noticing this change in behaviour, the facilitator commented that there must be something important they wanted to tell her. They said yes and explained that because it was school holidays, they would like a more informal session. The facilitator asked them what they would like to do. They mentioned that, instead of watching a video, they would prefer to go to the beach. The facilitator agreed and together with the group members changed the programme in such a way that it was still possible to fulfil the objectives planned for the specific session, namely to keep your area clean.

It is clear from the example that the group members felt accepted by the facilitator and it was therefore possible for the group to ask for a change in the programme and also to explore possibilities for coping with the change. If this process is repeated a few times, the group facilitator's job will become superfluous (this, incidentally, is how the group facilitator will feel), but the members will be empowered to do their own thing, which again will improve their experience and self-actualization.

1.4.3 Proposition 4 and the community

In the Sepedi language there is an idiom *Kodumela moepa rutsa ga go lehumo le le tswago kgauswi*. Freely translated, it means that 'people naturally strive and dig for what they want, no matter how difficult it may be'.

People's tendency to self-actualize is one of the core concepts of the person-centred approach. This proposition implies that every community is in a continuing state of growth and development towards self-actualization as determined by themselves. This is linked with proposition 5, according to which behaviour is intentional and directed towards self-actualization. Meador and Rogers (1973: 132) describe the actualizing tendency of all people as the inherent tendency of the organism (read community) to develop all its capacities in ways that serve to maintain or enhance the organism. They continue by saying that this process entails development toward autonomy and away from heteronomy, or control by external forces.

Example 1.6

An example provided by Menike (1993: 181) is of a programme organized for the women in a particular community comprising mainly Buddhists. The value system of the Buddhists prohibits the taking of any form of life. She wrote: 'The lecturer taught us about poultry keeping and how we could rear thousands of chickens and sell them for meat. He taught us how to generate thousands of rupees in 45 days. Next he taught us how to rear fish in the lakes where we bath, and how we could kill them and sell them for money.' Shaw, as cited by Rogers (1987: 59), comments that a situation or procedure like this 'is psychologically unsound because it places the residents of the community in an inferior position and implies serious reservations with regard to their capacities and neglects the greatest of all assets in any community, namely the talents, energies, and other human resources of the people themselves. It does not facilitate their growth'.

Example 1.7

A facilitator was employed by a mining company. (See also example 4.2.) The mine community lived in an informal settlement: corrugated iron, one-roomed shacks, winding dirt roads with potholes and puddles, very few water taps where the women fetched water in drums. The facilitator discovered that most of the people working at the mine came from rural areas and many of them were not able to identify with life in an impersonal mine hostel. So they chose to live in the squatter area, which was a bit more like their villages at home. At least they felt they were living on the land. Here they could grow vegetables, have a goat or two, and the children could play on the ground. To support their efforts, the accommodating mine management then offered to provide funds to develop a tarred road. The community opposed the idea, since this would change the rural atmosphere they had tried to create.

Their self-determination and control quite clearly emerged. Rogers' (1987: 266) statement is thus applicable to this community: 'I cannot prove that the individual is most to be valued. I can only say that my experience leads me to place a primary value in him.'

This community was clearly creative, resourceful, and knowledgeable, although it might not look like this from outside the community. According to Rogers (1977: 6), humankind must be seen as possessing 'vast resources for self-understanding, for altering his self-concept, his attitudes and his self-directed behaviour'.

Our main task as facilitators is to *facilitate* the process of the *growth and development of the community*. In order to utilize the resources of the community, however, Rogers proposes that certain prerequisites have to be met to create the particular climate that is favourable to the client's growth and development. This climate, according to Rogers, is the prerequisite for change (see proposition 17). This particular climate can also be created with the community as a whole in order to 'liberate' its potential for growth, development, and self-actualization. Therefore, the community can make its own decisions and participate in all aspects of the process, namely doing, thinking, executing, and evaluating. This is, essentially, the only way in which to facilitate the community's pathway to independence.

One of the implications of this is that the facilitator will not be able to claim any honour or recognition for specific results of the project. Any credit will always go to the community itself because, increasingly, it will be the community that manages its own community affairs.

We quote James Yen's credo (Hersey 1988: 151–92):

> *Go to the people*
> *Live among the people*
> *Learn from the people*
> *Plan with the people*
> *Work with the people*
> *Start with what the people know*
> *Build on what the people have*
> *Teach by showing; learn by doing*
> *Not a showcase but a pattern*
> *Not odds and ends but a system*
> *Not a piecemeal but an integrated approach*
> *Not to conform but to transform*
> *Not relief but release*

The facilitator

When working with people, we have to reflect critically on our attitude and action to see if we are creating conditions, and using skills, that enhance growth and self-actualization.

CHAPTER 2

Experiences that fit with the self

2.1 Introduction

In this chapter we will discuss those experiences that fit with the self of a person. They pose no problem and can be allowed into the conscious mind, or filed away as unimportant or irrelevant for now (proposition 11 [a and b]). Mostly, our behaviour also fits with this self (proposition 12).

2.2 Proposition 11 (a and b): Dealing with experiences at a conscious level

This approach assumes that our experiences manifest at two levels, namely the conscious and unconscious. In both instances, the difference lies in the *self*: whether a particular experience fits with the self or not.

Although Rogers (1987: 503) deals with both these kinds of experiences in one proposition, we think that the difference between these experiences becomes more apparent if this proposition is discussed in two parts. In this chapter we explore the process of symbolization and how we deal with experiences that do *not* threaten the self, but rather fit with the self.

> '*As experiences occur in the life of the individual, they are either (a) symbolized, perceived, and organized into some relationship to the self, (b) ignored because there is no perceived relationship to the self structure ...*' (Rogers 1987: 503)

There are two important aspects to this proposition: the process of symbolization as well as the relationship to the self.

> *'The human being deals with much of his experience by means of the symbols attached to it. These symbols enable him to manipulate elements of his experience in relation to one another, to project himself into new situations, to make many predictions about his phenomenal world.'* (Rogers 1987: 144, 145)

During our lifetimes, we have different experiences and begin to attach particular symbols to them. These can be any kind of sensory experience, like a parent who shows the child a picture of a tree. The child sees a tree and attaches the symbol or word 'tree' to it. Linking feeling to symbols is a bit more difficult: if a child falls down and hurts his or her knee, the mother will probably say a pain word, like 'hurts' or 'sore'. In this way, we learn to differentiate between what we like and don't like. We combine an experience with a symbol for like/not like.

We thus make sense of our experiences by attaching symbols to them. In the case of our conscious experiences, we have to place them in some kind of relationship to the self, or we can ignore them because they are not relevant to us at present.

2.2.1 Proposition 11 (a and b) and the individual

The first way that individuals deal with experiences is that the symbolized experience is integrated with the self. As a rule, these experiences are congruent with and affirm the self-structure. Thus individuals tend to admit to their consciousness (symbolize) those experiences that affirm the self.

Activity

Check which visual stimulation (books or films) you understand and remember best. Is it the material that corresponds with your own ideas and needs, or that which differs from these?

The second way of handling experiences means that certain experiences do not even register. Consider what happens when you go through a supermarket with a shopping list. Of all the available commodities, you usually notice only those that you need to buy. If people were to ask you afterwards which other commodities were available and on which shelves they may be found, you would probably not be able to tell them at all.

Figure 2.1 *Selective shopping*

2.2.2 *Proposition 11 (a and b) and the group*

Any programme presented, or information made available, to the group depends in the final analysis on what the group does with it. It is, therefore, truly impossible to predict the outcome, especially in the long run. In group work it is important, therefore, to involve members of the group in planning the programme. A programme that may be useful to a particular group with family problems, for instance, may be useless for another group because of certain different experiences. Similarly, a programme may be useful at a particular point in time, but completely useless for the same group two weeks later. The only people who can ensure the usefulness of a group programme are the group members themselves.

Example 2.1

Members are often coerced into joining groups, especially in institutions like prisons. Such groups may be for people who have been found guilty of driving a motor car under the influence of alcohol, or juvenile delinquency. Members are often compelled to become part of a group in terms of a sentence that is being enforced. Usually, structured programmes developed over a period of time and based on the experience of professionals are used. The groups are furthermore often required to complete the programme within a given time in order to proceed to the next programme. As a result of this inflexibility and because the experiences of the members have not been taken into account, it has happened that certain members have been prepared for their release from the institution up to two years prior to their release.

2.2.3 Proposition 11 (a and b) and the community

As the proposition indicated, the community can deal with experiences that are symbolized experiences. This implies that the community will make decisions congruent with their self-perception, as we will see with the elderly women who refuse to ride bicycles in example 2.5.

If people have to make choices or are trying to decide on ways of dealing with issues, they will probably choose ways that they know or feel comfortable with. In communities we will find that women's income-generating groups will often choose activities known and related to them, for example sewing, baking, crocheting, making polish, or manufacturing candles. They will seldom choose male-orientated or more challenging activities. This does not mean that the women should only choose activities known to them. When facilitating the *process* of symbolization of their context and needs they can take on more challenging activities to which they can relate and symbolize.

Members of a community, therefore, make decisions based on their own perceptions about their own 'self' and its values and what is considered useful for this self. The decisions we, as facilitators, make might be against the self and values of the community. An example of disregarding a community's situation is an incident that occurred during the Gulf War in 1991 when, as part of their emergency aid programme, a big Western country sent pork sausages to Saudi Arabia (where the population is mainly Muslim)!

Example 2.2

A social worker worked in a semi-rural area. The community's income was extremely low. The problems that were referred to her as a social worker were mainly those of child abuse and neglect. She was told by her superiors to start a child abuse prevention programme. Through the primary school, she managed to contact and visit some of the parents. They told her horrific stories about the children having to walk long distances to school every day, being picked up, raped, and abused on the way. Some of the children never reached the school. The parents asked the social worker to call a meeting with the other parents so that they could discuss the problem as parents and with the school. The parents were extremely concerned. Before meeting the parents, the social worker thought she would experience a very negative, apathetic community that didn't care about their children. Her experience was totally the opposite. Close to the school was a well-known bus company and the parents felt that this would be the point where they could start dealing with the problem. Some of the parents were working for the bus company and they felt that it would be possible for them to start negotiations with the company. With the helper's facilitation, the parents started to negotiate for transport for the children to school. After their experience of success, other projects soon followed.

The facilitator

Think about your experiences. Are they symbolized? Distorted? Denied? This may help us when making decisions, reacting to situations, and reacting to people.

Figure 2.2 Different symbolizations

2.3 Proposition 12: Self and behaviour

> *'Most of the ways of behaving which are adopted by the organism are those which are consistent with the concept of self.' (Rogers 1987: 507)*

Symbolized behaviour is usually consistent with the individual's self-concept.

2.3.1 Proposition 12 and the individual

Here we see, once again, that the self plays an important part, this time regarding our behaviour. Behaviour is not merely directed at need satisfaction (proposition 5); it also has to agree with the individual's self-perception. In other words, we usually behave in ways that fit with our sense of who we are, and avoid behaviours that do not fit with our self.

Example 2.3

All people eat (behaviour) when they are hungry (need). But how and what they eat depends on how the individual experiences the self and his or her culture. Some people use a knife and fork; others use only a fork or only a knife; some eat with their hands or use chopsticks. In addition, people have preferences; however hungry people may be, not everyone likes the same kind of food. Person A may not like spinach (it is not to his or her taste), while person B adores spinach (it is to his or her taste). People and their tastes (i.e. what they believe to be in line with their self) differ. Observe how people's tastes in clothing differ. This applies to all human experience and behaviour.

Figure 2.3
Like/dislike

Consequently, behaviour can be viewed in terms of both needs and self-perception.

Example 2.4

Another example is the situation within a family. The behaviour of everyone in the family needs to be understood in this way, not just for example that of the abused child or wife. The behaviour of the wife-beating husband also reflects a particular need and self-concept that has to be explored and understood. This may be difficult, particularly if the facilitator finds the behaviour unacceptable.

2.3.2 Proposition 12 and the group

This proposition emphasizes that each individual in a group as well as each specific group is unique. Therefore, a programme that was a success with one specific group may be a failure with the next. This may be due to two factors, namely a programme that does not fit with the uniqueness of the group due to its self-concept, and the composition of the group. It may, for example, be difficult to have equal participation in a group consisting of males and females if women are expected, in that specific society, to play a minor role in the presence of men.

Furthermore, a group of unemployed men may show resistance, opposition, and disinterest in a group-work programme that will improve their working skills. It may be better (if it is their need) to develop their self-concept first.

2.3.3 Proposition 12 and the community

If we see behaviour as driven by needs (proposition 5) and self-perception (proposition 12), then a project will be owned by the community if it addresses their needs and if it is consistent with the self and the values of the community – meaning if it develops from 'inside' the people of the community. The projects that people take on are also linked with abstract gains that become internalized with the self of the community and the decisions the people in the community make will be decisions that are consistent with the self and values of the community. The community in Polela, KwaZulu-Natal where people did not eat eggs, is a good example (example 4.7).

Example 2.5

An international aid organization bought bicycles for the carers of a home-based care project for terminally ill patients. The aid agency was concerned about the care workers who were walking long distances to reach their patients; hence the agency introduced the bicycles. Most of the care workers were elderly women and could not see themselves riding around on bicycles. They did not regard it as dignified. They gave the bicycles to the schoolchildren.

We often find that agencies with good intentions will start a feeding scheme providing soup to people simply because they regard soup as 'nutritious' and economical, only to find that the people do not really want the soup. The soup might not be regarded as food. Is it food they need? What does food mean to them? What kind of food do they regard as significant? Is the soup consistent with the self and values of the community?

The facilitator

You as facilitator have a perception about your self. The choices you make are consistent with your own self-perception and value system. What are the implications of this for practice?

CHAPTER 3

Experiences that do *not* fit with the self

3.1 Introduction

This chapter deals with experiences that are *not* in line with the self and therefore cannot be allowed into the consciousness, or only in a changed (distorted) way (proposition 11 [c and d]). Also, we look at how this affects our behaviour (proposition 13), psychological adjustment [or maladjustment and tension] (proposition 14), and the need to defend the self against these experiences (proposition 16).

3.2 Proposition 11 (c and d): Dealing with experiences at an unconscious level

In this part of the proposition we will focus on what happens when our experiences do not fit with the self.

> *'As experiences occur in the life of the individual, they are either ... (c) denied symbolization or (d) given a distorted symbolization because the experience is inconsistent with the structure of the self.'* (Rogers 1987: 503)

Rogers (1987: 147) distinguishes between differentiation of the symbols we attach to our experiences and the differentiation of the perception of our experiences:

> *One of the most characteristic and perhaps one of the most important changes in therapy is the bringing into awareness of*

> *experiences of which heretofore the client has not been conscious.*
> *What, psychologically, occurs when the individual thus deals with*
> *'repressed' material? Our experience would indicate that it is best*
> *described in terms of greater differentiation of perception, and*
> *more adequate symbolization ...*

As this proposition indicates, some experiences (specifically those that do not fit with the self) are not conscious and therefore we cannot attach any symbols to them. This could be expressed in many ways, like clients saying 'I don't know what is happening to me' or 'I don't know why I am behaving like I do'.

Some experiences, though conscious, are too threatening to the self for us to allow ourselves a clear idea of what it is we are experiencing, that is, what is it exactly that I am seeing, thinking, attaching so much value to or wondering about. Clients would, for instance, say something like 'I don't really know why I am upset' or 'why this upsets me so'.

Other experiences are threatening to the self and then we cannot allow ourselves to attach the appropriate symbol to them. The symbol we do attach might serve as a protective measure, but because the symbol does not fit what we are experiencing, it creates discomfort and stress.

The following chapter discusses the conditions under which experiences might be denied consciousness or full awareness, denied clear perception or denied symbolization, and the relationship of these experiences to the self, and how this may influence one's behaviour.

In Section D we discuss the conditions under which all experiences can be explored and dealt with.

3.2.1 Proposition 11(c and d) and the individual

As mentioned above, any experience that is perceived as threatening to the self in any way may be blocked out, either consciously or unconsciously. The following response by a client illustrates the point (Martin 1983: 144):

> *Well, ... I feel very much like I'm cornered. 'Cause I think that I'm*
> *going to find out something about myself that I don't like. Some-*
> *thing I'm not facing. You know, like I want to avoid a whole bunch*
> *of things, I think, around that ... and what that says about me ...*
> *something that isn't going to be some ... I want ... that I'm trying*
> *to be somebody I'm not, or something ...*

In addition, some experiences that cannot be symbolized or blocked out completely, are distorted to fit in with the self. For instance, people who do not experience themselves as unduly aggressive may refer to intense feelings of aggression as tension or frustration, which are more acceptable to the self. (This is not dishonesty or manipulation, as an outsider may perceive it. It is the only 'reality' that such people can permit themselves to experience.)

Such distortion may also apply to positive experiences. For instance, someone who believes in modesty may find it difficult to say, after a successful examination or interview: 'I've done well and I can be proud of myself'. Instead, the experience might be distorted into something like: 'I was lucky' or 'The examination (interview) was easy'.

3.2.2 Proposition 11 (c and d) and the group

Using proposition 11 (c and d) it can be stated that in example 4.12 on page 60 of this book, the teenage boy has to decide whether he is going to adopt the values of the community, which are based on the survival of the fittest, or the values of the group and the group members, which are based on group participation, to develop his self. In this specific case it took six sessions for the boy to make a voluntary decision in favour of the group's self. In other words, in the first six sessions the boy resisted symbolizing the experiences and the values of the group or saw them in a distorted way because the experience in the group was inconsistent with his self-structure and that of the community.

This also illustrates why the forming of groups must not be forced.

3.2.3 Proposition 11 (c and d) and the community

In the community, experiences can be unsymbolized because they are not part of the self-structure or not part of their frame of reference. This proposition implies that we need to facilitate the process of symbolization of unsymbolized experiences with the people. Freire (1972) will refer to this process as the process of conscientization. This process will assist the community to decide on ways of dealing with the issues in the community that will be consistent with their self-concepts.

Example 3.1

In a certain rural town there were a few mentally and physically disabled adults and children who were not looked after well. Some of the members from the community contacted the social worker to assist them in starting a care centre for these people. She assisted the group of women to get hold of a building and sponsors for a care centre where they worked as volunteers. One section of the care centre also developed into a feeding scheme where around 250 children were fed on a daily basis. To the social worker's surprise, the volunteers resigned from all the hard work they had been doing. Reflecting on what had happened she realized that the women actually saw this project as an income-generating project and, when they did not get any income from it, they left the project. She failed to explore their real needs with them before starting the project. They themselves were poor and were hoping that income would be generated from the project.

3.3 Proposition 13: Behaviour and unconscious experiences

> *'Behaviour may, in some instances, be brought about by organic experiences and needs which have not been symbolized. Such behaviour may be inconsistent with the structure of the self, but in such instances, the behaviour is not "owned" by the individual.'*
> *(Rogers 1987: 509)*

Unsymbolized experiences and needs or distorted symbolization may also motivate behaviour. If such behaviour does not correspond with the individual's self-concept, the person will deny the behaviour.

3.3.1 Proposition 13 and the individual

When an individual with a certain self-perception (of who he or she is and of what is consistent with his or her self) manifests behaviour (motivated by unsymbolized experience) inappropriate to that self, the individual will deny such behaviour rather than change his or her entire self-perception (the latter being a drastic and painful process). A husband who beats his wife, but cannot reconcile this behaviour with his self-image, for example, will deny that he is beating her. He is literally unable to believe that he is capable of doing such a thing. Confronting such a person with the behaviour will merely lead to further denial and defences (see proposition 16 below). The person is, moreover, not aware of the needs and experiences motivating this behaviour, because these, if symbolized at all, have been symbolized in a distorted way. A possible response in such a case would be: 'I am a decent guy. All my colleagues at work respect me and I can't believe that I would do such a thing. It's simply not me!'

3.3.2 Proposition 13 and the group

It is important to remember that groups can put additional stress on a group member, for example, by changing the role he or she must play in a group. These changes may cause stress because they do not fit with the self of the member. This in turn can cause a member to behave in ways that are not expected of him or her. It may, for example, happen that a timid and self-controlled person becomes aggressive in the group, or an honest member may deny things he or she has said. Some of the women mentioned in the discussion in 4.7.2 on page 67 may refuse to attend any further sessions if they are forced to participate on an equal level with men. It is therefore important, when dealing with stress issues, that the facilitator enables the member and group members to understand the change in behaviour. Taking propositions 11, 12, and 13 into account, it is easy to see why the groups in example 2.1 don't really have therapeutic value.

This proposition also stresses that the facilitator must, through active listening, try to identify the intrapersonal and interpersonal needs of the group members. The emphasis should be on the discovery of these needs by the group members themselves and not by the group facilitator.

3.3.3 Proposition 13 and the community

Certain events are denied within particular communities because they cannot be identified with the community's self, or they may have a different perception of their behaviour.

'We are not violent, we protect ourselves.'

Example 3.2

A member of a particular community died in her house. Her body was only discovered several days later. Her brother was very concerned about her death as he was under the impression that the community was a very 'caring' community. The members of the community were describing themselves as a caring community. Why then did nobody notice her absence if they claimed to be caring?

Example 3.3

A research project was undertaken with farm workers. On all the farms they described themselves as 'good people', people who loved other people, people who would like to do more, religious people who would like to give their children a better future, etc. However, when they were asked to describe the factors that could ruin their dreams, they described their heavy drinking and beating their wives, despite the claim to love people! (Compare Du Plessis 2000.) Deeper discussions with the community brought out their unsymbolized experiences of desperation, disempowerment, isolation, and no hope and vision. The process of symbolization/conscientization of experiences is, therefore, of utmost importance, as will be discussed later.

The facilitator

Are there experiences that you deny, that you feel uncomfortable with, and that are inconsistent with your self-perception? Do you display behaviour that makes you feel 'this is not me'? Who or what assists you in symbolizing your unsymbolized experiences?

3.4 Proposition 14: Psychological tension

> *'Psychological maladjustment exists when the organism denies to awareness significant sensory and visceral experiences, which consequently are not symbolized and organized into the Gestalt of the self-structure. When this situation exists, there is a basic or potential psychological tension.' (Rogers 1987: 510)*

Unsymbolized experiences or distorted symbolization of experiences that cannot be incorporated into the self create tension.

3.4.1 Proposition 14 and the individual

The psychological tension Rogers refers to in this proposition is not to be confused with everyday tensions and stress. This distinction needs to be clarified to avoid any confusion and possible misunderstanding. In terms of this theory, it can be explored by looking at the difference between emotional and/or *symbolized* tension or pain, conflict, fear, and confusion, and *unsym-bolized* experiences that create tension and why this is the case. In the first instance, we are aware of the source of our tension, as it is symbolized, while in the latter case, we are unaware of the source, as it is not symbolized.

We can have symbolized emotions that, in everyday language are also called 'stress', or, as some people maintain, these experiences create tension or stress. Whichever way you look at it, this kind of tension deals with symbolized emotions, that is, if you are afraid that you will not pass the exams and are aware of this, one could say that you are 'stressing' about the exam.

But, and this is confusing, the way Rogers perceives tension is more psychological and has to do with the self. If you are experiencing any thought, need, or emotion, that is, any kind of experience that does not fit with your symbolized self, then you may experience psychological tension. This implies inner conflict (in your psyche or self, as it were) on an unsymbolized level. So, if we link it to the example of the exams, if you have a self-concept that defines you as always doing well (or being perfect) and you think you will not be perfect this time, but cannot admit this thought as it does not fit with your self, you might, for instance, to protect your 'self', blame the lecturer for not helping enough. Now it is not just the tension of the exams that you are experiencing, but also the inner conflict of fearing failure, while not allowing your 'self' to harbour such fears.

Let us look at another example.

Example 3.4

A man hears intruders in his house. He is afraid for his life and his possessions. This is at a symbolized level. He calls the police, but before they arrive, the intruders assault him and his family, and rob them of some of their possessions. This is a very painful (stressful?) experience for them all. They are aware of this and therefore the accompanying tension is experienced on a symbolized level.

However, a few months later, this man begins to experience undefined tension and stress that he cannot really explain. He says he just feels restless and depressed, not as strong and in control as he used to be. This last statement implies a person who perceives himself as strong and mostly in control. During the assault, this self was threatened. He now wonders whether he is, or can still be, this person. So, besides the physical threat, he also experienced a psychological threat to the self, of which he is unaware. After becoming aware of this inner conflict, he decided that he still is a strong person, and then took various actions to make his home and neighbourhood safer for everybody. The locus of control reverted back to himself, although he had believed that the intruders had taken it from him.

Lack of symbolization impedes conscious control of behaviour that is directed at the satisfaction of needs of which the individual is unaware. The husband who beats his wife, after an incident of abuse, may well promise that he will never do it again. But the moment the needs or unsymbolized experiences surface again, the behaviour will most probably be repeated. Fear that this might happen exacerbates the sense of poor control, and leads to further psychological tension. But because the man is not conscious of the exact nature of the motivating experiences, he cannot be on his guard against them or handle them in a different, less stressful way.

3.4.2 Proposition 14 and the group

Unsymbolized or distorted experiences within a group not only give rise to *psychological tension* for the particular member involved, but also create problems for the group, because the member consciously or unconsciously denies that there is a problem. As a result of such denial, the member cannot act naturally within the group, which causes frustration and psychological tension for the member as well as other members because they can sense that something is wrong. The member may also endeavour to focus communication on other members and their problems. In so doing, he or she becomes an adviser (as in the example where the elderly man assumed such a role).

Group facilitators should guard against attempts simply to change the behaviour of members by acting rigidly instead of paying attention to all experiences and new perspectives. Only the members are able to develop new experiences and perspectives, and therefore each member should be given the opportunity to participate actively in the group. This is done by creating an environment in which members can focus on their experiences. If the facilitator demonstrates genuine acceptance, respect, and understanding, the members may loosen up and lower their defenses and rigid perceptions.

It is important to realize that members may need time to work through their doubts. The next example illustrates this need.

Figure 3.1

Example 3.5

In a group where acceptance behaviour between different racial group members had been successfully practised, for example having tea together and calling one another by first names, one of the members responded as follows during the last group meeting:

Pete: John (the group facilitator), if we meet one another next week and I say hello to you, will you greet me?

John: Pete, yes.

Pete: John, can I ask you another question? If I invite you for a cup of tea, will you accept?

John: Yes. Pete, I notice that you have doubts whether what we have done in the group is feasible in practice.

Pete: Yes, that's it.

(In Rogers' words, what happened in the group was, for Pete, still 'a distorted symbolization of the real life experience'.)

3.4.3 Proposition 14 and the community

Helpers or facilitators can create (unsymbolized) psychological tension if they introduce or impose change in communities that is in conflict or incongruent with their self-perception and values. This also implies that the community does not have control over the changes. Parkash and Esteva (1998: 52) gave the example of the teachers who came to teach at a school in Guatamala wanting the children to wear school uniforms in order to look the same. The children usually wear very colourful dresses and parents take pride in weaving this colourful material. What angered the parents even more was the fact that the teachers expected the parents to buy the uniforms. This was against their distinct custom of making their own clothes and other goods and then trading with each other. To buy something is to undermine their 'economy of gifts'. There was such uproar in the community that the teachers were forced to leave the community. The parents refused to allow their children to wear clothes made only of one colour!

The anger is symbolized but the experience of humiliation, lack of control of their children's education, not being respected, and feeling that their values were not appreciated were unsymbolized and created psychological tension.

Paolo Freire's work (1972/1994) facilitated the process of symbolization or conscientization with communities and assisted people in communities to act in congruence with their self-perception and to realize that the locus of control resides with them.

The facilitator

Facilitators also experience psychological tension due to personal unsymbolized experiences as well as unsymbolized experiences in the work situation. For example, you may feel that you are not coping and do not have control in the work situation, while your perception of yourself is that of a competent, hard-working person. How can we deal with these unsymbolized experiences? What will assist us in the process of symbolization? Where is the locus of control?

3.5 Proposition 16: Defence of self

> '*Any experience which is inconsistent with the organization or structure of self will be perceived as a threat, and the more of these perceptions there are, the more rigidly that self-structure is organized to maintain itself.*' (Rogers 1987: 515)

Experiences that conflict with the individual's self-perception are considered threatening to the self. The greater the number of such experiences, the more intent the self-structure becomes on self-preservation.

3.5.1 Proposition 16 and the individual

This principle may be readily observed and accepted in respect of the physical self. A person threatened by a lion will act very promptly to protect the self by screaming, running away, climbing a tree, or whatever is possible at that moment. No facilitator observing this or hearing about it will find it peculiar or deviant. Yet if a person becomes scared, angry, evasive, or rebellious when the psychosocial self is under threat, some facilitators tend to regard this behaviour as abnormal (describing it as resistance, poor prognosis, or poor motivation). Of course, facilitators do not enjoy experiencing themselves as threatening (a roaring lion). Yet this might be how some clients experience them. Facilitators are, in fact, threatening when they behave in a way that does not accord with the client's self.

3.5.2 Proposition 16 and the group

Proposition 16 may also be modified to read that experiences that are in conflict with the group's perception of itself are experienced as a threat to the group and its survival and must be counteracted. The implication of the proposition is that the facilitator who describes a group as 'unmotivated,

Figure 3.2 *Are you running or roaring?*

difficult, uncooperative and aggressive' may do so from his or her perspective and not from the perspective of this proposition or of the group.

Groups will often act aggressively, etc., if group facilitators are not willing to acknowledge that their actions are contrary to the group's perceptions. This does not mean that group members will not change their perceptions under any circumstances. Instead, it means that perceptions are not changed suddenly, but that change is a slow process in which the existing perceptions need to be accepted. During this process, it is necessary to understand the group's perceptions and experiences of, say, fear of change and the loss it might entail (see Sections C and D for the recommended actions).

Example 3.6 .

This is an example of a situation that has been experienced by a number of group facilitators. The group facilitator had a sound relationship with the group members and the group was making good progress. During a particular meeting, the facilitator became impatient with a member who, according to the facilitator's perception, was slowing down the progress of the group. Without trying to establish the reason for the behaviour, the facilitator scolded the member. The other group members immediately sided with the particular member and refused to participate further in the group.

Example 3.7

A group meeting aimed at improving the situation of married women was attended by both the husbands and wives. During the second meeting the group facilitator sided with the wives and started blaming and attacking the husbands. As a result, the men soon got up and left. They did not attend any subsequent group meetings.

3.5.3 Proposition 16 and the community

This proposition shows that the individual and the community will protect themselves from whatever appears to threaten their self-concept, values, and continued existence. This is exactly what happened to the teachers in the Guatamalan community. They were literally driven out of the community for violating the community's idea of self, values, pride, culture, and economy (see proposition 14).

Outsiders will then describe communities as unmotivated, resistant, apathetic, and dependent. What this may imply is that the outsider is threatening the community's self-perception. Let's look at another example of how community members defend themselves.

Example 3.8

In the example of the Richtersveld, the community defended themselves by refusing to work collectively and by simply doing nothing about the communal garden until the social worker discussed the matter with them, and they decided instead to assist each other in establishing their own individual gardens. This worked well and they could continue with their 'economy of trading'.

This proposition implies that any change or development that occurs must have more (what they regard as) benefits than (what they regard as) disadvantages for the community and must cohere with the 'self' of the community. If not, the community will defend the self by not turning up, resisting, or even destroying the development effort of the outsider. We cannot refer to a community as a 'resistant' community any more. We have to think *what* or *who* they are resisting. In this sense defensiveness or resistance are an attempt at retaining control over their own situation (i.e. self-determination).

Ownership of projects depends on being consistent with the self of the community as well as the previously mentioned needs-based and emotionally felt projects.

The facilitator

Think of your reactions when something threatens your own self-perception and values. Often we have difficulty in working with certain people. Why? When do you resist change? Where is the locus of control?

CHAPTER 4

Specific experiences

4.1 Introduction

As said before, the self derives from all our experiences. Human beings have many different kinds of experiences, which will be discussed in more detail in this chapter. All of these experiences also form part of the self, and none can be ignored when we try to understand the self of a person. This wholeness will be discussed in greater detail under proposition 3.

Furthermore, all of these experiences can manifest at a conscious and/or unconscious level. So, when we consider which experiences fit with the self and are thus symbolized, all the client's experiences need to be considered. In the same way, any of the experiences discussed below can be perceived by clients as not fitting with their self (and therefore threatening the self) and thus be denied symbolization or distorted to fit in with the existing self.

4.2 Proposition 1: Human experiences at a conscious and unconscious level

'Every individual exists in a continually changing world of experience of which he is the centre.' (Rogers 1987: 483)

There are three important elements to this proposition:
- for every person their experiential world is central, unique, and personal
- this personal world is continually changing, and
- the experiences that constitute this world can be conscious and/or unconscious.

Rogers uses the word 'experience' as an umbrella concept for all possible experiences. He does distinguish between particular experiences, but this distinction is not to be confused with separation. In other words, although particular reference is made to experiences like needs, behaviour, emotions, and values, this does not imply that one experience can be separated from the other, or from the person experiencing them.

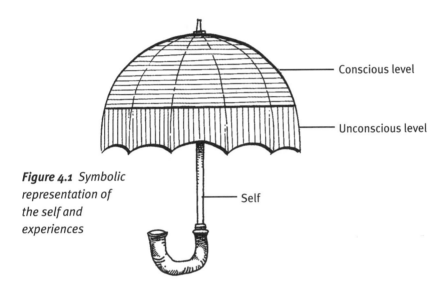

Figure 4.1 *Symbolic representation of the self and experiences*

One of these experiences is perception, that is, how people perceive themselves and their world, and how this perception constitutes their reality.

4.2.1 *Proposition 1 and the individual*

The experiential world includes both conscious and unconscious experiences. This is knowable only to the individual, which means that outsiders can only form an idea of an experience if the individual tells them about it. Think of going to the doctor because you have a stomach-ache. The doctor cannot know what you are experiencing simply by looking at you. Doctors have apparatus, such as X-ray machines and ultrasound, which they use to probe people's physical attributes. Sometimes surgery is performed for this purpose.

Figure 4.2 We cannot fathom people's inner worlds mechanically

Unfortunately, we cannot fathom people's inner worlds mechanically. Neither can the experiential world be 'cut open' while the client is under anaesthetic. Only the individual can give an outsider a glimpse of what is going on inside his or her private world.

Example 4.1

A mother and daughter consulted a facilitator because they could not get along. Each felt that the other did not hear or understand what they were saying. The above proposition will help the facilitator to understand that each of the two people is living only in terms of her own experiential world. This will enable the facilitator not to become impatient or judgemental. It is the facilitator's task to attempt to understand, and become part of, the experiential worlds of both mother and daughter.

The mother is central to her own world. Her perception of herself, of her task as mother, and of her daughter, changes continually. The way in which the daughter is experiencing herself, her friends, and her mother is also changing continually. Such changes are not synchronized, and changes in the one may give rise to anxiety in the other. The facilitator should ask himself or herself how each individual is experiencing her own world, including the changes and even the unconscious experiences. The facilitator's communication skills are the only tools available for this task. (Propositions 7 and 17 indicate the direction the facilitator could take. We will return to this example in the discussion of these propositions in Chapter 5.)

WHO CAN CRAWL INTO MY SHELL WITHOUT HURTING ME?

Figure 4.3

4.2.2 Proposition 1 and the group

The implications of this proposition for group work are twofold. First, the group itself, and not the group facilitator or any outside person or institution, determines which issue needs to be addressed. The group facilitator, therefore, explores the nature of the experiential world of each individual and of the group as a whole by means of individual interviews and pre-group meetings. *Often group facilitators refer to a specific session as 'difficult' because the members did not want to participate and listen to one another. This may, however, be due to facilitators not recognizing the human experiences of each member.* (Refer to example 4.1.)

Secondly, because each member's experiential world and the experiential world of the group as a whole may change in seconds, the group facilitator will find that long-term programme planning for the group is fraught with difficulties. In other words, the group facilitator may find that programmes originally decided on are rejected at a later meeting. One of the reasons for rejection may be that the experiential world of the members and group have expanded during the week between meetings. Such expansion may also have been stimulated indirectly by the previous group meeting. Group facilitators should, therefore, always be prepared to change pre-planned programmes. This should not be difficult if the facilitator uses the skills discussed in Section D and if the facilitator accepts that a group belongs to its members and that they themselves should decide on the functions of the group.

4.2.3 Proposition 1 and the community

In this proposition, Rogers looks at the uniqueness of a person's continually changing life-world. A community, too, is unique and continually changing, since people move in and out of the community and new technology is developed when there is environmental, political, or economic change. Along with the changes that take place come new experiences, perceptions, challenges, problems, needs, resources, and relationships within the community.

There is a Pedi idiom *mollo ofisa baori,* which means that 'only the person exposed to the fire can tell how hot it is'. Only the community or the people in the community can tell how they perceive and experience their continually changing world.

This proposition therefore implies the following:

- Firstly, it is impossible to determine what the community's unique experiences are from outside the community itself. There has to be continuous dialogue with individuals and groups in the community in order to get to know the people, their perceptions, needs, emotions, knowledge, skills, traditions, values, ideas, experiences, and meanings. This dialogue will also help to establish and understand their concerns, the way they perceive and experience these concerns, and the meaning they attach to them. Furthermore, dialogue will generate ideas with the community about how to address these issues. Working in communities is, therefore, a dialogical or participatory process. That is, a process where we continue to listen to the changing experiences and perceptions of the people.

Example 4.2

A mine provided housing for the mine workers, just to find, after some time, that an informal settlement was erected next to the empty single and family quarters the mine provided. They discovered that the mine workers preferred staying in the informal settlement. Originating from rural communities, the miners preferred their homes to be on the ground and more like a village. The double-storey flats did not feel like home to them. (Also see proposition 8, which deals with the self of the people or community.)

- Secondly, different individuals and groups in the community can have different perceptions and experiences. To talk only to the so-called leaders in the community, or the men in the community, will not elicit all of the community's concerns. The women and the children, for example, may perceive the situation differently and among the men, women, and children there may also be differences.

Example 4.3

A rural community was concerned about its water supply. The women regarded the water from the perspective of domestic use and clean drinking water, so they preferred the water supplied by tankers because it was clear and clean. The men preferred the running water as they could water their crops more easily with running water.

The facilitator

You as facilitator are unique and have unique perceptions, experiences, and realities that change continually. What does this imply for you as a facilitator regarding your own development and regarding your interaction with individuals, groups, and communities?

4.3 Proposition 2: Human perceptions

'The organism reacts to the field as it is experienced and perceived. This perceptual field is, for the individual, reality.' (Rogers 1987: 484)

Like experience, perception (or observation) of the world (or reality) is an individual matter. People respond in terms of both experience and perception.

Figure 4.4 Different lenses result in different views

4.3.1 Proposition 2 and the individual

Below are three figures. What do you perceive in each of them?

(From Hanson 1961:13)   (From Compton and   (From Parnes 1981:37)
                         Galaway 1984:110)

- The first picture could be a small buck with long horns, or a bird with a long beak, or …
- The second picture could be a vase, or two profiles facing each other, or…
- The third picture could be an aeroplane in the process of landing, or possibly taking off?

None of the above perceptions is either true or false, unless one believes that one's own perception is the only admissible one.

Example 4.4

A mother and her fifteen-year-old son are watching the film *2001: A space odyssey* together. She asks him whether he recognizes the background music and he answers that it is a waltz. She remarks that it is interesting that such an old tune should be so appropriate in a modern film. 'Modern?' her son responds, questioning her comment. 'That film was made way back in 1968!'

The experience or notion of what is 'modern' is relative to the individual's perception and it is futile to try to judge who is right or wrong, the mother or the son. For both of them, their experiences are real and relevant, and they are entitled to their own experiences. Facilitators often find themselves in situations where one member of a family is complaining about another. This is when it is especially important to remember that all parties have the right to their own experiences and that we cannot judge or condemn anyone. Everybody experiences their world in a uniquely individual way.

Example 4.5

When a facilitator has to deal with a mother and her adolescent son who, for instance, argue over rules and liberties, it is important to bear in mind that mother and son are individuals with their own perceptions or experiences of rules and freedom. The facilitator has to find out how each of them sees the issue, without taking sides with one or the other. This is somewhat difficult because the facilitator also has his or her own perception and experience of rules to contend with. He or she may, for instance, believe that the parent is always right and that children are obliged to obey their parents until such time as they leave home. Or the facilitator may feel sorry for the son, and may believe that he should be supported, or believe that adolescents are entitled to more freedom. Can you guess how these ideas may influence the facilitator's actions, regardless of the contribution made by the clients? It is important to hear, however, how the mother and son, respectively, perceive and experience their situation, because it is *their* reality that is at issue.

Here it is also important to keep in mind that, if you speak to one person, and that person talks about another, it is only the frame of reference, or experience, of the person speaking to you that you are hearing. These experiences do not tell us anything about the person spoken about, because that person will have his or her own experiences, known only to herself or himself. A facilitator cannot get to know one person by talking to another about that person. Let's consider the example of the mother and daughter mentioned above: if the mother should come to see you alone, without her daughter, and talks about her daughter, it is important to keep in mind that it is her experiences we are dealing with, and not the daughter's. If, for instance, the mother says something like: 'My daughter is very naughty these days. She does not listen to me any more and wants to do everything her own way,' the facilitator cannot then assume that the daughter is naughty, or know anything else about the daughter, as the mother is sharing *her own* experiences, which are unique to her, and reveal something about her mother-self and the changes taking place in this self. The way in which these dilemmas can be dealt with will be discussed in Chapter 17.

4.3.2 *Proposition 2 and the group*

Each person is unique and every group is unique. You may already have come across this statement. The unique nature of a person and a group is brought about, among other things, by the way in which the person and the group perceive reality. It would, therefore, be wrong to base group work on a single member's perception of a problem. This dilemma is further aggravated when the programme is planned according to the perceptions of the group facilitator, or the organization or institution the facilitator is working for. The following example shows the danger of dealing with groups according to the perceptions of one or two people or the perceptions of organizations and institutions such as schools.

Example 4.6

The management of a firm decided to instigate problem and growth-orientated groups for employees. The purpose of the groups was to give employees the opportunity to discuss anything that influenced their functioning in the work and social environments. The group consisted of five members, namely two adolescents, a married couple, and a man who had recently been appointed as a control manager of 500 employees. The group decided that they wanted to discuss relationships. The facilitator had, however, found out during the first meeting that the members had different ideas about what 'relationships' entailed. For example, the adolescents understood relationships to mean relationships with the opposite sex, while the manager thought it implied that attention would be paid to building up relationships with employees.

If the group facilitator had been unaware of these perceptions, the group sessions would have failed, despite the fact that attention had been paid to certain relationships. Group facilitators should be especially sensitive when raising broad concepts that could lead to different perceptions. They should always find out exactly what group members want and then identify shared experiences, perceptions, or themes.

Activity

1   A group was asked to identify the element that did not fit into the following collection, namely dog, cat, and television. Do you know the answer?
    Answer: I do not know because I am not familiar with the group's perception. Should their perception focus, for instance, on animals, the answer would be television. On the other hand, if their perception is focused on licences, the answer would be cat. The group may even have a perception that indicates dog as being the correct answer.
2   Can you think of more examples where the group members' perceptions can influence communication in the group?
3   Look at the picture on the cover page. What is your perception? Asking colleagues the same question their perceptions varied from 'it illustrates depth' to 'flying saucers'.

4.3.3 Proposition 2 and the community

This proposition is about reacting to reality as it is experienced by the person or people in the community. You cannot understand the actions of the community unless you get to know them and learn how they experience things.

Individuals and groups within the community have different experiences, attach different meanings to their experiences, and also react differently to these experiences and, for them, realities. They may have shared or similar perceptions and experiences. Rogers (1989: 425) also said that 'reality is basically the private world of individual perceptions, though for social purposes which have a high degree of commonality among various individuals. The desk is real because most people in our culture have a perception of it which is similar to my own'. People may have different as well as shared experiences. We will not know the shared experiences if we do not talk to many different people in the community. Nobody in a community can talk on behalf of others. For example, men cannot talk on behalf of women or on behalf of children.

Rogers (1989: 428) promotes the appreciation of differences: 'If I accept ... that we live in different realities; if we can see these differing realities as the most promising resources for learning all history of the world; we can live together in order to learn from one another without fear; if we can do all this, then a new age could be dawning'. This links with Chambers (1997) who emphasized the diversity and complexity of communities. They consist of people with different perceptions, experiences, and meanings. These differences should be respected and 'celebrated'. The richness of the diversity can be seen as their biggest resource. This viewpoint, however, reflects on the perception of the facilitator. If the facilitator perceives the community in this manner, then his or her way of working in a community will be participatory and people-centred. Regarding the similarities and differences in perceptions and experiences of the individuals and groups in the community, it is not about who is right or wrong, but about what we can learn from each other.

Example 4.7

To illustrate the different viewpoints of professionals and the community Jackson (1979: 1–3) has shown how professional people identified serious health problems within a particular Zulu community in the Polela district near Pietermaritzburg. These were ascribed to malnutrition and specific dietary problems. Interviews with the community revealed that the community's attitude towards particular types of food seemed to be influenced by their perceptions and system of values. For instance, it was thought to be uneconomical to eat eggs because they could instead be used to produce chickens. Their value system prescribed that if young girls ate eggs, this could cause them to have loose morals. It should be emphasized that this perception of one subcommunity of the Zulu community or culture cannot be seen as generally applicable to all Zulu people and their attitude to eggs.

Activity

It might be interesting to share and *compare* some of your answers to the following questions with others:
1 What meanings do you associate with food/shelter/water?
2 What do you regard as sufficient food/shelter/water?
3 What are your dislikes regarding food/shelter/water?

The facilitator

You as the facilitator are the centre of your own experiences. The experiences you have are real for you but are not realities for other people or for your clients. How will you deal with that? How can we learn from other people without fear? Do you see other realities as the most promising resources for learning?

4.4 Proposition 3: Wholeness/Unity

> 'The organism reacts as an organized whole to this phenomenal field.' (Rogers 1987: 486)

The response to the experiential world is that of the person as an organized whole.

4.4.1 Proposition 3 and the individual

People, complete with all their ideas, feelings, behaviour, needs, values, and physical attributes, may be regarded as contained in the circle in Figure 4.5. Ask yourself where the human being begins and ends in this picture, or which part is not connected to every other part.

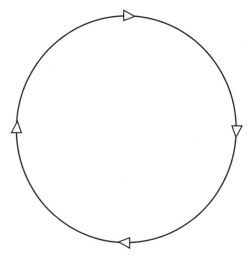

Figure 4.5 *Wholeness/unity circle*

Does one act exclusively in terms of one's perceptions, or of what one feels or thinks? Can these dimensions of the self be considered separate, or are they all integral to the person? Although we are not constantly aware of all these dimensions, they are always there, part of what we do and what we are.

Facilitators should therefore be open to all dimensions of human nature and not focus on just one aspect of a person. When considering the mother and son in example 4.5, or the mother and daughter in example 4.1, in terms of this proposition, the facilitator needs to attempt to see each of them in the light of *all* of his or her experiences.

Some people are under the misconception that person-centred theory deals only with emotions. When all the propositions have been explored, it becomes evident that this theory is far more comprehensive. Only one of the nineteen propositions deals specifically with emotions. The propositions examine needs, behaviour (proposition 5), emotions (proposition 6), the self (proposition 8), and values (proposition 10). All of this, together with the observations or perceptions discussed in proposition 2, should be taken into account when attempting to understand people. For instance, the mother in our examples should be understood in terms of the way in which she experiences her self (proposition 8), the values that she attaches to parenthood (proposition 10), her needs as mother and as an individual (proposition 5), and how she expresses such needs (proposition 5), how she feels about these needs (proposition 6), and how she perceives herself and her son or daughter (proposition 2). The same demands are made of the facilitator's understanding of the children, of how they themselves experience all these aspects.

4.4.2 *Proposition 3 and the group*

In terms of this proposition, the facilitator should regard each individual and group as a whole and not concentrate only on one aspect, such as behaviour. This implies the need to determine during the pre-group phase which other characteristics of a member, such as emotions, desires, aspirations, attitudes, perceptions, and values, may become part of the group.

Behaviour within the group should not be viewed in isolation either, but should be seen within a particular context. All personal characteristics and influences of the community should also be taken into account.

Example 4.8

One of the boys in a group of teenagers always carried a hunting knife. During the third meeting, the facilitator asked him about the purpose of the knife. He replied that he carried it to defend himself. The facilitator was shocked and asked him to dispose of the knife. He refused because he came from a rough neighbourhood where every man carried a knife to defend himself. It is interesting that the boy, during the eighth session, told the group of his own accord that he had decided to dispose of the knife, which he did after the session.

We often hear people say that they misjudged someone or a group. This is because people focus on only one aspect of the person, which they judge to be good or bad, or right or wrong. In the above example, the facilitator wanted to deny the boy further access to the group. Once she had taken the boy's needs, values, aspirations, desires, and functions into account, however, she allowed him to remain in the group. Due to a change in his own experiential world, it was possible for him to change his mind during the eighth session. Upon termination of the group, the facilitator found the progress made by this boy to be most exciting.

Activity

How would you, as a group facilitator, explain the boy's behaviour, taking the first three propositions into consideration?

4.4.3 Proposition 3 and the community

The community can be seen as a whole from different angles:
- The community forms a whole that includes values, attitudes, behaviour, emotions, ideas, desires, aspirations, meanings, perceptions, and experiences. They all interlink with each other. Change in one aspect will bring about change in others. If my values change, meanings, perceptions, experiences, and actions may change.
- The community is a whole consisting of individuals and groups and forming part of a larger environment. Change in sections of the community

may affect the rest of the community. Development efforts often have great impact on the physical environment.

Example 4.9

This is a little story of a phenomenal woman who really affects the larger community around her:

Her name is Mrs M. She is 46 years old. She lives in an informal settlement. Most of the houses in the settlement were made of mud and others were made of cardboard boxes. One summer, when it was raining, the house next to hers collapsed, two children were killed instantly, and the others were left in a serious condition in the hospital.

This incident served as a wake-up call to Mrs M. She could not sleep at night thinking about what she could do to prevent this in future. She came to the conclusion that the only way to prevent this was to build houses made of bricks. She managed to get hold of a brick-making machine and she and her *stokvel* (spontaneous credit union) group and their husbands started to make bricks. Some families came to join in with the brick-making and building of houses. Not all the families living in the informal settlement joined. Others would look down on this group saying 'They think they can do what government has failed to do!'

The important point here is that whatever she did had an effect on the community in one way or another.

- The process of change is also holistic. If you change something here it will have an effect in another place, as in the case of Mrs. M. The people making the bricks also had an impact on the environment (maybe for the worse) by using the sand from the river for brick-making.

This proposition implies that we cannot look at the community as an entity consisting of isolated and unrelated components. Rogers (1987: 487) puts it like this: 'The outstanding fact which must be taken into theoretical account is that the organism (community) is at all times a total organized system, in which alteration of any part may produce changes in any other part.'

Wholeness is also important when we facilitate the process within a community at a very practical level. For example, when a group of women would like to generate income for themselves it is not just the activity of generating income but also the market, the running costs, the product, and the resources that have to be considered.

The following example may also illustrate the concept of wholeness in communities.

Example 4.10

In a suburb of one of the bigger cities in South Africa (as in other developing countries), many people from outside the community were coming to look for jobs. Every morning they would stand next to the road indicating with an upward second finger that they were looking for work. The community started to get very worried about people flocking to their areas, for various reasons, including safety, as crime was rising at the same time and affecting their property values.

The community started to demand that the police should remove the people. A social worker started to talk to the people waiting along the road. What she learned from them, among other things, was that they came to this community because people here paid well – better than the people in the suburbs closer to them. The area was still growing and lots of construction was underway, giving them plentiful opportunities. Similarly, the social worker discovered that many churches with good intentions had started soup kitchens that provided food for these people. Job seekers could literally get a meal on a daily basis if they moved from one church to the other. They also made friends with the domestic workers in the community, which gave them access to places to sleep, to food, and to water. Therefore, we cannot look at the problem in isolation. The community actually provided the ideal context for jobless people to survive.

The facilitator

You as a facilitator are also a whole, with your own feelings, experiences, values, and actions, interconnected with each other. You are part of a family, a community, groups, and organizations. You have an impact on the lives of people and on the environment and in turn they impact on you. The fact that we may throw a piece of paper on the ground, instead of into the wastepaper bin impacts on the environment and other people. The way we approach people may have an impact on them. Whatever we may do or say may have an effect on people and the environment.

4.5 Proposition 5: Needs and behaviour

> *'Behaviour is basically the goal-directed attempt of the organism to satisfy its needs as experienced in the field as perceived.' (Rogers 1987: 491)*

Behaviour essentially consists of purposeful endeavours by individuals to satisfy their needs as experienced in their life world.

4.5.1 Proposition 5 and the individual

In terms of this proposition, behaviour is associated with needs. Individual needs motivate behaviour. If one bears this in mind, it becomes clear that all behaviour (however odd it may appear to an outsider) has some motive, reason, or goal.

Figure 4.6 Nest in shoe – motive?

Example 4.11

A teenage girl from an average income home engages in shoplifting. At face value, this is perplexing. When one looks more deeply into the matter, it turns out that she is giving the stolen items to her friends. In such a situation, the underlying need (whether symbolized or not – see proposition 11) may be to gain the approval of her peer group. Possibly, she does not believe that they really like her (self-perception, propositions 8, 9, and 12) and therefore tries to 'buy' their friendship and acceptance. Once her underlying need is understood, the apparently peculiar behaviour becomes more understandable.

4.5.2 Proposition 5 and the group

An unknown educationalist once said that children in schools are forced to exhibit naughty or problem behaviour. According to him, the reason for such behaviour is to gain recognition (and therefore need satisfaction). Because the average child receives no attention in class, he or she has to aspire to be included in the gifted group, which is really impossible. The child consequently moves downward to join the group of 'problem children', where he or she will receive attention or recognition, even if such attention is negative (such as punishment). In view of this, behaviour in groups and group behaviour should not (immediately) be identified as simply problematic. The facilitator should rather establish the advantage that such behaviour offers the member or group, or find out what the member is trying to tell him or her, or the group, through his or her behaviour.

Example 4.12

A teenage boy always tried to be the centre of attention in the group. When the group played cricket, for instance, he had to bat or bowl. This behaviour had a negative influence on the group and the facilitator felt it best to exclude him from the group. After an in-depth discussion with the supervisor, the facilitator realized that the boy was seeking recognition. Once he was granted recognition by the group, who put him in charge of certain activities (such as being captain of the sports team), he became more sharing and even started voluntarily assuming a subservient role to other members. This proposition warns group facilitators never to label or judge their observations of clients during group sessions as 'good' or 'bad'.

4.5.3 Proposition 5 and the community

Ngwana a sa llong a swela tharing 'a child cries to get attention', according to a northern Sesotho idiom. The child's crying is purposeful. So the behaviour of the people in the community is also goal directed.

This proposition suggests that Rogers does not see behaviour as something 'mad' or 'bad', but rather as an attempt to satisfy needs or to self-actualize. There is another northern Sesotho expression *Manna o dira ka boomo*. Directly translated it means 'man acts with intent'. In other words, it differs from other approaches that may view behaviour as pathological or deviant. This proposition again takes a positive stance towards people and their behaviour.

Example 4.13

In some communities, shebeens might be regarded as a social problem. However, they are one of the largest sources of income in these communities, and cannot therefore simply be dismissed. In the same way, the mine community's behaviour in example 4.2 was difficult for the mine's management to understand. But the mine workers, coming from rural areas, had a need to live in a more rural atmosphere.

Behaviour is therefore purposeful and although it may appear to be peculiar, it remains an attempt to satisfy certain needs and attain self-actualization.

The facilitator

Your behaviour is also intentional. Whatever you do or however you react towards your client is intentional. You can either try to convince a client of something, or you may try to create a warm, safe atmosphere. We can also try to act in a way where we try to prove to people that we are good helpers or good facilitators. The importance of this is that we as facilitators must be aware of, and accountable for, our behaviour.

4.6 Proposition 6: Emotions

> *'Emotion accompanies and in general facilitates such goal-directed behaviour, the kind of emotion being related to the seeking versus the consummatory aspects of the behaviour, and the intensity of the emotion being related to the perceived significance of the behaviour for the maintenance and enhancement of the organism.' (Rogers 1987: 492)*

Emotion accompanies and facilitates the purposeful behaviour mentioned above. The intensity of the emotion correlates with the importance that the person attaches to the behaviour in terms of self-preservation and self-enrichment (proposition 4).

4.6.1 Proposition 6 and the individual

The intensity of emotions varies from one person to another and from one situation to the next. For instance, when you are alone at home and you hear a strange noise, you will probably experience some measure of anxiety. The resultant behaviour may vary from keeping quiet and listening, to getting up and investigating. If you were to see someone climbing in through the window, the perceived threat to the self would probably be even greater and your behaviour would be correspondingly more strongly directed to self-preservation.

Thus, the girl in example 4.11 may experience anxiety at the thought of being caught shoplifting, but may feel even greater (more intense) fear of being rejected by her peers.

4.6.2 Proposition 6 and the group

When taking proposition 6 into account, the group facilitator will also concentrate on the emotions expressed by the group members and the group as a whole. These feelings will be expressed both verbally and non-verbally. A client may, for instance, express emotions non-verbally by bringing a hand up to his or her mouth in an expression of surprise. Non-verbal behaviour may also be used to confirm verbal communication of emotions, for instance making agitated gestures while talking. The group facilitator will therefore have to both listen to, and observe, the clients.

Figure 4.7
Shoplifter

By intensely observing the emotions of all members, the group member will also note to which issues attention should be paid within the group. Such issues may then be successfully incorporated into the group process. This can, in fact, provide the basis for group communication. In example 4.12, the responsibilities of the teenage boy were only changed after emotions such as frustration and anger had been observed by the group and facilitator.

In group work, strong feelings can be expressed and demonstrated during the closing phase. Such emotions may vary from anger to despondency. If the group or facilitator does not deal with these feelings, it may undo the success achieved with the group.

However, group members will only express or demonstrate their feelings if a climate of acceptance and trust prevails in the group. Such a climate can be achieved only if the group facilitator acts empathetically (see Chapters 14 and 15 for a more detailed discussion of empathy), in other words he or she should display an attitude 'of genuine caring and the sincere desire to understand the world of another' (Corey 1990: 295). According to Corey (1990: 293), the group facilitator should 'also be able to communicate this understanding to the client'.

By being in full emotional contact with the group members, group facilitators improve

- unity between the members, and
- lay the foundation or basis for good group communication.

4.6.3 Proposition 6 and the community

This proposition is one of the most important propositions for the facilitator working with communities, an idea that Paolo Freire (1972/1994), the Brazilian pedagogue, also stressed. Freire referred to 'generative themes' in the community, meaning exploring those experiences that the community feels strongly about. Freire (Hope and Timmel 1984: 6) refers to the direct link between emotion and motivation to act. People will only act upon something if they have strong emotions about it. If they do not have a strong emotion about a certain issue they will not really make an effort to do something about it.

Bawden (1991: 17) refers to Rogers, saying that:

> *much of what we know has nothing to do with the sort of logical, rational, reasoned, scientific knowledge that comes from propositional or practical learning. Each of us has a store of knowledge which we have gained in non-rational ways; our intuitions, our aesthetic likes and dislikes, our cultural beliefs and traditions, and so on.*

Example 4.14

Let us go back to the example of the mining community. Logical, rational, reasoned thinking, from the management's perspective, would be to stay in the living quarters provided by the mine. The needs and feelings or emotions of the miners (including the urge for freedom, rural life, and family life) motivated them to create their own rural community life in the informal settlement.

Example 4.15

A social worker worked with farm workers with the aim of 'informing' them about HIV/Aids. She spent ample time with the community, listening to their stories, wishes, hopes, and dreams. The aspect that they (men and women) felt most strongly about was domestic violence between husbands and wives, but also fighting and beatings occurring among the members of the community. After they had dealt with the issue of fighting, they were ready to deal with the HIV/Aids 'monster' that also threatened them, as one couple in the community had been diagnosed positively. Included in this process was the empowerment of the women, who could not refuse sexual intercourse or demand the use of condoms. The husbands have the 'power' to beat them, force them, or chase them away from home.

Emotions accompany our behaviour. To understand the behaviour of the people in the community, the facilitator has to listen to the intensity of their experiences, emotions, beliefs, meanings, and traditions. What makes the community feel angry, happy, exploited, frightened, hopeful, or sad? What are their hopes and dreams? The issues about which the community feels most strongly, at that moment, will most probably be the issues that they would like to act upon first.

The facilitator

Our emotions also lie behind our actions. We as facilitators also act upon our emotions. We also experience emotions about our clients that influence our actions towards the people we work with. Critical self-reflection is important as is the symbolization of our emotions, experiences, and actions.

4.7 Proposition 10: Values, own and adopted from other people

> 'The values attached to experiences, and the values which are a part of the self structure, in some instances are values experienced directly by the organism, and in some instances are values introjected or taken over from others, but perceived in distorted fashion as if they had been experienced directly.' (Rogers 1987: 498)

Values attached to experiences and forming part of the self may be shaped by the individual's own experience, but they may also be taken over from others and assimilated into the self as if they had been experienced personally.

4.7.1 Proposition 10 and the individual

Initially, the child's self is shaped mainly by interaction with the parents. Later, the peer group and teachers also play an important role. Other significant others (as illustrated in proposition 9) become part of our lives as we grow older. It cannot be emphasized enough that the critical issue here is how the child (individual) *perceives* or experiences the interaction and the values of the significant others. Thus a mother may give both her children porridge for breakfast (she may value a healthy breakfast for her children). One of the children likes porridge and feels good about himself and his mother. The

Figure 4.8 and 4.9 *Understanding of parents in children*

other one does not like porridge and might experience a sense of being punished, so that she will feel less good about herself and her mother. Thus parents may have good intentions (values) that are not experienced as such by their children. (This also applies to children who want to give their parents a treat by bringing them breakfast in bed, but in the process turn the kitchen upside down.)

A mother may encourage her son to take part in athletics because he is a good runner. She believes in his potential and wants the best for her child (her values include being a good and encouraging mother). The son, on the other hand, may feel that he is under pressure to achieve and may wonder whether he will still be accepted if he fails to achieve (like the girl in example 4.11 who wondered whether she would be accepted if she did not produce presents). Consequently, the boy may import the value that he has to achieve in order to be accepted. Then, if he fails to achieve, he may resort to steroids or drugs because he fears rejection if he were to fail.

In interaction with the facilitator, both the self of the client and the facilitator are influenced. (As mentioned above, you are only a facilitator in relation to a client, and a client is only defined as such, in relation to you). This can be seen as the motivation for our professional interaction with clients, that is, that their self can change (be re-structured) in interaction with a significant other. In this case, the facilitator becomes that significant other. Clients can therefore also be tempted to take over values from facilitators. It is thus very important for a facilitator *not* to praise (or condemn and criticize) a client. Since this is done in terms of the facilitator's values and frame of reference, clients may act in a particular manner merely in order to gain the facilitator's acceptance and not because this behaviour reflects their own values.

In Section B of this book, you will be introduced to some of the professional values that are associated with being a professional facilitator. These values are introduced to you by the authors and lecturers and you could feel that you have to take them over from these others, without making them your own. That is why it is important for you to think about these values, and see whether they fit with your (developing) professional self, and whether you can really own them. If not, your behaviour might reflect this inconsistency. More about experiences that are inconsistent with the self, are discussed in propositions 11 and 13.

Values attached to experiences and forming part of the self may therefore be shaped by the individual's own experience, but they may also be taken over from others and assimilated into the self as if they had been experienced personally.

4.7.2 *Proposition 10 and the group*

The main issue highlighted by this proposition is that no group exists in isolation, but continually interacts with other groups. A group of teenagers, for instance, comes into contact with various family groups, peer groups, school groups, and formal groups such as welfare organizations. These groups may alter a particular member's or group's perception of himself or herself or itself by means of pressure or comparisons. Unfortunately, the various groups are often in competition with one another and in the process assign certain labels to one another. This may occur in particular in long-term groups.

Labelling of groups can be reduced by paying increased attention to the values of the group and group members. These values are frequently also influenced by the groups mentioned in the paragraph above.

The implications for the group facilitator are as follows:

- The group facilitator must realize that values may influence the functioning of groups. In South Africa, for instance, young Zulu women may say very little in a group if older Zulu women or men are also present, even when they disagree with what is being said. This is out of respect for their elders and for the men.
- The group facilitator may be able to determine the influence of values on the functioning of the group to a large extent if he or she knows the groups with which the group members have contact.
- Because groups and group members do not exist in isolation, their attitude towards the group and themselves may change from one group meeting to the next.

4.7.3 *Proposition 10 and the community*

We have already referred to the importance of the values of the community. Communities have values and traditions that were developed over years, centuries, and generations. When working with communities to facilitate change, these values should be respected, but can also change in interaction with other people. Values give an indication of the self of the people.

The facilitator

It is important to be aware of our own values and why they are important to us. Why do we hold certain values and how does it affect our interaction with people?

CHAPTER 5

Conditions for facilitation

5.1 Introduction

> 'Individuals have within themselves vast resources for self-under-
> standing and for altering their self-concepts, basic attitudes, and
> self-directed behaviour; these resources can be tapped if a definable
> climate of facilitative psychological attitudes can be provided.'
> (Rogers 1980: 115)

Here we discuss the theoretical requirements for how facilitators could be (as whole people, in interaction with others) in order to create the necessary climate for their clients to grow towards being more of themselves, and why this is necessary.

In Section B we explore the ideas of respect and being non-judgemental in greater detail, while in Section C the attitude and 'way of being' of empathy is explored. In Section E, Chapter 18, we take a more concrete look at the self of the facilitator and whether the ideas discussed in the book can become a congruent part of himself or herself.

5.2 Proposition 7: Frames of reference

'The best vantage point for understanding behaviour is from the internal frame of reference of the individual himself.' (Rogers 1987: 494)

The best way to understand behaviour is to view it in terms of the individual's frame of reference.

Example 5.1

A story is told in Malawi about the monkey that landed in a river. Eventually, after some struggle, the monkey managed to climb out. When the monkey saw a fish splashing in the water, he assumed that it too needed to be rescued from the water. Obviously this led to its death.

5.2.1 Proposition 7 and the individual

Since behaviour is motivated by needs and accompanied by emotion, these three dimensions (i.e. behaviour, needs, emotion) are best understood in terms of the individual's frame of reference.

Example 5.2

A woman described an incident that occurred when she was buying her mother a birthday present. The present was a few bushy trees for her mother's garden. The trees were a fair size and in order to avoid damaging them, she let down the roof of her convertible car and transported them on the back seat. As a result she was effectively sitting under an umbrella of foliage as she drove along! While she was waiting at a red traffic light, the motorist in the adjoining lane stared at her in disbelief and called to her, 'Lady, wouldn't it be easier just to put up your roof if you want some shade?' Clearly, outsiders do not always understand our behaviour unless they enter into our life world.

In all the examples already mentioned, each individual's behaviour needs to be understood in terms of his or her frame of reference: the behaviour of the mother and children, of the teenage girl who shoplifted, and of any client you may encounter, is best understood from within the particular individual's own frame of reference. Empathy accordingly means that while facilitators recognize and retain their own frames of reference, they also respect the right of clients to their own frames of reference and allow them to express it.

Figure 5.1. *Tree roof*

The client's behaviour (and needs, which motivate behaviour, and emotions, which accompany and facilitate behaviour) makes more sense if it is understood in terms of his or her own total frame of reference. This may sound easy, but facilitators encounter several obstacles. (Empathy and its application are discussed in more detail in Chapter 13.)

5.2.2 Proposition 7 and the group

Proposition 7 emphasizes the following two issues for the group facilitator:

- The facilitator has to talk to the members of the group in order to determine their frame of reference. This process can be time-consuming and group facilitators are often tempted to try to speed up the process. This may happen when group facilitators listen only until they think they understand the situation, or until they hear something that fits their perspective and believe it presents a solution. Group members may respond to this behaviour on the part of the facilitator by saying, 'You did not listen to me', by throwing their hands up in desperation, or simply by acting passively or aggressively.
- Group members may also attempt to gauge the group facilitator's frame of reference. If they can establish what it is, members may try to communicate within the facilitator's frame of reference in order to be accepted by him or her. This occurs more often in the initial phase of groups.

To explore why the members are attempting to communicate in terms of your frame of reference, make sure that you listen carefully. You should not only hear what the members are saying, but also establish whether you have heard correctly by restating what has been said. In other words, you must communicate within the group's communication process.

> **Example 5.3**
>
> A group facilitator entered the venue where he was supposed to work with a group on the topic of 'separation from the sheltered home'. He noticed that the members were depressed. He discovered that a friend of the members had died during the preceding week. He allowed the members ten minutes to talk about their friend and then started with the formal programme. The group facilitator commented that the meeting had been difficult because the members were unwilling to participate.
>
> One of the reasons why the members would not participate was that the programme did not fall within their frame of reference (needs) at the specific time.

This happened because the facilitator did not follow the communication process of the group members who clearly wanted to talk about the death of their friend. By accepting the members' frame of reference and using the communication process creatively, it still would have been possible for the facilitator to fulfil the objectives with the group.

5.2.3 Proposition 7 and the community

When a community works alongside or with a facilitator, it is a learning process for the community as well as the facilitator. At one level, the learning for the facilitator takes place when he or she discovers how the community perceives situations, what they experience as their concerns, how they plan, how they create solutions for their problems, what their aspirations are, and how these can be fulfilled. In other words, the facilitator constantly listens and explores to facilitate the community's sharing of their frame of reference.

Example 5.4

This example is taken from Meyers (1994: 3–4). One afternoon a researcher was standing under a tree with a small group of Senegalese villagers. They were watching a hydrologist studying a hydrological survey map that was draped over the bonnet of the project vehicle. Nearby, fiddling with his soil science survey kit, another man was running tests with a variety of test tubes and chemicals. Meyers suddenly wondered what the villagers thought these two men were doing.

He explained:

... the villagers ... felt they were watching two outstanding witchdoctors at work. They explained to me that the one with the test tubes was consulting the spirit of the earth and asking it where the spirit of the water was. The one studying the survey map was like their *marabout* (Islamic religious leader) who reads the religious language (Arabic) and does magic. Together they would determine where the water was. I asked if these two witchdoctors were any good. 'Oh yes,' they said, 'they are better than our witchdoctors. They always find water.'

Sometimes agencies plan projects according to their frames of reference, only to find that the projects cannot get off the ground as the people are not interested in what they offer. Menike (1993: 177) explains from a community member's point of view: 'Those who plan their ... interventions clearly do not understand our reality, our practices, our wishes, our thought processes, our constraints and our needs.' There may be shared frames of reference but the different people or groups of people may have different frames of reference.'

People share their experiences and perceptions with us if we really and congruently try to understand their experiences, perceptions, and meaning from their frames of reference. In Venda there is the saying that 'you can open a pot but you cannot open a person's heart unless that person opens it for you'.

5.3 Proposition 17: Conditions for facilitation

> 'Under certain conditions, involving primarily complete absence of any threat to the self-structure, experiences which are inconsistent with it may be perceived, and examined, and the structure of self revised to assimilate and include such experiences.'
> (Rogers 1987: 517)

5.3.1 Proposition 17 and the individual

In certain circumstances, especially ones that pose no threat to the self, experiences that conflict with the self (proposition 11) can be symbolized and explored. In this case, the self-concept can be reorganized.

This proposition provides a guideline for facilitators' intervention in situations where people are experiencing stress and pain (proposition 14). A climate must be created in which clients are accepted unconditionally, without judgement or condemnation. The facilitator tries to perceive and accept the self as it is experienced by the client. Then the client has no need to fight for the preservation of the symbolized self or to defend it (proposition 16). As the symbolized self comes to be accepted, unsymbolized experiences are gradually admitted to consciousness.

It is not easy, however, to create such a climate.

Example 5.5

While walking in the veld, a nature lover comes across a pupa. The pupa has already changed into a butterfly that is thrashing around desperately to escape from the cocoon. Out of sheer kindness and very gently, the man picks up the pupa and makes a small hole in it to help free the butterfly. But once freed, the butterfly is unable to fly and wriggles around on the ground without any coordination. The struggling inside the cocoon was essential for the butterfly to strengthen its wings sufficiently for flight.

Clearly, then, good intentions are not enough. It requires great skill to treat people in accordance with their own self-structure and frame of reference (i.e. empathetically).

This is especially difficult when the client shares dark or painful experiences with the facilitator, like depression or anger. One's first reaction would probably be to lighten the depression or calm the anger, but that is the facilitator's need. It is not where the client is now. To enter the world as experienced by the client in the here and now takes a lot of courage and security in the self on the part of the facilitator.

The experience of depression can metaphorically be linked to that of a deep, dark hole in which the client finds himself or herself. The facilitator must decide whether he or she is able to climb into this hole with the client (believing that it is possible for the facilitator to get out again) or whether to stand at the top of the hole and try and pull the client out of it. This would also require a lot of strength, as something is keeping the client rooted to the bottom of the hole. If the facilitator gets down into the hole, he or she might help the client explore the hole, its depth, and what keeps the client anchored down there.

5.3.2 Proposition 17 and the group

This proposition may be regarded as a guideline for the group facilitator to treat group members who are experiencing stress and pain. (See comments on proposition 16.) It is important that the group should hold no threat for its members. Members should not only not feel threatened, but should feel that they are being accepted totally. To accept a group member, the group facilitator needs to enter and deal with the member's life world. Treating members within their own self-structure and frame of reference requires skills such as empathy on the part of the group facilitator.

If the group members are accepted and respected in a genuine, open, and honest way, an atmosphere may develop that will, among other things, enhance self-evaluation. By practising the aforementioned the group members may also use it in real life situations.

Activity

Describe how you would treat the case study in example 5.3 by using proposition 17.

5.3.3 Proposition 17 and the community

If we believe that people attempt self-actualization, are self-determined, and have the need for self-regard, then the main task of the facilitator in the community is to create a warm, congruent, accepting, and understanding context in which people can grow, risk, learn, make mistakes, and change in a way that is consistent with their self-structure. This context will facilitate growth (and liberation) from within the person and the community. There should be no threat for the people. This non-threatening context includes no judgement and no top-down, inappropriate projects from our own frames of reference.

The important principles that are valid for the individual, the group, and the community are acceptance of, and respect for, the community and all its experiences, and validation of their frame of reference. Therefore, the facilitator tries to act within and respect the community's frame of reference. Well-intended projects may threaten the community self. Conditions and values are created and skills applied that will allow people to grow and develop.

In Sections C and D we describe how this proposition may be applied in practical situations by means of the appropriate use of the different levels of empathy.

The facilitator

Are we creating conditions for change and growth? Do I reflect critically on my thoughts, values, and the skills I use as a facilitator? Why do we use skills? What is the effect of the values and skills we use? What is the effect of our thinking?

CHAPTER 6

Reorganization of the self and its implications

6.1 Introduction

If the conditions for facilitation have been met, it is probable that clients can experience the self in a different way. They might perceive that how they view their self now includes more of their experiences on a conscious level. Their experiences and their self are thus more congruent with each other and they feel more in control of themselves.

Rogers (1987: 135) also found that there was '...movement from symptom (problem) to self ... from environment to self'. This means that clients can become more aware of themselves in relation to their problems and also that, where previously they sought control over their problems in the environment, now they become more aware of the locus of control lying within themselves.'

Once the restructuring of the self has occurred, various other changes can follow. For instance, clients are not only better able to accept themselves, but they can also accept others as separate people (proposition 18) and can also develop their own valuing system, which fits with this newly found self (proposition 19).

6.2 Proposition 15: Reconstruction of self

'Psychological adjustment exists when the concept of the self is such that all the sensory and visceral experiences of the organism are, or may be, assimilated on a symbolic level into a consistent relationship with the concept of self.' (Rogers 1987: 513)

A person becomes well adjusted (with concomitant tension reduction) when all or a maximum of experiences can be symbolized congruent with the person's self-perception.

6.2.1 Proposition 15 and the individual

The new self-structure is able to symbolize a wide range of experiences. Now behaviour is not motivated by experiences that have not been symbolized (or that do not accord with the self-structure).

Such experiences include negative or painful experiences as well as positive ones that have been symbolized and integrated with the self. This enables individuals to express their experiences in a more controlled way, so that the experiences accord with their self-perception.

When unsymbolized or distortedly symbolized experiences are allowed full symbolization, various changes can occur. On the one hand, the self could be restructured to fit with these experiences, or, on the other hand, the behaviour could change to fit with the existing self.

Figure 6.1 '*I can also paint – with my feet.*'

Example 6.1

An example of the first would be a woman who has always been (to her) physically beautiful. Much of her sense of self had always been associated with her physical beauty, as she won many beauty contests, worked as a model, and thus saw herself and her interactions with others in terms of these experiences. Then she was in an accident, in which her face and body were badly scarred. She was very depressed and wanted to die. For her, the essential part of herself had in fact died.

During the helping process she explored her own belief or value that she was only alive or of worth if she were beautiful, in greater depth. She realized that much of this was taken over from her perception that she had to participate in all the various beauty contests as a child, to be accepted and loved, and her fear that, if she lost these competitions, she would also lose her parents' love.

She began to question these beliefs and was able to symbolize that she and her parents also had fun together when on a picnic, with her hair full of sand and toes stubbed on the rocks of the seaside. She began to see herself also as a person who had fun, who could see the lighter side of life. This led to wondering whether she could share some of her vast experience regarding the world of beauty competitions and modelling with others who were struggling to survive. From this emerged a whole new career and sense of self.

Example 6.2

The example regarding the second kind of change, that is, where behaviour changed, rather than the sense of self, can also be related to an accident. The man was a professional person who could not continue with his chosen profession after an accident. He too became very depressed and feared the loss of his family's love, if he could not provide for them financially. When he explored this perception, that is, that he was only acceptable if he had money to give, he began to realize that his family love and need him for other things that he still could provide, like being there when they are afraid or lonely or confused. He could accept that he meant more to the family than a meal ticket, but he could not see himself as totally unoccupied and dependent on a maintenance grant from the state for his own income. He started exploring other possibilities for generating money and later went into business for himself.

Thus, he changed his behaviour (way of generating an income) to maintain the sense of self as an active, financially contributing member of society.

The facilitator cannot prescribe or predict what changes will occur in the client's world, but can only walk the road of exploration with him or her.

6.2.2 Proposition 15 and the group

Proposition 15 recognizes the importance of certain situations, including the group situation. According to this proposition, group members will be able to deal with the group situation if it is in agreement with their own perspectives and reconstruction of the self. This emphasizes the importance of the maintenance objectives in the group, in other words the objectives that attract members to the group.

As far as the task objectives are concerned, the group is precisely one of those places where people can share their experiences – both positive and negative – in a safe environment.

6.2.3 Proposition 15 and the community

This proposition means that the community can identify and symbolize most of their experiences in line with their idea about the self of the community. On the one hand, this means that some experiences confirm their idea about their 'self'. On the other hand, events happen in a community that may be painful or difficult, but the community is able to restructure these as something useful for the community.

Example 6.3

In a rural community, a crèche was erected for the community by an outside agency without consulting the community about the need for the crèche. It was also built in an area that was not really accessible to the children. The community was furious about this project. After some discussions among the members of the community, they restructured the 'problem' as an asset, using it for more meaningful purposes. This also links to the example where the bicycles were given to the aged care givers in a community. They, however, gave their bicycles to the children in the community who could use them more appropriately by arriving at school in time instead of walking long distances.

This process also takes place at a much deeper level in communities where we sometimes have to make painful shifts in our own thinking – symbolizing and integrating experiences into our self-structure.

6.3 Proposition 18: Acceptance of self

> *'When the individual perceives and accepts into one consistent and integrated system all his sensory and visceral experiences, then he is necessarily more understanding of others and is more accepting of others as separate individuals.' (Rogers 1987: 520)*

When the individual is able to symbolize most of his or her experiences and to integrate them into a total self-concept, such an individual will display greater understanding of others and be able to accept them as separate, unique individuals.

6.3.1 Proposition 18 and the individual

Individuals who are conscious of most of their experiences and have integrated them into a self that contains no contradictions are not threatened by other people's experiences, even when these differ from their own. They are able to say, 'I know who I am' ('I'm OK', proposition 15) and 'I can allow you to be who you are' ('You're OK').

Together, propositions 18 and 19 present the long-term goal of client-centred therapy. However, these propositions presuppose that the facilitators themselves have reached a stage in their lives where they are able to permit and enable other people (especially the clients) to be themselves – even though they differ from the facilitator!

Prospective facilitators may benefit by testing themselves against this thesis. Ask yourself:

- 'What do I experience when people differ from me?'
- 'What do I want to *do* with such people?'
- 'What will happen to me, in interaction with them, if the other parties do *not* change, and what will happen if they do change to become like me?'

Figure 6.2 *We are both OK*

The self of the facilitator is discussed in greater depth in Section E in Chapter 18.

6.3.2 Proposition 18 and the group

The application of this proposition will contribute to the realization of the general objective, which is to assist members to grow or to develop in terms of their self-actualization. Groups could, therefore, help members to develop enough confidence to empower themselves.

The process of developing self-confidence may be hampered in group work if the group facilitator pursues his or her own specific objectives in respect of the group, not allowing members to do things on their own. Such behaviour by the group facilitator may result in:

- group members becoming passive and dependent during group sessions. This again may hamper the communication process in the group because the communication will not be between the group members, but between the facilitator on one side and the group members on the other side.
- members never becoming self-sufficient and therefore never becoming self-empowered. On the other hand, if the facilitator demonstrates a belief in the potential of the members, the members will start to accept themselves. As they become more at peace with themselves, recognizing their so-called good and bad points, they may start to accept one another in the group and because of the acceptance, a climate conducive to communication in the group may occur.

6.3.3 Proposition 18 and the community

The more you become aware of your own self and accept yourself the more you will be able to accept others. The more the people in the community symbolize their experiences and integrate them into their self-concept the more they will accept each other and people from other communities. If the men, the women, or groups of people, for example gay people, 'straight' people, poor people, rich people, people of any colour, etc. symbolize their own experiences, the more they will accept the other groups of people. We often find that 'straight' people will make nasty remarks about gay people or vice versa. It may be unsymbolized fears, anxieties, etc. that make them uneasy. This proposition again stresses the importance of the process of symbolization or conscientization.

The facilitator

One of the main criteria or conditions to facilitate change is regarded by Rogers as the unconditional acceptance of the person or the people. It is, therefore, of the utmost importance that we need to work on our own process of symbolization of our experiences to be able to accept other people and, in particular, our clients.

6.4 Proposition 19: Developing your own valuing process

> 'As the individual perceives and accepts into his self-structure more of his organic experiences, he finds that he is replacing his present value system – based so largely upon introjections which have been distortedly symbolized – with a continuing organismic valuing process.' (Rogers 1987: 522)

As individuals come to perceive and symbolize more of their sensory experiences, integrating these into their self-concept, their value systems hitherto based mainly on distorted symbolization of other people's values (proposition 10) will make way for a process of determining their own values.

6.4.1 Proposition 19 and the individual

The first part of this proposition is linked to propositions 15 and 18. The rest of it indicates another advantage of an integrated, symbolized self (the outcome of therapy). Individuals now decide for themselves what they consider to be important. They do not need to adopt other people's values (including those of the facilitator, proposition 10). It no longer matters all that much whether other people praise them, and they become less dependent on others. Such individuals embark on a process of evaluation, continually testing and examining their values.

Following the discussions in the example provided under propositions 2 and 10, the mother and son may decide on their own norms, regardless of whether these agree or disagree with those of her parents and of his friends, according to that which they themselves consider important.

6.4.2 Proposition 19 and the group

This proposition is the final result of group work. The members have developed their own value systems, and they are capable of working independently

Figure 6.3 *Weighing up the pros and cons for yourself*

and of evaluating their own functioning. In addition, the members are able to solve, manage, and control their own problems. As soon as group members display these attributes, it is an indication to the group facilitator that he or she has become superfluous and should or may leave the group. You may have noticed that it is not a question of terminating or dissolving the group. As far as the facilitator is concerned, the group has been terminated, but for members of the group the working phase may only just have started, because the formal group may now become an informal group.

To summarize, this section on the proposition and the approach reminds one of the crank in vintage cars. The crank is merely the 'facilitator' of the engine. It is the engine that has the potential or mechanics to run or move. Once the car is cranked up or started, the engine kicks in and starts the car running on its own. In a group work situation, the group worker, with his or her skills, can be seen as the facilitator of the communication and group process. Through communication, the members (engine) are facilitated to identify the group's needs as well as how they are going to fulfil them.

6.4.3 Proposition 19 and the community

Adopted values are now replaced by internal 'homegrown' values and actions indigenous to the community. (Compare with 'levels of awareness' from Hope and Timmel (1995 (3): 78).) Homegrown values and actions or the appreciation of homegrown values and actions will be the result of people accepting and appreciating themselves. The African Renaissance movement is an example of this process of moving away from Western standards and values as the only accepted ways to believing and appreciating their own values and ways of doing.

In communities we can see this usually when the members of the community really take ownership of the projects and proudly show them to others. They can, for instance, invite their sponsors, other community members, or their leaders to tell them 'this is ours, we did it ourselves'.

As indicated in proposition 18, the community will indicate when they feel sufficiently adequate and well equipped to continue, and the facilitator actually becomes redundant. According to Swanepoel (1992: 3–4), certain growth, development, and empowerment have occurred through the learning process that took place in the community, causing them to become self-sufficient, to develop self-esteem, and to maintain their own values. They do not look to other people as the experts. They see themselves as experts and value their own knowledge and skills: 'We can do it ourselves.'

The facilitator

As facilitators we are trained to adopt certain values that may not be congruent with our own value systems. This may cause some psychological tension as discussed previously. If you learn from, or integrate a theory and its implied values into your own self-structure, those values will become part of you. Take the value of respect. If you work with a person and find it difficult to act respectfully toward that person, it is important to symbolize why this might be the situation. Until you can symbolize your experience of the person, you will not be able to act congruently in a respectful manner towards that person.

The facilitator's values

Introduction

In this section we are going to explain the meaning of values and the role they play in the process of rendering assistance; define the values of respect, individualization, self-determination, and confidentiality; and explain how the said values are operationalized in working with individuals, groups, and communities.

Although specific values have been identified they are all inter-related. *Values reflect the facilitator's entire attitude towards humankind.* Professional values more particularly reflect the attitudes of facilitators towards their clients, the people in need they are involved with. Such values are applied (or operationalized) in practice and form the basis of the total process of rendering assistance.

The value bias may not be consciously symbolized, yet still influence the facilitator's behaviour (proposition 13). It is, therefore, important for all facilitators to try to examine their own values in terms of the people they are

Call a plumber when you have plumbing problems

involved with. For instance, many people (including facilitators) feel awkward when reference is made to people in need – mixed feelings of pity and superiority are often experienced towards people who cannot cope with their situations or with life. It is somewhat peculiar that such sentiments are felt particularly towards people in psychosocial need. For example, when people experience problems with the plumbing in their homes, it makes sense for them to call in the services of a qualified plumber. People who cannot cut and style their hair themselves visit a qualified hairdresser and people who are physically ill see a qualified physician. We do not pity them or think less of them for asking for help. Why should it be any different for people who are experiencing psychosocial problems to consult a qualified facilitator?

Activity

Analyse (as honestly as possible and for your own edification only) your attitude towards your clients.
1   Do you respect them?
2   Do you believe in their potential to grow and to function independently? If not, why not?
3   If you do believe in their potential, how do you demonstrate these sentiments to your clients?

In practice, the facilitator faces many obstacles which may hamper the application of professional values. These obstacles are discussed in detail by Boy and Pine (1983: 93–95) and can be summarized as follows:

- The values that facilitators internalize in a programme of studies do not seem operable in the real world.
- All groups that pressure the facilitator to do more and to do different things are well intended. They identify certain needs.
- Groups insist that the facilitator is in the best position to meet their needs.

According to Boy and Pine (1983: 95), the problem is that institutions and pressure groups that influence the organizational behaviour of institutions often identify human needs that are *not* the actual needs of clients within a community. Such institutions and groups often identify needs that are politically expedient, needs that flow into the interests and competencies of staff, needs that are in concert with the interests of funding agencies, needs that have a certain ethical or moral bias, and needs that have become popularized by the mass communications media. According to Boy and Pine (1983: 94), such demands and pressures not only place a heavy burden on the facilitator's time and energy, but they create a psychological burden for the facilitator. The pressured and harassed facilitator becomes easily confused regarding professional identity, mission, and role. The question is whether you as facilitator attach sufficient importance to the issue of professional values and whether you still have the energy to take a stand and even to take on the authorities and other professions on this issue.

What exactly are these values and how do they relate to the person-centred approach? Authors such as Glassman and Kates (1990: 21) place such emphasis on the value of the human being that they refer not merely to values, but speak of human values. They furthermore emphasize aspects such as support, cooperation, voluntary participation, and respect for differences between people.

In this section we will give the theoretical background as well as examples of how to use the values of respect, individualization, self-determination, and confidentiality in working with individuals, groups, and communities.

In closing, it is useful to remember this statement by Wood (1995: 18): 'The person-centred approach is not a psychology, a philosophy, a school, a movement, not many other things frequently imagined. It is merely what its name suggests, an *approach*.'

Therefore it is a psychological posture, a 'way of being' – a way of being towards individuals, groups, and communities. This 'way of being' is realized through 'living out' the values of the approach. The values should become part of the facilitator's value system and not something that we apply when necessary or needed. It is a way of being when moving alongside the individual, group, and community.

To demonstrate these values in practice the facilitator needs certain skills. These skills are discussed in Sections C, D, and E.

CHAPTER 7

Respect

7.1 Introduction

For all those who really believe in the person-centered approach and who want their clients to experience it, the use of respect is central. Rogers (1987: 19), however, warns against the habit of using respect only as a method or technique. According to him, respect is more an attitude that is supplemented by certain techniques and methods. In other words, if you show respect to clients you allow them to decide what they really want to do. By using the communication process clients are enabled to be their own 'judges'.

This is only possible if you as facilitator believe in the abilities of your clients and try to understand your clients (whether the client is an individual, group, or community), their self-definition, and their purpose in life.

7.2 Respect and the individual

Rogers (1951: 24) describes the facilitator's basic hypothesis concerning humankind as respect and the belief:

> *that the individual has a sufficient capacity to deal constructively with all those aspects of his life which can potentially come into conscious awareness. This means ... a meaningful demonstration of the counsellor's acceptance of the client as a person who is competent to direct himself.*

This hypothesis or assumption reflects an attitude and belief that every person is worthy of our respect and esteem. Without such respect, facilitators cannot communicate empathetically or facilitate growth because they will not be able to create an atmosphere of acceptance and freedom in which clients can reveal their deepest, darkest, and most painful experiences without fear of rejection. Boy and Pine (1983: 83) agree with the above when they state that 'the creation of a liberating counselling relationship requires that the counsellor not only have a fundamental belief in the client's tendency toward health, but that the counsellor create a counselling atmosphere in which this tendency is nourished'.

In order to facilitate the client's growth, it is necessary to believe in his or her potential for growth and to create the conditions in which growth can take place freely.

Figure 7.1 *Creating conditions in which growth can take place freely*

Many of you may regard such an attitude as wishful thinking, something that is not possible in practice. You may be thinking that it is easier said than done, for how is one supposed to respect someone, for instance, who has raped a child, or who has committed murder, or who is very poor or old and confused?

When facilitators no longer believe in the client's striving for growth, the true purpose of any helping process may be questioned. Does the mission to help people to help themselves still remain plausible? This is a most important issue that all facilitators must resolve for themselves. As far back as 1964, Rogers (in Boy and Pine 1983: 80) addressed the dilemma of developing one's own value system:

> *Even more important, perhaps, is the fact that the modern indi-*
> *vidual is assailed from every angle by divergent and contradictory*
> *value claims. It is no longer possible, as it was in the not too distant*
> *historical past, to settle comfortably into the value system of one's*
> *forebears or one's community and live out one's life without ever*
> *examining the nature and the assumptions of that system.*

The following are suggested ways for the facilitator to implement respect in practice.

7.2.1 Refrain from judgement

Facilitators are there to help their clients, not to judge them. It is not the facilitator's role to judge clients as being good or bad and guilty or innocent and to apportion blame. The facilitator's task is rather to understand clients and their pain and to help them grow.

The concept of unconditional positive regard is important in this regard. It relates to clients' thoughts, needs, behaviour, feelings, self, and values. They must feel that the facilitator accepts them even when they do not yet accept themselves. Thus, the facilitator must demonstrate consistent willingness to extend understanding, irrespective of the client's behaviour and of whether the facilitator approves of that behaviour or not. This does not mean that the facilitator gives up his or her own values, but only that during the facilitation process, the values and pain of the client come first. Putting the client first thus becomes one of the facilitator's own values or aims.

According to Hepworth and Larsen (1990: 53), facilitators are confronted with the need to retain their own values without imposing them on others and to refrain from the tendency to condemn people whose behaviour is offensive to the facilitator. This is linked to the injunction to remain serene and imperturbable and not to react with embarrassment, shock, or disapproval when people discuss painful situations. Facilitators will be able to accept people whose behaviour conflicts with their personal values only if they have developed openness and self-acceptance (see propositions 18 and 19).

Failure to do so may reduce their effectiveness, for it is impossible to hide negative feelings or to camouflage them so well that the client does not become aware of the facilitator's incongruence.

7.2.2 Enable the client to work through pain

The helping process is likely to be painful. The facilitator shows respect for the client by empathizing with the pain rather than by avoiding it. This is done on the assumption that the client is prepared to pay the price for more effective living. Thus, respect makes demands on the one hand, and on the other hand it offers the client someone who will be there while it is happening. (See also proposition 17.)

7.3 Respect and the group

According to Gordon (in Rogers 1987: 338), group facilitators show respect when they accept the values of group members and also accept the differences in their values. Group facilitators also realize that they cannot use (abuse) influence or lead members to achieve their own objectives or values. Gordon (in Rogers 1987: 338) also mentions that group members are people who do not want someone with superior qualifications and values to prescribe to them. The group-centred facilitator sees the group as an organization that exists for its members. It offers members the opportunity to express themselves and to satisfy their needs. The group facilitator furthermore believes that the group itself should indicate the direction of the group work.

Furthermore, Gordon (in Rogers 1987: 338) gives group facilitators guidelines according to which they can determine for themselves whether they have respect for the group and its members or not. Questions they have to answer are the following:

- Do I trust the capacities of the group, and of the individuals in the group, to meet the problems with which we are faced, or do I basically trust myself?
- Do I free the group for creative discussion by being willing to understand, accept, and respect all attitudes, or do I find myself trying subtly to manipulate group discussion so that it comes out my way?
- Am I willing to be responsible for those aspects of action that the group has delegated to me?

- Do I trust the individual (group member) to do his or her job?
- When tensions occur, do I try to make it possible for them to be brought out into the open?

Respect is present in a group when the group facilitator:
- listens carefully to what the members are saying. Experience has shown that group facilitators are generally good listeners. Readers who need more guidance on how to listen in a group can refer to Chapter 12
- tries to understand what is said by the group members. This means that the facilitator views that which group members say within the appropriate context or in terms of the group members' frame of reference
- understands what group members are saying
- accepts what members are saying
- communicates a non-evaluative attitude
- communicates and demonstrates empathy
- uses the members' resources in the communication process.

Therefore, an attitude of 'listen most carefully to members, but never believe a word they say' cannot be regarded as respect for group members.

Example 7.1

In a group, where the members were discussing what respect means in practical terms, one of the members said it means that one has to stand in the shoes of the other person. Another member was not satisfied with this explanation, and said that a better example would be that a person has to stand *on* the shoes of someone else while the particular person is still wearing them. The group members and facilitator were surprised and asked the member to explain his metaphor. The member explained that people often listen until they hear what they want to hear and then follow their own train of thought. If the facilitator were wearing a member's shoes, he or she could easily follow his or her own train of thought. However, if a person was to stand on the shoes that the other person was wearing, he or she wouldn't be able to move if the person wearing the shoes was not prepared to move.

The implication of this example is that in a group, the facilitator will not be able to change the pattern of thought unless the members are prepared to change it. Listening that is aimed simply at confirming the group facilitator's ideas and programme is, therefore, not acceptable to the members.

Example 7.2 (Example where respect did not occur.)

In a mixed group of teenagers (boys and girls), the group facilitator decided at one of the meetings that group members should work together in pairs. She also decided that each pair should consist of a boy and a girl. This decision caused moans and groans in the group. However, the facilitator insisted that the pairs consist of a boy and girl. The result of her insistence was that one of the girls decided to leave the group. The facilitator even allowed her to leave the group since, according to the client-centred approach, the girl had the right to do so. As further motivation for allowing the girl to leave the group, the facilitator mentioned that the girl was experiencing personality problems for which she first had to undergo individual therapy.

Another example of respect is respecting people's traditions and customs.

Example 7.3

In a group of traditional Zulu people, the facilitator did not take into account their culture and traditions, and both young Zulu women and elderly Zulu men were included in the same group. Communication proved to be a problem from the outset because, traditionally, a Zulu woman is not permitted to contradict a Zulu male. Furthermore, a young person is required to respect older people, and one of the ways of showing such respect would be not to contradict them. The facilitator could clearly see that some of the Zulu women were not happy with events in the group, but they had to keep quiet because of their age and gender. The women only started participating in the group after special support from the facilitator. Comments such as 'I notice that you are smiling' by the facilitator and later by group members helped them to communicate.

Even disregarding a less obvious aspect such as the venue in which groups meet may cause problems in the communication process.

Example 7.4

A number of patients with various mental problems were included in a group in order to be prepared for release. A lounge with an informal atmosphere was used as a venue. As the lounge was not available for the fifth meeting, the facilitator decided to use the therapy room without obtaining the consent of group members. The facilitator found the group session to be a problem. The members would not cooperate and would not communicate as in previous sessions. The change in the pattern of behaviour and communication was because some members had unpleasant memories of the therapy room.

If the facilitator respects the group and each individual group member, the members will experience the facilitator as real, caring, understanding, and flexible in his or her viewpoints. The aforementioned is a prerequisite for a safe climate that again will help the members to communicate freely, focus on themselves, and to take risks when needed in the group. Flexibility also means that facilitators will be compliant in their use of communication in the group. Rogers (Corey 1990: 300) identified fifteen characteristics that may be perceived during any communication process. To make it easier for the facilitator Rogers (1974: 126) reduced the fifteen characteristics to six phases, namely:

- Phase 1 in which the members focus on external and impersonal factors
- Phase 2 in which the members sometimes describe some of their feelings
- Phase 3 in which the members describe their feelings in the here and now
- Phase 4 in which the members describe the feelings and experiences they are experiencing now
- Phase 5 in which the members describe all the feelings in personal terms in the here and now situation, and
- Phase 6 in which the members accept the feelings and experiences as their own.

In 1987 he reduced the six phases to three steps, namely

- Step 1 catharsis or ventilation, that is, the members express their personal feelings about their situation
- Step 2 development of insight into the origin and nature of their difficulties or situation, and
- Step 3 the making of positive choices and decisions in regard to their difficulties or situation (1987: 23).

Facilitators who force the group members during their first contact to communicate in the framework of Phase 6 or Step 3 have no respect for the members.

Warning: Rogers does not want facilitators to work with recipes when communicating. It was with hesitation that he identified the six phases and three steps. We must, therefore, treat this theory cautiously.

Activity

You are facilitating a group of elderly people to function independently within their community. A visit by a group of community leaders and the Minister of Health has been planned for the next meeting. The group has decided to serve tea and cake for the visitors. They also made the arrangements as to who would bring what. You as facilitator are aware that some of the members are forgetful and may forget to bring cake or tea. Discuss how you will ensure that those members meet their obligations without prejudice to their self-respect in the group.

7.4 Respect and the community

Respecting the community is the gateway to the community and the facilitation of the participatory process. Respect means that the facilitator regards people as human beings, believes in the potential and abilities of the members of the community, respects and trusts them, and separates the behaviour from the person. Respecting people means to trust them, to listen to them, and to accept them with a non-judgemental attitude. Respect also means respecting their values, traditions, and ways of doing things. We also respect the plurality of voices, the variety of discourses, and the different meanings.

Treating the community with respect therefore refers to the way in which the facilitator sees, believes, acts, or behaves towards members of the community. Our respect for the people we work with must permeate every facet of our work with them. It will be shown in seemingly small matters such as our punctuality for appointments, our reliability about times, the returning of phone calls; and in promptly obtaining information that we have promised. How we address people and whether we pay attention to their views and perceptions also shows our respect. The principle of facilitating their active involvement in the helping process is of itself an expression of respect. It conveys that we do not see them as helpless but it gives a message that we see them as having the capacity to share with us in the work of reaching solutions and finding new, more rewarding paths of action (Hancock 1997: 32).

The facilitator

Every action we take and every skill we use should demonstrate our respect to people. Respect should be expressed in everything we say and do – and our manner of saying and doing – throughout the helping process. This means that we have to look critically at everything we do and say – even in the smallest actions such as returning a phone call and the other things that were mentioned.

CHAPTER 8

Individualization

8.1 Introduction

If the facilitator accepts the value of individualization, he or she, according to Rogers (1987: 29) 'assumes the internal frame of reference of the client, to perceive the world as the client sees it, to perceive the client himself as he is seen by himself, to lay aside all perceptions from the external frame of reference while doing so, and to communicate something of this empathic understanding to the client.' To illustrate this, Van der Kolk (1985: 235) discusses the difference in the interpretation of the word 'individualization' between the Americans and certain Asian cultures. While the Americans put great emphasis on individualization, certain Asian cultures put more emphasis on the group and the community. This difference in interpretation will definitely affect the facilitation process.

Taking this into consideration, it will only be possible for the facilitator in a country like South Africa with its different cultures to make a success of facilitation if individualization is taken into account.

8.2 Individualization and the individual

In terms of propositions 1 and 2, each person's experiences and perceptions of life and himself or herself are *unique*. This includes needs, behaviour (proposition 5), emotions (proposition 6), the self (proposition 8), and values (proposition 10). It is not always easy to implement these ideas or values, especially when the facilitator is active in a specialized field. One can very easily generalize (seeing people as stereotypes) and label, for instance, by believing that all 'alcoholics' are the same. And yet people with a drinking problem differ even physically: one may drink only a bottle of wine before losing control, whereas another may be able to drink two bottles of liquor before losing control. People also do not react the same when under the influence of alcohol: one may become weepy and sad, another may become angry at everyone around him or her, while a third may wish only to sleep. If even the physical reaction to the same substance differs, why is it sometimes so hard to accept that the personal aspects will also differ? Similarly, everyone with such a problem will have a different perception of who they are, and what needs are being satisfied by such behaviour. They themselves may not even be aware of such needs at a conscious level (see propositions 11 and 13). Saying that all alcoholics are the same is like saying that all women or all men are the same. Do you think that you are the same as all others of the same gender? In spite of certain similarities (your gender) you are certainly unique in other respects, just as people with a particular problem (such as alcohol dependency) differ considerably in spite of certain similarities.

Ignoring or disregarding this uniqueness means that the unique potential, forces, and direction of the person one is dealing with are also being lost. Both the facilitator and the client may start believing that the client is just one more 'alcoholic', who will necessarily follow the same route as all others before. This may discourage both the facilitator and the client, and the facilitator's task will become tedious. The contrary is also true. The facilitator who approaches each client as a unique person will find a challenge in each new situation, like a lucky packet that simply has to be opened to reveal the surprise.

Activity

If you already find yourself in practice (or have in the past), consider the nature of your approach to clients:

1 How do you regard and treat them?
2 How do you experience the work you do? Do you still enjoy it?
3 Are you still confident that you and your clients will be able to achieve something? If you are not, why not? If you are, to what would you attribute your optimism?

Figure 8.1 Surprise, surprise!

If you are still studying to be a facilitator, ask yourself:
1 How do you react to people who have transgressed the country's laws?
2 Are there any people you will truly never want to understand?

8.3 Individualization and the group

It is interesting that, although Rogers emphasized the uniqueness of individuals, he also mentioned a few basic abilities that each individual human being possesses. These abilities are that human beings are basically:
- rational
- responsible
- realistic, and
- have the potential to grow (Farber, et al. 1996: 6).

Rennie (1998: 2) put these abilities in person-centred language with the following quote:

> *'We are human beings. As human beings we have the ability to*
> - *think about ourselves*
> - *think about our thinking*
> - *treat ourselves as objects of our attention, and*
> - *use what we find there as a point of departure in deciding what to do next.'*

Although each individual possesses these abilities, we must remember that everyone uses them in their own unique way.

Individualization of group members and the group is stressed by virtually each and every author on groups:
- According to Douglas (1976: 26), one of the basic principles that can be formulated from the philosophy and knowledge of group work is 'a genuine acceptance of each individual with his unique strengths and weaknesses'.
- Corey (1990: 201) states that 'thoughts, feelings, beliefs, convictions, attitudes and actions are all expressions of the uniqueness of the person'.
- Glassman and Kates (1990: 114) are of the opinion that interaction showing respect for differences between group members is a prerequisite for a democratic communal help system such as a group. Glassman and Kates (1990: 114) add that 'this interaction is reflected in the members' abilities to listen to, to respond to, and to incorporate different opinions, values, cultures, and personalities without requiring adherence to a narrow ideology or to a narrow spectrum of permissible behaviours. Veiled reactions or avoidance of differences is brought to the members' attention'.

- Konopka (1972: 67) says 'he (the group facilitator) must realise that each member is different from everyone else or from any other group, in past, present, and future'. According to Konopka, no teenager is 'just another teenager'. Similarly, an elderly person is not 'just another elderly person'. Both are unique individuals with specific behaviour, needs, and so forth. Konopka (1972: 68) explains that group facilitators are inclined to be inflexible in their application of theoretical knowledge and to cling to the average characteristics for a group of people. This does not imply that we should ignore knowledge or theory because it does present a framework of possible human behaviour as well as possible explanations for such behaviour. However, theoretical knowledge should be applied circumspectly because certain theories can only reflect the average and general behaviour and explanations of individuals and groups.

In group work, facilitators should bear in mind that they cannot apply generalizations, but should work with the specific characteristics, behaviour, and needs of each individual or group, in other words individualization. It is the task of the group facilitator to identify and acknowledge the uniqueness and specific nature of each member and group. According to Konopka (1972: 126–127), the group facilitator needs to possess certain skills in order to see individuals and groups in their totality and in the light of their individuality. These skills will be discussed in Sections C and D. How individualization is manifested in groups is illustrated in the next three examples.

Example 8.1

In a group of bulimia sufferers, the group facilitator established that one of the girls had been moved to a boarding school. According to the facilitator, the bulimia may have been caused by the fact that the girl had to leave her parents' home. The facilitator consequently planned a group session dealing with the feelings and consequences associated with leaving home. The particular girl was very passive during the meeting. At subsequent meetings, it transpired that the girl's problem was not that she had to leave her home, but that she did not know how to cope with anger. The culture within which she had been raised dictated that anger could not be expressed. What was required, therefore, was for the group to focus on coping with anger rather than on dealing with the feelings associated with leaving home.

Example 8.2

When a member always arrives late for group meetings, it may be a sign that he or she is threatened by the group, but it may also be that the member has other responsibilities that make it impossible for him or her to be on time.

Example 8.3

The behaviour of a group of teenage girls attending a group meeting in sloppy clothes may be attributed to various factors. It may be a sign of rebellion against their mothers and the community, rejection of the existing values and norms of the community, rebellion against the group or facilitator, or even a case of the group wanting to look the same.

Activity

Various programmes have been constructed for groups. Taking individualization as a value into account, would you use such programmes in your group? If so, explain how. If not, substantiate your answer.

8.4 Individualization and the community

This value means to respect, show appreciation for, and encourage the uniqueness of the community. As in the case of an individual or group, the emphasis falls on the uniqueness of each community member, with his or her own frame of reference, experiences, and realities.

Each community is unique because it consists of unique individuals. Often, and mistakenly, the uniqueness of communities is ignored because generalizations are made, for instance, by referring to black communities, white communities, sub-economic communities, rural communities, poor communities, squatter communities, and so forth. This is also a form of labelling.

Each community differs in respect of the values and meanings attached to particular situations. When the facilitator is getting to know the community, the uniqueness of the community is illustrated in particular by the values and meanings attached to specific things and situations.

For instance:

- If the community talks about food, clothes, income, housing, relationships, etc. what does it mean to them?
- What type of food, housing, clothes, income, relationships, etc. are they talking about?
- What are the rituals around these concerns?
- What are their perspectives, experiences, emotions, thought patterns, traditions, ideas, myths?
- Can we listen to them without any value judgement?

We as facilitators therefore have to listen to, and learn from, the people in the community to be able to recognize and discover their uniqueness. The unique experiences of individuals and groups provides a multiplicity of ideas that can be used by the facilitator to create or generate more unique ideas. The community doesn't have to agree on certain issues, but rather must work with the richness of the diversity and utilize and appreciate this diversity. In interesting research done by Du Plessis (2000; 2002) all the different groups of people in a small rural town were interviewed, for example the white aged, farm workers, farmers, coloured aged, unemployed people in the coloured community, unemployed people from the black area, the black aged, etc. Each group related different stories and perceptions, but also shared stories and dreams. The stories from the farm workers from different farms also differed. She showed respect to the community members by listening to them and acknowledging their uniqueness.

The biggest issue regarding the uniqueness of the community comes in when we want to implement and work with preconceived ideas and plans. We tend to listen superficially to the community. Fortunately, some communities are extremely creative despite agencies and developers trying to impose their ideas, as seen in the following example.

Example 8.4

While evaluating a sanitation and toilet project in certain African villages, the manager of the projects noticed that the toilets in one village had not been built according to the specifications. He found that the dividing wall had been built only halfway up, instead of to the roof, so that the men were able to look into the women's toilets and vice versa. When the manager asked his interpreter to explain, he said that the people preferred their toilets without walls because it is cooler. Traditionally, the community would have built the men's and women's toilets in completely separate areas, far apart. The community thus came up with the lower walls as a compromise – meeting the prescribed rules, while trying to value their own way of doing things (Bradshaw 1993: 5).

The facilitator has to listen to, and learn from, the community to be able to know and value their uniqueness embedded in their value systems, experiences, and perceptions.

Example 8.5

Often we come across mothers expressing the need (solution) for a crèche. If the building of the crèche is seen as the need, we can easily replicate the project in different communities. If the crèche is seen as a solution (implied message) to the need, the individual needs of the mothers must be listened to. For example, do they need the crèche for stimulating their children, or for babysitting? A day mother may be the solution to their need.

At an informal settlement, the facilitators came across mothers expressing the 'need' for a crèche (solution). Why a crèche? They were concerned about the safety of their children. In this community, some people believe that if a man rapes a child under the age of five, he will prevent or even cure HIV/Aids. The mothers thus felt that looking after the children at a crèche collectively would provide more safety than individual mothering. The crèche therefore offers a *solution* to their concern. The actual need is the protection of their children and their striving to be good mothers.

The facilitator

According to Hancock (1997: 154) the most important capacities a facilitator should have to be able to *individualize* every community, group, and person are the following. The ability to:

- be free from bias and prejudice. This involves self-awareness in facing and identifying our prejudices and biases
- listen
- move at the client's pace
- be empathic, warm, and non-judgemental, and
- be flexible.

CHAPTER 9

Self-determination

9.1 Introduction

According to Angyal, as quoted by Rogers (1987: 489), 'Life is an autonomous dynamic event which takes place between the organism (client) and the environment. Life processes do not merely tend to preserve life but transcend the momentary status quo of the organism (client), expanding itself continually and imposing its autonomous determination upon an ever increasing realm of events.'

Rogers (1987: 489) adds that the human organism (client) tends to move forward, or as the client will see it, in a direction of growth. To be of assistance to clients, this belief in growth and self-determination is an essential aid in person-centred therapy.

9.2 Self-determination and the individual

As we mentioned in the discussion of respect, the person-centred approach requires faith in humankind's pursuit of growth and self-actualization. This relates to proposition 4. This pursuit needs to be viewed in terms of the *client's* frame of reference. The facilitator cannot decide what the client's goals should be, or what would be best for the client. (This would imply greater belief in and respect for himself or herself than the client.)

Self-determination therefore means that clients determine for *themselves*:
- what they wish to discuss
- how they wish to discuss it
- whether they wish to discuss it (dealing with silence)

- how they experience and perceive themselves and their world (propositions 1 and 2)
- what their needs are (proposition 5)
- how they wish to satisfy their needs in line with that which corresponds with their 'self' (propositions 5 and 8)
- what their own values are and will be (propositions 10 and 19)
- what the threatening experiences are (unsymbolized or distorted, proposition 11) (in this instance it is imperative that facilitators should not think that they know better than the client what is painful or problematic)
- the direction in which to move in the exploration of painful experiences (propositions 17 and 15).

If we accept the principle that each person knows the self better than anyone else, and is therefore in the best position to explore, expose, and understand the self, we see that counsellor direction of a counselling session is non-productive (Boy and Pine 1983: 9, 10).

Figure 9.1 *Each person knows the self better than anyone else*

9.3 Self-determination and the group

In the human sciences, clients are often portrayed as passive, isolated, and unable to help themselves. In the person-centred approach, however, it is believed that human beings are experts on themselves and they are more aware of their own needs and abilities than any therapist could ever be. Therefore, if people are allowed to speak for themselves, social science can reveal, rather than mask, the members' realities. In working with groups it may be possible that we as facilitators too often 'mask' the reality of the group members because we ignore or incorrectly apply the important value of self-determination.

According to the existentialists, self-determination means that one has the freedom to choose between two possibilities (Corey 1990: 261). People are therefore responsible for the pattern that their lives follow. Rogers (in Corey 1985: 250) also believes in the group and group members' right to self-determination: 'The group will move – of this I am confident – but it would be presumptuous to think that I can or should direct that movement toward a specific group goal.' However, it is not necessary to wait passively for the group to move. By using the communication process and phrases such as 'you're angry about ...' or 'you're confused by ...' or 'you think you're bad because ...' it may be possible for the members to develop and to move in a direction that is still their own.

Glassman and Kates (1990: 176) agree with Rogers that group members cannot be forced to change their behaviour or to participate in a group programme that does not interest them. Members' right to self-determination and to make their own decisions must always be taken into account at group sessions.

Peggy Natiello (Farber, et al. 1996: 132) found that since Rogers' death 'the commitment to, and trust in, the self-determination of the client is at risk in the ranks of the client-centered therapists. It (self-determination) is the radical aspect of the approach and the most difficult to practise in a world where lures of expertise and authority are so pervasive'. If we want to facilitate self-determination we must remember, as Rogers (Farber, et al. 1996: 131) said, that 'the therapist becomes the "midwife" of change and not its "originator" '. The group facilitator will therefore not:

- take control away from the group members
- interpret facts and behaviour to the group members
- guide or manipulate the group members, or
- change the direction of the session on his or her own.

Activities

1 Refer to example 7.2 and explain how you would deal with the group, taking the value of self-determination into account. Think of how self-determination and the group process are hampered if the group facilitator makes decisions on behalf of the group.

2 A group of mothers said that they would like to discuss the disciplining of children at the next meeting. The facilitator had an American programme on discipline at her disposal and decided to present this programme. The meeting was a failure. In view of self-determination as a value and the group facilitator listening selectively as a hindrance, explain why the group did not succeed.

3 See example 3.6. In the specific example the facilitator noticed the change in the process. Taking the self-determination of the member and group into consideration, how would you handle the situation? What if the group facilitator does not observe change in the group process?

4 In a group of teenage girls, the facilitator focused on the development of social skills with strong emphasis on self-determination. The group had to decide for itself which issues were to be discussed. For the sixth session, the members decided to discuss relationships with boys. The facilitator established that seven of the ten girls were sexually active. During the session, the three girls who had not been sexually active decided to start experimenting with sex. The group had been presented under the auspices of a school that had conservative values about standards of behaviour between boys and girls. Discuss:

   a) Which factors will you take into account in further dealing with the group?

   b) How will you handle the situation by taking into account the value of self-determination?

9.4 Self-determination and the community

Rogers (1987: 488) states in this regard that:

> *We are talking here about the tendency of the organism to main-tain [and self actualize] ... to achieve the goal of self-maintenance even when the pathway to that goal is blocked ... it moves in the direction of greater independence or self-responsibility ... in the direction of increasing self-government, self-regulation and autonomy, and away from the control of external forces ...*

Self-determination is therefore more than the *choice* made by the people in the community itself. It includes the protection of their self, their values, their traditions and that which is known to them. Self-determination is part of their attempt to self-actualize and grow. Their decisions might be needs-driven, in line with their self-concept and their emotions. It will not necessarily always be the 'best' decision.

Wood (1995: 30) emphasizes that self-determination must not be confused with the myth that individuals control their own destiny. All people are part of a social system and cannot always control what is happening around them. According to Wood (1995: 30), the governing mind does not fully grasp the complete reality in which it functions. Individuals therefore cannot *decide* cognitively what is in their best interests only, but the total organism is capable of self-healing far beyond our current comprehension.

Self-determination is built on the respect we have for the autonomy of the person as being able to heal himself or herself, and as facilitators we create a context for people in which we facilitate the healing and growing process. An implication of this process is that the facilitators need to have a tolerance for uncertainty because *the outcome of the process cannot be predicted*. Wood (1995: 23) comments: 'We tried things that we understood and they did not work. We did things that we did not understand and they did work.'

Freire also believed strongly in the autonomous power of self-determination, which means that people can be trusted to take responsibility for their own decisions and actions. Again the decisions, plans, and responsibilities rest on the participatory way of working between community and facilitator. If we remove their decision-making power we reduce people to objects and show disrespect for their unique knowledge and abilities. Our responsibility, however, is to facilitate a process of critical reflection after which the community can make *informed* decisions based on symbolized experiences. For example, if a community wants to protest against something, they can choose different ways of doing so. They can send a small delegation to see the mayor, they can picket to make their wants known, they can 'toyi-toyi' dancing and singing down the street, disrupting traffic and work, or they can call for strikes. The final decision lies with the community, after the facilitator has taken them through the process of thinking thoroughly about why they want to do that, possible results, what will be most effective, what the consequences will be, what the risks will be, what the consequences for other people will be, etc.

The facilitator

The client's rights are an essential component of sound professional helping. Limitations on this right are, however, imposed by legal requirements, the agency's mandate or policies, and the rights of others. Genuine choice for clients requires a process of symbolized experiences/reasons and that they be fully informed about the choices. The facilitator creates a climate of trust in which clients can explore their experiences, needs, and perceptions and be properly informed, so as to make choices that they can be accountable for. The belief of the facilitator in the Northern Sotho expression *Naka tsa go rweswa ga dikgomarele hlogo*, which means 'One cannot stick the horns of one cow on another – The horns have to grow from within!', also forms the basis for self-determination and individualization.

CHAPTER 10

Confidentiality

10.1 Introduction

Confidentiality is a debatable and controversial issue. In this chapter, we try to highlight some of the dilemmas for your continued consideration.

10.2 Confidentiality and the individual

According to proposition 17, the facilitator should create a climate within which the client feels completely unthreatened, allowing the client to consciously acknowledge and explore painful experiences that have not been symbolized (or that have been distorted) because they threaten the self (proposition 11). The facilitator therefore facilitates the acknowledgement of painful material by the client. This gives rise to two issues: what should we do with this material, and will the client entrust us with such material if he or she is not entirely certain that it will not be repeated to others or used against him or her? Would you share your deepest experiences with someone if you were not certain that they would not be repeated to others? If you were to discuss a sensitive issue with someone and then found that it had been repeated to someone else, how would you feel about it? Is there any reason why the client would not feel the same way or, even worse, should not be allowed to feel the same way? People may be unique, but one can nevertheless expect a negative reaction, such as disappointment, shame, or anger if confidentiality is broken. It is also very unlikely that the client will again trust the facilitator.

According to Odendal et al. (1987: 1273), trust includes believing in someone's honesty and loyalty. Confidentiality means that what has been said will remain private and will not be repeated to someone else. What are the practical implications of this confidentiality? Think about these scenarios:

- Once you have, for instance, conducted an interview with a married woman, are you entitled to tell her husband about it?
- Or to tell the wife about a conversation with her husband?
- Are you entitled to inform parents of conversations with their child?

We often say 'Yes' in the above situations, believing that breaking confidence is in the best interest of the client. But who should decide what is best, the facilitator or the client? How can we be sure that we know what is best? (See propositions 1, 2, and 4.) Responsibility towards the community raises another dilemma. When we hear something that poses a threat to others, we have to make it known. Does your client know this? Could it be that he or she has a need to report something of this nature? If the client has shared such information with the facilitator, it may be an indication that it is no longer possible to keep things bottled up (even if this is on an unsymbolized level). According to propositions 17, 18, and 19, we can help the client to change the way in which he or she deals with needs and his or her behaviour.

The key to solving this dilemma is the *client*. The facilitator has to decide on any action *together* with the client. You and your client are therefore involved in a partnership, and if you bear that in mind, it may be easier not to feel overwhelmed by the client, or your own sense of responsibility. This will make it possible for you to respect the client and will enable clients to respect themselves (and you) as well.

The above discussion already gives you an idea that confidentiality is not an easy value to uphold. You need to be continuously aware of making it happen. In this sense then, it is also a skill, something that you have to *do*, in order to create the necessary conditions for effective facilitation. Some of you might expect your future employer to make facilities available where confidentiality can easily be maintained, but this is not always the case. For instance, you might be expected to interview clients in an

Figure 10.1 Confidentiality

open-plan office, or one in which the doors cannot close, or close completely. In any of these situations, your conversations might be overheard, which nullifies confidentiality.

Activity

Imagine you find yourself in the situations mentioned above: In each case, describe what you could do to maintain or create a sense of confidentiality.

10.3 Confidentiality and the group

To maintain confidentiality in a group, the group facilitator as well as the group members must be confidants. In other words, they must have the ability to keep the information that has been shared in the group. To truly maintain confidentiality, it is necessary to believe in the worthiness of group members as human beings and to respect them.

Even group facilitators who do respect the group members sometimes unconsciously breach confidentiality by:

- using the names of group members in reports
- asking members too soon after the group has been formed to reveal personal information to the other members
- not obtaining members' consent to make reports available to other institutions
- not obtaining members' consent for discussing their actions in the group with other professionals, such as a case facilitator
- passing on group information on minors to the parents without the consent of such minors
- not obtaining a member's consent to reveal certain information to a group (it often happens, for instance, that a group member provides the group facilitator with information between two meetings. The group facilitator conveys the information to the group by saying: 'Mandla, may I tell the group what you told me yesterday, or do you want to tell them?')
- making audio and video recordings of groups without the consent of members
- putting pressure and even group pressure on members to reveal personal confidential information about themselves to the group before they are ready to do so.

Example 10.1

During the first meeting, Agnes was one of the most outspoken members in the group. Due to illness, she could not attend the second group meeting, during which the members consented to an audio recording being made of the third meeting. At the third meeting, Agnes was very quiet and did not participate in the group discussion. The group facilitator noticed this and asked whether she was still feeling ill. She placed her left index finger on her mouth and pointed to the tape recorder with her right hand.

This example, which actually happened, clearly shows how important it is that group facilitators at all times take into account the confidentiality not only of the group, but also of each individual group member. In the example, the group facilitator should first have obtained the consent of members who had been absent from the second meeting before starting the third session.

Example 10.2

In a group consisting of women experiencing marital problems, the group facilitator expected members to discuss their marital problems as early as the second meeting. One of the members suggested that the group should rather discuss the behaviour of a well-known person who experiences problems in her marriage.

In the example, the facilitator was wrong to expect the group members to reveal personal information that they did not want to discuss. Because the particular member wished to remain in the group, she made a counter-proposal that she did not find too personal. A member who did not attach much value to the group would simply have left.

Confidentiality is especially important in certain group situations, for instance:

- where the group members are in regular contact with one another outside the group
- where people are in institutions, where the release of confidential information may be misused not only by other residents, but also by the staff of the institution
- where the group occurs in a work situation where management may use confidential information against the facilitators or group members.

Example 10.3

Facilitators are sometimes regarded as part of a company's management. In a company where management intended to retrench certain employees, the facilitator was requested to release to management certain information that the group regarded as confidential. The facilitator refused, but management pressured her by, among other tactics, asserting that she was disloyal to the company and its management. Management again demanded to be given access to the confidential information.

Activity

Consider how you would deal with the situation described in example 10.3.

10.3.1 Developing confidentiality in the group

Some group facilitators (such as Van der Kolk 1985: 190) experience no difficulty with confidentiality. According to these group facilitators, the group members know exactly how much to say without exposing themselves or the other group members. Van der Kolk (1985: 15) further points out that if group members and facilitators share a mutual trust, this improves the group's functioning. However, Konopka (1972: 89) cautions that confidentiality should not be forced on members, but should develop from 'a voluntary effort on the part of the group members'. Confidentiality, even when as part of a contract, may therefore never be enforced by the group facilitator.

Van der Kolk (1985: 15) states that confidentiality should receive attention as early as in the pre-group phase. During this phase the group could be asked whether they would like to discuss the exact meaning of confidentiality in the group, how confidentiality will be applied, why confidentiality is important to the group, and also how difficult it will be to apply confidentiality at all times and to strengthen mutual trust. Corey (1990: 30) agrees that confidentiality should be negotiated in the group.

Confidentiality and trust are reinforced when group facilitators show that they are serious about confidentiality. The facilitator can do so, for instance, when a member asks for permission to share something that has happened in the group with his or her spouse. It would be easy to grant permission, but if the facilitator takes confidentiality and self-determination seriously and wants the group to assume responsibility for maintaining confidentiality, the group should be allowed to decide.

Establishing confidentiality is not a single event, but forms part of the group communication process. That is why members should be reminded of confidentiality from time to time as the process develops and should think about it as the climate becomes more open and members become prepared to divulge personal and confidential information more easily.

10.3.2 Is confidentiality a myth?

In the discussion so far, it has largely been assumed that confidentiality should be maintained at all times. Schwartz and Zalba (1971: 20) point out that it is more difficult to control confidentiality in working with groups than in working with individuals. Group members themselves often tell their friends, parents, and spouses what happened in the group. Schwartz and Zalba (1971: 20) quote a group facilitator who said that confidentiality is a myth.

Although various group facilitators have said that confidentiality must be maintained at all costs, Corey (1990: 31) also feels that the group facilitator may breach confidentiality under certain circumstances, such as the following:

- If a member's behaviour poses a danger to himself or herself or to the community, the group facilitator may release information for the protection of the community. This information may, however, only be revealed after consultation with, and with the consent of, the group member.

Activity

What would you do if the group member refuses to give consent in the above situation? Before you answer the question, also read Section E.

Information may be released to the parents who have consented to their children attending the group sessions. According to Corey (1990: 32), however, such information may never be released without the consent of the child, and the child should also be present when the information is conveyed to the parents. Corey is nevertheless of the opinion that children should be encouraged to tell their parents what happens in the group. Parents should also be informed during consultation that group facilitators intend telling the children what is said during telephone conversations. This is not only of significance to confidentiality, but also may prevent parents from providing children with inaccurate information in respect of telephone conversations.

Activity

How would you act in each of the following three situations, taking confidentiality into account? Substantiate your answers:

1 The headmaster of a high school asks the group facilitator to provide him with the names of group members who may be using drugs. The headmaster needs the names in order to take disciplinary steps against the pupils.
2 A probation officer calls and asks the group facilitator to evaluate a group member. The information will be used to determine whether the group member needs to continue serving a jail sentence.
3 A member admitted to the group that his parents were supplying him with drugs. He then sells some of the drugs to other children.

If the values of respect, individualization, and self-determination are handled correctly by the facilitator in the group, confidentiality may not really become an issue. We believe that this is the reason why books on the person-centred approach seldom refer specifically to confidentiality.

10.4 Confidentiality and the community

Confidentiality means that the information that the client reveals to the facilitator is confidential and may not be released to any person or organization without the consent of the person. The question is how this can be achieved within a community. Is the information that communities provide in any way confidential? After all, the issues are not personal, but concern communal interests.

Activity

1 Is confidentiality a value that applies to the community?
2 If you are working in a community, ask different groups or individuals their opinions regarding confidentiality and how you as facilitator and community should deal with information shared with each other.

A facilitator who communicates with a community attempts to build a relationship with the community based on trust. Trust is developed by acting *respectfully* and working in participation with the community and treating its members as worthy of human dignity. When the community allows the facilitator to enter the community, this implies that they trust him or her to protect their dignity, value them, and treat them with respect. It is important for the community to experience that they as people, their values and beliefs, are being respected. That is their security and the guidelines of their existence. These values may not be judged or criticized.

Confidentiality also means that the community trusts that what they reveal to the facilitator will be validated and respected.

Example 10.4

Isaac had been appointed as a developer in a village. On the recommendation of someone in the community, he went to talk to Mr Gideon*, the bartender, who was in close contact with the community and especially with the young people. After his conversation with Mr Gideon, Isaac called the person who had sent him to Gideon and the following conversation took place:

'Why did you send me to Gideon?' asked Isaac.

'You mean you've already been out there? I must say you are dedicated, Isaac ... Well, to tell you the truth, I had some workers working on the back road here at the farm and they were all talking about what a character Gideon was. I had taken them some lunch and they asked me to join them. Gideon was like a boss from what I could gather. I've never met him but that gang of workers spoke well of him. How was your trip?'

'It was a wild goose chase. It's a good thing we're friends ... He's too much of a businessman and only thinks of his bar. He seems to be some kind of a trouble-maker and I wouldn't be surprised if they don't like him over at the school. From what the principal told me, the teachers are a pretty conservative bunch and I would think that any man who sells liquor to kids is low in their estimation. And Gideon has had some kind of run-in with the local authorities. He's just interested in making money, I'll tell you.'

* All names have been changed in the case study.

Activity

1   What does this conversation tell you about trust, respect, and confidentiality and Isaac's value system?

2   If Isaac's friend should repeat to Gideon what the community developer had said about him, what do you think the outcome could be?

3   The information that Gideon provided concerning the community was not confidential, so why should it not be repeated?

Feedback to the donors, agencies, or people involved should be done in participation with the community or preferably by the community itself. The following are the golden rules relating to confidentiality in communities:

- Be aware of the value, conviction, and attitude with which the information is conveyed. Is human dignity being respected?
- Never link the information to the person *unless* the person has consented to that being done.
- The community or people in the community share and decide which information should be revealed and how it should be shared. For example, if a proposal for funding a project has to go to a donor agency, the community (if necessary with the assistance of the facilitator) draws up the proposal, deciding which information can go to the particular agency or donor.

The research of Du Plessis (2000) is a good example of how to deal with confidentiality in communities. She was (and still is) a facilitator as well as a researcher in the rural community. She respected the community by treating every bit of information with confidentiality and would not bring other professionals, donors, or interested people into the community without their consent. After the completion of her research paper she submitted it to the community for their consent before publishing it. Confidentiality is also about transparency to the community and confidentiality to the outside world at all times and in all situations.

The facilitator

Confidentiality is central to the helping relationship and in professional practice is governed by the code of ethics. Confidentiality is, however, not cut and dried, but has many grey areas. We need to think critically about every situation before we take action. When are situations private affairs and when are they social matters or events? When do we protect a client and when do we protect the community? Are we at all times acting in a respectful manner towards the clients?

Activity

Discuss this matter with social workers, psychologists, nurses, and other professionals to get clarity on difficult issues regarding confidentiality. List them for yourself in preparation for practice. Here are some to start with:

- What do you do if you start working and you find that your office walls are not sound proof and that the people sitting next to your office can hear what you and your client are discussing?

- In a rural town people see Mrs W go into your office. They know the circumstances. Someone stops you in the street and asks you how she is. What would your response be?

Continue collecting these incidences. Breaches of confidentiality are the main reason that clients report social workers and other professionals to their governing bodies.

Putting thinking and values into practice: Dealing with symbolized experiences

Introduction

We hope that, after reading these chapters, you will be able to use the following skills in communicating with individuals, groups, and communities within the framework of the person-centred approach:

- attentiveness
- listening
- empathy.

Communication with individuals

Rogers (1951: 5, 6) is not particularly concerned with the techniques of rendering assistance. In his opinion, the facilitator's entire attitude and action should be such that it facilitates the growth of the client as a person. In time, the facilitator assimilates the theory and values and is able to implement these aspects in *his or her own unique way*. (See proposition 12, to find action that fits with the facilitator's 'professional' self.)

Nevertheless, it is initially not easy to convert this theory into action. Because the theory focuses largely on understanding the client as a person, a newcomer may get the impression that the facilitator is not being active. The theory defines clients as the experts on their own lives, so that clients are the ones who determine the direction and rate of the facilitating process. The facilitator's role is therefore non-directive, in other words facilitators do *not* decide on behalf of their clients what their experiences are or should be.

This does *not* mean that the facilitator is passive.

> *'This misconception of the approach (that it is merely passive and has a laissez faire policy) has led to considerable failure in counseling – and for good reason. In the first place, the passivity and seeming lack of interest or involvement is experienced by the client as rejection, since indifference is in no real way the same as acceptance. In the second place, a laissez faire attitude does not in any way indicate to the client that he is regarded as a person of worth. Thus, (with) the counselor who plays a merely passive role ... many clients will leave both disappointed in their failure to receive help and disgusted with the counselor for having nothing to offer.'*
> *(Rogers 1987: 27)*

Inexperienced facilitators often have this kind of experience, as it can be hard to find the difference between doing nothing (being passive), and giving advice or solutions (suggestions) to a client's problems. Being actively non-directive is not easy. On the contrary, understanding clients and facilitating their growth requires intense concentration and considerable skill. For instance, if a client is unemployed, it may be easier to pick up the phone and arrange employment than to *enable* the client to find ways of earning an income. And yet it is the aim of the facilitation process to enable people to help themselves, therefore to facilitate an independent and, for them, satisfying lifestyle.

Operationalizing the person-centred approach is one way of realizing this objective. The communication skills provide the basis for all forms of assistance and for the total facilitating process. The skills are applied not only during the initial contact, but continually, until the termination of the process.

Three skills are discussed in more detail below. Because many of you are perhaps not familiar with the implementation of this theory, the relationship between the propositions and the implementation will be indicated at the start of each technique.

Communication with groups

Working with groups does not take place only within the offices of welfare organizations, but also in classrooms, on sports fields, under trees, in the homes of group members, in hospitals, institutions, factories, and even in restaurants or on hotel verandas.

Group members are also traced and involved in various ways. Most commonly, potential members are identified by studying the files of the organizations, institutions, and firms. Potential members may also be identified through advertisements, or may also approach the facilitator and request for groups to be established.

Facilitators also receive frequent requests from other professionals, managers, line supervisors, and doctors to undertake group work with people whom they perceive to be experiencing problems. If the facilitator should approach potential group members on the basis of the professionals' perceptions, such a group may never succeed. By using communication skills such as empathy, listening, and attentiveness, however, even the most 'difficult' members may agree to group work, as illustrated in the following examples.

Example 1

A facilitator received a request to help six homeless children with their problems. The people who made the request had already tried to help the children, but because they attempted to prescribe to the children, the children always ran away when these people came to the hostel. The group facilitator therefore decided that he was not going to force his ideas on the group, but to listen to the group and to pay attention to what the group members said. By fulfilling the said requirements, it was possible for the facilitator to communicate with the members within their frame of reference. After three visits, the children agreed to participate in group work.

Example 2

The group members were identified by the headmaster of the school who also told the group facilitator what the members' problems were and what the programme should cover. The members attended the first session, but after that always made excuses not to attend any further meetings. The group facilitator again visited the members and then found out that they did not want to participate in the group because the headmaster had forced them to join the group. They also felt that the headmaster had judged them unfairly and, more importantly, that the group facilitator believed him because the group facilitator was following the proposals of the headmaster.

The above examples show that group facilitators should not allow themselves to be influenced by the referral agents, but should instead attempt, by using the pattern of verbal and non-verbal communication between the group members (that is, the communication process) and skills of attentiveness, listening, and empathy, to work within the frame of reference of the group members. This is, however, easier said than done. Still, the last example shows that communication is possible if the facilitator uses the skills and the communication process creatively.

Example 3

A group of young men sat drinking at a certain hotel every evening. The group facilitator was instructed to try to help them to use their free time more creatively. Rather than obtaining a lot of information from the referral agent, the group facilitator wanted to know only the name of the hotel where the men gathered. The following evening the facilitator visited the hotel and sat listening near the group to try to find out what their interests were. When they started discussing motorbikes, the group facilitator passed a comment that led to a conversation between him and the group. After a while, the group asked him to join them. By using the communication process, the facilitator was able to determine that the group members were visiting the hotel every evening because they were frustrated and bored. By organizing better leisure activities, the members started visiting the hotel less frequently and the group facilitator was able to start with more intensive group work.

Activity

Considering the issues on value dilemmas discussed in Section B, would you say that the group facilitator's behaviour was ethical?

Communication with communities

Somebody once said that God put people on earth because He loves stories. People are story-tellers. You cannot work with people in communities without communicating with them, listening to their stories, or facilitating the story-telling process. When facilitators, (health workers, social workers, development workers, engineers, etc.) enter the community, get to know the members, and so forth, they perform these tasks by communicating and conversing with the individuals and groups within the community, and by listening to what the individuals and groups within the community have to say, in other words listening to the stories they have to tell. At the same time, facilitators share their experiences and perceptions with the community, empathize with them, and so forth.

Paolo Freire (in Thomas 1994: 52), who was influenced by Martin Buber, refers to this type of relationship as the 'I-Thou' encounter. This encounter is one of dialogue, mutual respect, openness, and give and take. In contrast, the 'I-It' relationship is one of monologue, inequality, objectivity, and detachment, and is sometimes seen as the root of the alienation of human beings from one another.

Hope and Timmel (1984: 35) say that communication is not only about sharing problems but that the facilitator needs to hear what pleases the community, what makes them happy, what makes them unhappy or angry, what makes them feel anxious or hopeful. The facilitator's task in the community is thus to facilitate a process in which the community reflects on local concerns through discussions, listening, trying to understand and creating a learning process (context) (Yaccino and Yaccino 1994: 15). Rogers (1990: 32) himself made the link between the person-centred approach and community development by saying that workers in the field of community development have drawn upon this approach, on the theory and the practice to facilitate the independent growth of the community.

The communication skills relevant to work with individuals and groups are therefore also applicable to work with the community. Working in and with a community means that we are in a constant dialogue with the individuals and groups of people and the people in the community with each other.

Rahim (1994: 12) adds:

> *Communication acts take place in a social space of a particular time and moment of history. There is no communication without community and no community without communication. The communicating subject is constituted by self and others. The individual voice is inextricably linked to other voices. The individual communicator is always already engaged in dialogues with himself and others.*

Rahim goes further to say that the dialogical process is the process of production of meanings and the process of conveying values in human communication. This is the sharing of ideas and world views in order to create change and transformation in the community. Most of these are shared via the stories they tell us.

Communities are thus communication systems, and working in communities is a dialogical process. More specifically from a person-centred perspective, communication with the people in the community is a participatory process in order to symbolize experiences and create new frames of reference about the community's self and situation. How this participatory communication takes place will be discussed in the rest of this section.

Working in a community is not social engineering. Communication is the most important factor in facilitating change and transformation. Dialogue takes place from the first contact until the withdrawal of the facilitator.

Participatory communication also means respecting and using indigenous communication systems, namely folk media and traditional media. According to Ayee (1993: 57), folk media refers to the performing arts, for example puppetry, shadow plays, folk drama, folk dance, ballads, story-telling, crafts, mime, rituals, and games. These folk media provide a reflection of the values and world view of a society. Traditional media, on the other hand, refers to indigenous modes of communication such as meeting places, market-places, religious centres, and community halls. Ayee (1993: 58) gives examples of indigenous communication systems in West Africa, including both folk and traditional media: the gong man or traditional news man, the village market-place, village festivals, drums, songs, folklore, folk drama, dance, mime stories, riddles, parables, and even mask forms.

These media should not be used to promote your own top-down programme, but can be used by the community itself in the development process. The community will decide when and how these methods can be used appropriately.

Above all, in our communication with the people in the community, we must remember that people are not passive recipients of information. They consciously interact with it and weigh it carefully and then decide whether it is meaningful and useful.

Everything said here adds up to what Chambers (1994: 1) refers to as the 'new professionalism' in participatory development. The new professionalism reverses the values (as already described), roles, and power relations (as will be described in this section) of the 'normal professionalism'. According to Chambers, the new professionalism puts people first. The 'last-first' paradigm includes learning from the community, decentralization, empowerment, local initiative, and diversity. Development is therefore not by blueprint, but by a flexible and adaptive learning process. According to Chambers, the 'last-first' people-centred paradigm is now the greatest challenge facing the professions. This means that facilitating growth and development is built on sound, respectful, and trusting relationships and thorough communication.

CHAPTER 11

Attentiveness

11.1 How does attentiveness relate to the person-centred approach?

When facilitators are attentive, they enter the client's total life world (propositions 1, 2, and 3). The message to clients is that facilitators are accessible to them as people. This helps create a safe space (proposition 17) in which clients will not be threatened (judged) (proposition 16).

11.2 Attentiveness in communication with individuals

Attentiveness may be described as the way in which facilitators orientate themselves physically and psychologically towards clients so that the clients will feel sufficiently at ease to share their experiences, ideas, and emotions. The message is thus conveyed to the clients that the facilitator is open to them, that the clients can trust them, and that they can drop their defences in discussions with the facilitator. This enables facilitators to be 'with' their clients and to maintain continual contact with them through attentive listening.

Shulman (1982: 86) points out that attentiveness is a two-directional process during which facilitators attend to what they themselves say, do, and feel. This is the crux of attentiveness. On the other hand, the facilitator must attend verbally and non-verbally to the client.

On the personal level, facilitators can ask themselves before an interview whether they are emotionally ready to communicate with another person, that is, to focus all their attention and energy on the other, or whether there are any distractions that might impede this process. Distractions can be brought about by the physical setting, for instance when there is a high level of noise in the surroundings, or if the setting is too hot or too cold. Or the facilitator could still mentally be with a previous client whose world was entered into quite deeply. The facilitator has to 'clear the decks', metaphorically speaking, to bring his or her attention back from that client and focus it on the one to come. At another level the distractions could be associated with something personal in the facilitator's life: say a sick child or spouse about whom one is concerned and to whom the attention strays. Whatever the obstacle to total concentration might be, facilitators need to stop and take stock of where they are and whether they are ready to fully commit their energies to the person they are about to communicate with.

When the client is in the room, there are some hints about using your body posture and facial expression to indicate that you are there for him or her. Please keep in mind that these are just some ideas to make you aware that one communicates with one's whole being (proposition 3) and not just with one's voice. The way your body is used will depend on what you are familiar and comfortable with. Facilitators also have to learn what clients will be comfortable with by observing their posture. For example:

- *Arrangement of physical setting for the communication process:*
  - If you see the person in an office, how are the chairs arranged and how does the client respond to that arrangement?
  - Is there a desk between you and the other person and if so, why?
  - Do you need to write notes while you are talking to the client? If yes, can this be done in such a way that you remain respectful of, and attentive to, the client? Are there any other arrangements you can make, like tape recording the interview (with the client's permission) so that you can make notes afterwards?
  - If you have two chairs close to one another, does the client push the chair back a bit when sitting down? If yes, what do you make of it? Do you feel rejected, perhaps, or compelled to move closer because you think it is necessary for the communication process? Can you allow clients to determine the most comfortable space for themselves and follow their lead?
  - If you have to speak to clients in hospital, do you sit on the bed? If so, are they comfortable with this physical closeness? If not, can you arrange a different setting? Is there sufficient privacy for a personal discussion?
- *Eye contact:* In some cultures, direct eye contact indicates attention and awareness of the other. However, this is not always the case, as in other

cultures direct eye contact may be seen as rude, as a challenge, or even as confrontation. Sometimes a younger person is not permitted to look directly at an older person. So there can be no 'recipe' that holds for every person you will talk to. The best guideline is usually the client. Observe clients and be sensitive to their eye contact and what is comfortable for them. If direct eye contact is perceived as threatening, then avoid it, because you want to create an atmosphere where no threat to the client is perceived (proposition 17).

- *Non-verbal communication (body language):* These messages are important in dealing with individuals. Consider interviews with children, with an extremely tense person, with a person who cannot maintain direct eye contact, and think about how you can physically adapt your attention. Facilitators can use their bodies deliberately as a means of communication by being aware of the signs and messages they receive and in turn send out while in contact with clients. In this regard, Middleman and Wood (1990: 49) point out that the facilitator can engage in the client's medium, by doing what the client does, which will probably lead to verbal interaction. For example, during the facilitator's visit an elderly lady sits reading a newspaper. The facilitator also takes a newspaper and pages through it, which gives the client the opportunity of deciding when or whether she will start speaking.

  Linked to this is the choice of a medium that suits the client, based on indications of the person's interests and/or the facilitator's observation of what is acceptable to a particular age group or situation. For example, a child may find that it is easier and less threatening to communicate verbally while busily involved in something else such as a ball game, stroking a pet, or drawing a picture. Sometimes this also applies to an adult. For instance, if the facilitator walks with an adolescent while they drink cooldrinks, the adolescent may feel more relaxed and inclined to talk. This could be the beginning of an interaction that will bind the facilitator and client together.

11.3 Attentiveness in communication with groups

Attentiveness in groups is aimed at two main aspects, namely what group members say and how and, secondly, the behaviour of members individually and the group as a whole. These two aspects are discussed in more detail in what follows.

11.3.1 Verbal communication in the group

Members of a group often say that the facilitator and other members are not hearing what they are saying. In the case of facilitators, the members often sense that they are not focusing on the group when they ask closed questions, when they talk too much, are quick to give advice, and force members to talk.

The facilitator and group members are also not attentive when they are only thinking of what to say once the present speaker has finished, if they listen selectively, in other words listen only to hear what they want to hear, or are busy developing counter-arguments. Under these circumstances, the facilitator and group members who speak next often change the subject and therefore don't follow the communication process.

11.3.2 The behaviour of group members

It is important for the facilitator to become familiar with the verbal and non-verbal behaviour of each member and of the group as a whole as soon as possible. Observation of such behaviour will immediately indicate to the facilitator when something is wrong. Examples of behaviour changes are:

- a friendly member who becomes grumpy
- a member functioning at the maintenance level all of a sudden functioning at the task level
- an active member becoming inactive
- a supportive member starting to behave rudely, for example interrupting the communication process, which he or she has not done before.

11.3.3 Measurement of a person's attentiveness

According to Gilliland et al. (1989: 77) a person's, and therefore also facilitator's, degree of attentiveness is measured by three criteria by the group members, namely his or her:

- facial expression, which includes aspects such as 'eye contact, smiling, mirroring the members' mood, seriousness of expression, genuine interest, and a deep concern about the members' situation'
- body postures, which indicate whether the facilitator 'is relaxed, respectful, uneasy, bored, accepting, anxious, puzzled, tired and receptive', and
- voice qualities such as 'modulation, tone, pitch, smoothness, diction, enunciation and variation'.

11.3.4 Advantages of attentiveness in the group

Attentiveness brings many advantages. Members trust their facilitator, care for one another, and are more receptive when facilitators show them that they are attending to them. Group facilitators can show this by shaking their heads, looking directly at the speaker, and by paraphrasing and reflecting what is being said. The following are some of the phrases that the facilitator may use:

- 'You are saying ...'
- 'You feel that ...'
- 'If I understand you correctly, you are saying ...'
- 'I am not sure that I follow, but do you mean ...?'
- 'Let's see if I understand ...'

11.3.5 Is attentiveness a myth?

Attentiveness is one of the skills that can be misused. Some people have learned techniques that make it seem as if they are attending even when they are not really doing so. Individuals, even children, soon notice if attentiveness is only a pretence, and facilitators should avoid it. An example of pretending to attend is the misuse of the word 'yes'. People who say 'yes' with every second step they take while talking to you may not really be attending to you. Another example is when you greet a person and they reply 'Morning, fine thank you'. That person did not necessarily attend to what you were saying, but might have reacted out of pure habit. That is, they were expecting that your next question would be 'How are you?' and answered it before you even asked the question. This type of communication creates negative feelings, such as 'Who does he or she think he or she is?' and 'Surely he or she can ask me how I am?' Such negative feelings can create discomfort in the group members, which again will harm the communication process in the group.

Gilliland (1989: 78) mentions further that 'many clients (members) come to counselling with feelings of vulnerability, apprehension, fear, caution and uncertainty. The counsellor (facilitator) who cultivates the attitude and the skill of attending can allay these negative feelings'. Because of Gilliland's comments, attending must be seen as an important skill to improve the communication and group process.

Activity

1 Give examples of situations where a person was not attending to you.
2 How did it make you feel?

3 How did this influence your communication with the person or group?
4 Do you agree that in the example that follows, the facilitator used the skill of attending correctly? Motivate your answer with the theory you have studied.

Case study

Mr X: 'I don't know why Ms Y (*teacher*) is bothering me. I really don't know.' (*Pause.*) 'I really don't.' (*Wringing his hands; some group members also nod their heads.*)

Facilitator: (*Leans forward towards Mr X.*) 'I hear what you are saying. Something in Ms Y is really bothering you. I noticed that Miss A and some of the other group members nodded their heads while you were talking. Let's hear whether they have the same feelings about teachers.'

11.4 Attentiveness in communication with communities

Everything said about attentiveness in communication with the individual and groups is relevant when communicating with the individuals and groups in the community. During the dialogue with the members of the community, attentiveness is the way in which the facilitator enters the life world of the individuals and groups and conveys to them the message of being receptive to their stories and to them as people.

One important factor in this instance may be culture. Egan (1994: 92) points out that 'people differ both individually and culturally in how they show attentiveness'. When facilitators are getting to know a community, they need to find a way to show receptiveness to the community and to act in such a way that members of the community feel that they are being attended to.

Before giving attention to the individuals and groups in the community, we have to meet them and find them. Where do we find them? Who do we start talking to? The first step is making contact.

11.4.1 Making contact

The contact-making in the communication process is crucial. This process is initiated with the members of the community in a way that fits their life world and is focused upon content that has meaning and purpose to them (Ayee 1993: 151). The initial entry is to build a relationship and create the opportunity for the community to get to know the facilitator and vice versa.

The contact-making is crucial in the sense that it legitimizes the facilitator's presence in the community.

When working with the community, the issues are not only how to apply the communication skills, but also *where, when,* and *with whom.*

- Where do we meet the individuals and groups within the community?
- Where do we conduct interviews with them?
- When is the most suitable time to meet and get to know the community?
- With whom should interviews be conducted and how should this be done?
- How do we listen to a community consisting of hundreds and even thousands of people?

What follows in this section are merely guidelines and ideas, not rules or a blueprint. People differ and communities have their own distinct ways of communicating with each other. *Let us listen to them and learn from them.*

11.4.2 *Where does contact take place?*

You already know how to introduce yourself to clients when they come to see you at the office or when you visit them at home. At first, the people in the community do not know the facilitator. To get to know one another, the facilitator usually moves about within the community and meets the individuals and groups in various situations. Introductions or initial contact are of utmost importance. The way in which this is done may determine whether the facilitator will have an open door to the community or not.

Interviews with individuals and groups seldom take place in the facilitator's office. Interviews usually take place on street corners, in people's homes, in offices, under trees, etc. Find out from the

Figure 11.1 *I just wanted to get to know your world/community!*

community the most appropriate places where you can talk to them and where they will feel respected and attended to. Certain places, such as your office, might be intimidating for certain people. For other people, meeting at your office may be empowering. Let the community guide you or indicate the most suitable places to meet them.

11.4.3 How can we communicate?

Feuerstein (1986: 90–95) highlights a number of aspects that facilitators need to be aware of when they enter a community. These aspects relate to respect for the community's self, values, traditions, rituals, and ways of communicating.

- *Age:* In certain communities, the age of the facilitator may play a role. Feuerstein (1986: 90–95) states: 'In parts of Africa a man under 25 is still considered to be a young man. Young interviewers may not have the status or confidence to ask questions of their elders.' In this respect, for instance, an elderly man may guess at the age of the facilitator. If he thinks that the facilitator is younger than he is and the facilitator does not act with dignity and greet him first, he will have no confidence in him and will not participate in any further conversations. Former president Nelson Mandela, for instance, often reminds young journalists that it is not appropriate for him to discuss marriage with them, according to his culture.
- *Gender:* In some communities, the gender of the facilitator may prove problematic, for instance in a particular community where the status of women is still very subservient to that of the men. May she talk to males? Which males may she talk to and where is she allowed to talk to them? Should she wear particular clothing?
- *Customs:* In some communities there may be certain customs that have to be respected, for instance the way in which a village is entered, or the way the leader of the community must be approached. Often, a community leader's approval must be gained before the facilitator may talk to anyone in that community. The way they open their meetings and the clothes that are regarded as appropriate may also have to be considered.

Example 11.1

Among a Setswana community, a male development worker would be required to put on a jacket or coat (whether it is winter or summer) when attending meetings at the *kgotla*. This is regarded as the appropriate form of dress for this formal occasion and is a standard requirement for all male participants. If it happens that a male person is without a jacket or coat, he needs to get special permission from the chief to attend the meeting. Females are required to wear appropriate dresses as no trousers are allowed (Ayee 1993: 293).

11.4.4 With whom should contact be made?

The facilitator often wonders where contact with the community should take place and who should be contacted or engaged in conversations. The answer is both complicated and simple, and differs from one community to the next. In some communities, such as certain African rural communities, the facilitator cannot make contact with the community without first talking to the formal leaders, for example the captain, Chief or *Nduna*, and obtaining their permission to speak to the community. The leader will often tell facilitators where and how they will be able to get to know the community.

It is sometimes recommended that the facilitator should contact the community leaders, such as ministers, headmasters, civic associations, and others, to gain access to the community. This may be very valuable, provided the facilitator bears in mind that their comments reflect only their own perceptions of the community, and do not necessarily indicate the different experiences and perceptions the other people in the community have. It is not sufficient to speak only with the leaders. The facilitator should get to know as many people as possible within the community and listen to the differences, but also common themes in their perceptions.

The following example indicates how the community can guide the facilitator in the best way to make contact with the members of the community. It also illustrates the fact that the community will not reject facilitators if they move into the community 'wrongly', but with respect, attentiveness, and openness. They will sense their honest intentions and show them the 'right' way.

Example 11.2

Within a particular community (a hostel for single men), the facilitator discovered through her conversations with the individuals that she should preferably not speak to the hostel residents individually, but rather at a mass meeting. She explains it as follows: 'They feel more comfortable in a big group than individually discussing projects or problems that involve most of them. They tend to be suspicious if issues are discussed behind closed doors.' The facilitator, by allowing herself to be questioned during a mass meeting, gained credibility.

Example 11.3

In a rural town the community consisted of different groups of people. There were the white people living in the town, the coloured people in their township, and the black community on the other side of the town in their own township. There were farm owners and farm workers. The facilitator met with all the groups of people on different occasions and in different places and at times that were suitable and accessible for each group, so that as many different people could attend as much as possible, excluding no group.

11.4.5 When does contact take place?

Making contact with the community is also about getting acquainted and building a relationship. The facilitator needs first to get to know the people in the community and become familiar with their values, views, history, what is important to them, their traditions, everyday existence, and so forth. The information that the facilitator receives from the community depends largely on those issues that are important to the community and will vary from one community to the next.

Facilitators should also find out *when* they may communicate with members of the community. In some communities, for instance, great value is attached to particular rituals when a person dies and is buried, and facilitators will not be allowed to contact the community until the period of mourning has passed and the community once again becomes accessible. In more traditional African communities, facilitators should also find out who they will be allowed to interview, because there are certain beliefs relating to the purity and impurity of particular persons that prohibit them from having contact with people.

Example 11.4

Ngubane (1977: 78) mentions the impurity (*umnyama*) of the Zulu woman after giving birth:

Of the *umnyama* that arises from reproductive situations, the most highly intensified point is associated with a newly delivered mother (*umdlezane*). She is dangerous to herself, her baby, and particularly to males, who not only become vulnerable because of her pollution but whose virility also suffers if they eat food prepared by her or share eating utensils with her. During the first three days she must not leave the house at all.

There are many more prescriptions as to what she may do or may not do and 'she remains an *umdlezane* until the flow of after birth emission stops'. This means that it will not be possible to make contact with her during this time.

The people in the community will have to guide the facilitator about the most appropriate times to move around in the community.

• When do they gather and where?

• When are the people in the community present or available? To be in the community during day time is not worthless, but most of the people in some communities are at work. In some of the rural communities any time might be appropriate. In other rural communities the employed adults might be migrant workers who are only in the community during weekends or the last weekend of every month when they bring their money home. In some urban areas, most of the community activities take place over weekends because the members of the communities work long hours and have difficulty with transport to attend the activities during the week. Certain communities have specific times for meetings. In a rural community, farm workers could meet after their work was finished at 17:00 in the afternoon, or during their lunch-breaks. In another semi-rural community, the mothers indicated that they could meet at 11:00 in the morning after they had finished with their housework and before the children came back from school.

Example 11.5

Ayee (1993: 264) gives an interesting example of the people of Makoupan who meet every Tuesday to listen to their councillor giving a report on any decisions taken by the Kopano Tribal Authority, which meets on Mondays. Three bells are rung in various parts of the village to call people to public meetings. The bells are rung first on Monday afternoon to announce the meeting for Tuesday. They are rung again on Tuesday morning to remind people of the day's meeting. The third time the bells are rung at the time of the meeting. In order to make contact with this community, this would be the path to follow and respect. Obviously facilitators cannot merely arrange a meeting in this community to suit their own programmes.

Activity

1 What is important, within your cultural context, in respect of attentiveness?
2 Can you provide examples of the way in which other cultures show attentiveness?
3 Ask people from different communities how they perceive a person as attentive or not attentive.

CHAPTER 12

Listening

12.1 How does listening relate to the person-centred approach?

In order to understand clients' experiential worlds (proposition 1), their perceptions and realities (proposition 2), we first need to listen carefully to what they are experiencing and how they are experiencing it.

One should therefore *listen* to what clients are saying in relation to the total person (proposition 3); in other words, in terms of their:

- experiential worlds (proposition 1)
- perceptions and thoughts (proposition 2)
- needs (proposition 5)
- behaviour to satisfy needs (proposition 5)
- emotions accompanying needs and behaviour (proposition 6)
- self – who the clients are as they experience themselves (proposition 8)
- values – those arising from own experience and those adopted from others (propositions 9 and 10).

All these experiences should be heard and understood from within the client's own frame of reference (proposition 7).

Firstly, it is necessary to listen to the symbolized experiences (proposition 11 (a and b)). Secondly, we listen to the unsymbolized and distorted experiences (proposition 11 (c and d)). To listen to the unsymbolized and distorted experiences requires a deeper kind of listening, beyond the obvious content of what the client is saying. It is sometimes called listening with a 'third ear'. This type of listening will be discussed in Section D.

12.2 Listening to individuals

Active listening is closely related to active attentiveness. It is a process of *observation* and *listening*. It is a prerequisite for all other communication skills and precedes all other skills. Listening may be regarded as the inverse of talking, and unfortunately we are all more inclined to talk than to listen.

Listening can be defined as the active process of receiving auditory stimuli, attaching meaning to what we hear, and making sense of the raw vocal symbols we receive. It is a deliberate, selective process in which the hearer selects the sounds the speaker makes, and pays attention to, recognizes, understands, and makes sense of them (Kadushin 1990: 244). Listening bridges hearing and understanding. Listening is a complex process consisting of different elements:

- *Hearing:* There is a difference between listening and hearing. Hearing is an automatic, physiological process in which auditory stimuli are received. Problems can arise even at this stage if the hearer has a hearing defect and cannot hear or can only hear imperfectly, or if there is so much noise that hearing is not possible. The speed of speech is a further problem since the hearer can process the message faster than the average speed of speech, with the result that the hearer's thoughts may begin to wander.

- *Understanding:* During the process of understanding, meaning must be attached to the words that are heard and the meaning must correspond with the message intended by the sender. The message must be *understood*, which means that we must at least understand the language, the intention of the message (e.g. serious, funny), the context of the message, the relationship with the person, the climate of the meeting, and the subject of the message. According to Tubbs and Moss (1991: 180), the process of understanding involves our associating the message with our previous experiences. At this stage we are inclined to evaluate and judge the message, to approve or to disapprove, to accept or to reject. Such evaluation is regarded as one of the biggest stumbling blocks in interpersonal communication. The attitude should rather be to receive the message as it was intended by the person who sent it.

    From the perspective of this theory, the facilitator also has to understand the *person* who is uttering the message. In other words, it is not just the message that should be understood (or the words or content of what is being said), but also what this conveys about the person who is uttering the message.

Example 12.1

A woman says that she wants to be a good wife, but her husband abuses her. The facilitator needs to understand not only the message of abuse, but also the person, the woman who needs to be a 'good' wife to this husband and seems uncertain of how to be a good wife under the prevailing circumstances.

- *Remembering:* Remembering takes place when information is stored for later retrieval. Part of the proof of how well we listen is how much we remember of what is said. Research shows that only 50 per cent of what has just been said is remembered, and after eight hours, only 35 per cent.
- *Listening to and understanding non-verbal behaviour:* What constitutes non-verbal behaviour? Communication without using words is the basic way of conveying information to another person. For example, long before a baby can speak, it expresses its dissatisfaction by crying and waving its arms around. Non-verbal communication comprises two-thirds of communication between people, as opposed to one-third verbal communication. Non-verbal communication is a continuous process that may or may not be accompanied by verbal communication and is the most important way of conveying attitudes and feelings (Brill 1990: 64). Cormier and Cormier (1985: 66) show that many 'leakages', that is messages that are valid, but are not intentionally sent, occur by means of non-verbal communication, and that often the non-verbal messages give a deeper, fuller picture of the client than the verbal.
- *Body language:* Body language (a type of non-verbal communication) relates to movements, gestures, and attitude and is constantly observed during the interview by both communicators. Shulman (1982: 88) makes the important point that the expression of feeling in particular occurs through body language and that the observant facilitator can perceive this in many ways. Equally, the client can gauge the facilitator's attitude by reading the facilitator's body language. A tense body and a relaxed body send out different messages. Crossed arms and legs while the interviewer is sitting bolt upright on the edge of the chair may convey a tense message.
- *The face:* The part of the body providing most of the clues is the face. Kadushin (1990: 284) says: 'The face is naked and so is open to observation.' Kadushin goes on to say: 'It is said that the most important thing we wear is the expression on our face.' The face is the part of the body expressing the most automatic signs of tension, such as blushing, sweating, and dry lips. Furthermore, the face is capable of thousands of different expressions and one can learn to adopt certain facial expressions

that one perceives as suitable for a certain occasion, for example, a funeral or a discussion with one's boss. There are certain categories of 'primary affect displays' (DeVito 1991: 161) such as joy, surprise, fear, anger, sadness, and loathing, which find expression in the face. Often it is the mixture of these emotions that makes it more difficult to read them. Different parts of the face can manifest a certain emotion for a fraction of a second, which can be followed by a reaction on another part of the face. It is only when they are filmed and played back slowly and moments are frozen that the full extent of the variety of facial expressions can be realized.

Listening is an active process and does not just *happen*; we have to make it happen. Kadushin (1990: 244) says that it is not an automatic process, but that 'we have to make a conscious, deliberate, and continuing commitment to listen. It almost requires that we occasionally command ourselves to listen, stop to listen'. It demands energy and dedication. Listening is a skill of critical importance to all forms of human communication (DeVito 1991: 70). It sounds easy, but from the cries of distress of so many people who say: 'You don't listen to me. You don't hear what I say', it is clear that listening is not so easy.

There are many reasons why listening is a *fundamental skill*:
- It shows respect for other people and demonstrates to clients that facilitators value them enough to give their full attention.
- Active listening removes the need to make assumptions about clients because they are giving the information. Because clients feel safe, they can remove the masks used to protect the self.
- It bridges differences in age, gender, and culture. How can facilitators know what it is like to be old, male, female, Zulu, white, dying, hungry, raped, and so on if they have not experienced one of these or are not one of these people? People with experiences different to yours can help you to understand them, if you listen well.

This was confirmed in a lecture presented by Carl Rogers in 1965 (Barret-Lennard 1988: 415): 'I think I know why I'm satisfied to hear someone. When I can really hear someone it puts me closely in touch with him. It enriches my life. It's also true that it's through hearing people that I have learned all that I know about individuals, about personalities, about interpersonal relationships ...'

Figure 12.1 *Different facial expressions*

12.3 Listening in groups

The objective of listening in group work is to help the members as well as the facilitator to explore and understand the ideas, feelings, and intentions of the speaker. The facilitator's intention with the group also plays an important role in listening. Such intentions are influenced by the theoretical approach followed by the facilitator. In the group-centred approach, for instance, the facilitator believes that the group is capable of improving its situation by communicating. The group facilitator therefore listens for aspects that may hamper or facilitate communication. The group facilitator does not focus only on the individuals in their totality, in other words on the group members' ideas, feelings, circumstances, and intentions, but also on the group process. In more direct approaches, on the other hand, group facilitators listen only until they hear what they want to hear, and then take over the group. The facilitators therefore listen selectively, *that is what satisfies or fits their frames of reference.*

When the group facilitator and members listen selectively, the speaker feels that the facilitator or group is not listening. The member's communication then changes to 'I want to say … Listen to me … Listen carefully … You are not hearing me.' Communication of this kind is not conducive to the group process. Even Rogers is blamed for 'blind spots' and biases. O'Hara in Farber et al. (1996: 297) mentioned that the client-centered approach has been created by 'white middle-class mostly North American males'. According to O'Hara, Rogers' case studies clearly indicate these biases and blind spots.

Rogers (in Johnson 1981: 90) states that the establishment of sound relations and listening are hampered by people's natural tendency to judge, evaluate, accept, or reject everything that is being said. According to Johnson (1981: 90), this happens when the speaker 'makes a statement – you respond silently or openly with "I think you're wrong", "I don't like what you said", "I think your views are right", or "I agree entirely".'

The question is how group facilitators can ensure that they do not listen selectively and can enable the members to listen. According to Martin (1983: 18), the first requirement is to enable members to pay attention to what the other members are saying. The second requirement is to make speakers feel that they are understood. This is done by using communication that is based on the experiences of the speaker and on the content of his or her communication. Examples of communication focusing on content are 'What I hear you saying ..' and 'I gather …'. Communication focusing on feelings is, for example, 'So you feel …' and 'You feel …'. The value of this kind of communication is that the members will stay in the communication process.

It will also help the group members to understand one another's frame of reference. It will also bring them closer together and into a more personal interrelationship.

More specifically, after evaluating Rogers' interviews Farber et al. (1996: 15–24) identified the following 'methods' according to which the facilitator can improve listening, namely to:

- provide an orientation
- affirm his or her attention
- check understanding
- restate
- acknowledge members' unstated feelings
- provide reassurance
- interpret
- confront (Rogers used confronting in his interviews when clients were avoiding painful issues)
- use direct questioning
- turn pleas for assistance back to members
- maintain silence
- use self-disclosure.

Another advantage of careful listening is that it communicates to members the feeling of 'I care for you and I want to understand'. When the facilitator is not listening well, the group members get the message: 'I do not care what you say and do not wish to understand.' The following example illustrates the consequences of poor listening.

Example 12.2

The main objective for a group of young girls was family-planning education. During one of the sessions, the use of contraceptives was discussed by the members. The facilitator also emphasized that the members should use contraceptives when they become sexually active. Some of the members said that they would never use contraceptives because it was prohibited by their religion. Another two members said that in their culture they have to prove prior to their marriage that they can bear children. An illegitimate child is therefore not considered to be a problem and they would consequently not use contraceptives either. The facilitator, who was not listening to the members, tried to persuade the group to use the contraceptives by discussing the consequences of extramarital pregnancies from her frame of reference. The group members listened passively. Not one of the members attended the subsequent meeting.

Activity

Discuss how the facilitator used the following propositions in the previous example. Motivate your answers:

1   proposition 1
2   proposition 2
3   proposition 5
4   proposition 8
5   proposition 10
6   proposition 16.

12.4 Listening in communities

Dean Rusk (in King 1965: 24) said 'One of the best ways to persuade others is with our ears by listening to others.' King (1965: 24) continues: 'How few of us are good listeners, particularly if we regard ourselves as experts, accustomed to tell others rather than let them tell us.' (See also Chambers' (1994) 'new professionalism'.) Louw (2002: 45) cites a community member who wrote about the facilitator who came to their community: 'Some time ago a young woman showed up at the gathering place (the pay-out point for the aged) where we waited in long queues for our pensions. She listened to our complaints (what else is there to talk about?). She asked questions. Here was someone who makes it her job to listen to old people's stories. We also started to listen more carefully to each other's stories.'

The person-centred approach is contained in the above because the objective of listening to the community is mainly to get to know the community's story, to learn about the self of the community, its frame of reference, emotions, experiences, values, meanings, dreams, hopes, etc. on which all further plans and actions will be based and also to facilitate listening among community members (Egan 2000). Although we may try to listen 'to everything' it is impossible. There are filters and biases that make our listening selective.

12.4.1 Filters that influence listening when communicating with the community

(a) Frame of reference filters

Feuerstein (1986: 92) points out that interviews are influenced not only by the cultural and religious background of the community, but also by that of the interviewer or facilitator. The religion and culture of facilitators thus determine whether they will be able to understand what the community is trying to convey to them: 'The culture and religion (values, theoretical frame, in fact his/her world view) of the interviewer may affect his/her ability to understand, be acceptable to, or even to question certain respondents or groups of respondents about certain topics.'

Being able to listen includes enabling the community to communicate with the facilitator. The facilitator has to create opportunities, within a safe, accepting atmosphere, that allows the community to tell their stories.

(b) Mission of the facilitator/organization/donor

These situations act as filters through which the facilitator listens to the community and in so doing does not hear what the community is actually saying. A person employed, for instance, by an organization dealing with alcohol and drug problems might only ask questions and hear issues regarding alcohol and drugs, and not necessarily in relation to other burning needs of the community. The facilitator's own personal mission will also determine the questions the person will ask and, to a large extent, what they will eventually *hear*.

Structured questionnaires, for instance, provide limited information on a particular aspect and, furthermore, are usually drawn up from the frame of reference of the researcher or investigator.

Example 12.3

A facilitator employed by an agency concerned with alcohol and drug abuse planned a project in a particular township aimed at reaching the youth and presenting a programme that would help prevent alcohol and drug abuse or glue-sniffing. A large number of children in the community had been reported for these transgressions. The facilitator initially put together a group known to the agency with whom she had been in contact. Contrary to the facilitator's expectations, the actual need felt by these young people related to learning skills to be able to obtain employment and not to abuse alcohol. The facilitator and the youth started negotiating for soccer fields, beautification of their community, knowledge on entrepreneurship in order to generate their own income, and so forth. This process gave meaning to their lives, indirectly preventing the abuse of alcohol.

(c) Chambers' six biases as filters

Chambers (1983: 13–25) set out six situations that influence what the facilitator *sees and hears* within the community. He calls these the 'six biases' and explains them in terms of rural situations, but they are equally applicable to urban situations. According to Chambers, these six biases are applicable to 'development tourists', researchers, and local-level staff who live and work in rural areas.

- *Spatial biases: urban, tarmac, and roadside:* 'Most learning about rural conditions is mediated by vehicles. Starting and ending in urban centres, visits follow networks of roads. With rural development tourism, the hazards of dirt roads, the comfort of the visitor, the location of places to visit and places for spending the night, and shortages of both time and fuel dictate a preference for tarmac roads and for travel close to urban centres.

  'Urban bias concentrates rural visits near towns and especially near capital cities and large administrative centres.'

- *Project bias:* 'Project bias is most marked with the showpiece: the nicely groomed pet project or model village, specially staffed and supported, with well-briefed members who know what to say and that is sited at a reasonable but not excessive distance from the urban headquarters. Governments in capital cities need such projects for foreign visitors; district and subdistrict staff need them too, for visits by their senior officers. Such projects provide a quick and simple reflex to solve the problem of what to do with visitors or senior staff on inspection. Once again, they direct attention away from the poorer people.'

- *Person biases:* 'The persons with whom the developer, tourists, donors, health care workers, and researchers have contact, and from whom they obtain impressions and information, are biased or give a biased perspective.'
  - *Elite bias:* ' "Elite" is used here to describe those people who are less poor and more influential. They typically include progressive farmers, village leaders, headmen, traders, religious leaders, teachers, and para-professionals. They are the most fluent informants. It is they who receive and speak to the visitors; they who articulate "the village's" interests and wishes; their concerns, which emerge as "the village's" priorities for development.'
  - *Male bias:* 'Most local-level government staff, researchers, and other rural visitors are men. Most rural people with whom they establish contact are men. Female farmers are neglected by male agricultural extension workers. In most societies women have inferior status and are subordinate to men. There are variations and exceptions, but quite often women are shy of speaking to male visitors. They often work very long hours, and they are usually paid less than men. Rural single women, female heads of households, and widows include many of the most wretched and unseen people in the world. This means that they

are often overlooked and the facilitator does not hear their contribution or their perspective to the issue/concern.'

– *User and adopter biases:* 'This bias applies to visitors who have a professional interest in, say, education, health or agriculture, to local-level officials, and to researchers. They tend to visit buildings and places where activity is concentrated, easily visible, and hence easy to study. Children in school are more likely to be seen and questioned than children who are not in school; those who use the health clinic more than those who are too sick, too poor, or too distant to use it; those who come to market because they have goods to sell or money with which to buy, more than those who stay at home because they have neither.'

• *Active, present and living biases:* 'Those who are active are more visible than those who are not. Fit, happy children gather round the Jeep or Land Rover, not those who are apathetic, weak and miserable. Dead children are rarely seen. The sick lie in their huts. Inactive old people are often out of sight; a social anthropologist has recorded how he spent some time camping outside a village in Uganda before he realised that old people were starving.'

• *Professional biases:* 'Finally, professional training, values and interest present problems. Knowing what they want to know, and short of time to find it out, professionals in rural areas become even more narrowly single-minded. They do their own thing and only their own thing. They look for and find what fits their ideas. There is neither inclination nor time for the open-ended question or for other ways of perceiving people, events and things. "He that seeketh, findeth." Visiting the same village, a hydrologist enquires about the water table, a soils scientist examines soil fertility, an agronomist investigates yields, an economist asks about wages and prices, a sociologist looks into patron–client relations, an administrator examines the tax collection record, a doctor investigates hygiene and health, a nutritionist studies diets, and a family planner tries to find out about attitudes to numbers of children.' It is impossible for a facilitator to listen without bias because of the fact that we have our own frame of reference from which we perceive and listen. We should therefore try to be self-reflective by looking critically at our own biases and frame of reference.

• *Politeness bias:* This refers to the tendency of professionals to refrain from frankly questioning informents. Hope and Timmel (1995) stress the importance to constantly ask the "why" question to be able to hear and listen to the people's real needs and experiences.

Activity

1 In your experience as facilitator, have you also come across these biases? Are there any others that you could perhaps add?

2 In view of these and other biases, can we share some ideas on what the facilitator can do to be able to listen to all the people in the community and more specifically the usually inconspicuous, voiceless people?

Example 12.4

The facilitator in a rural town that consisted of different groups of people really made an effort to visit the various groups. She had to drive many kilometres to get to those farm workers who are usually inconspicuous and unheard. In her report she wrote all the different stories and issues she heard from the different groups, e.g.

- history of the town
- unemployment
- education of the children
- lack of vision and motivation – of being trapped
- lack of facilities and infrastructure
- alcohol and drug abuse
- HIV/Aids
- crime and concern about safety
- isolation and the wish for friendship
- lack of leadership, and
- better care for the elderly.

She was able to hear a wide range of different stories from the community and tried to prevent biases. However, they would still be *selected* stories, as she probably selected them from her own frame of reference and following her own theoretical basis. At particular times and in certain contexts people will tell their stories differently.

Activity

What biases could she also have been subject to?

CHAPTER 13

Empathy

13.1 How does empathy relate to the person-centred approach?

Rogers (1987: 29) comments as follows:

> *This formulation would state that it is the counsellor's function to assume, in so far as he is able, the internal frame of reference of the client, to perceive the world as the client sees it, to perceive the client himself as he is seen by himself, to lay aside all perceptions from the external frame of reference while doing so and to communicate something of this empathic understanding to the client.*

Egan's (1994: 123, 124) view of empathy is as follows: 'Empathy as a form of communication involves both listening to and understanding the client.' In other words, I must be able to see, as it were with *the client's* eyes what *his or her* world is like to *him or her* and how he or she sees *himself or herself.*

This means that the facilitator temporarily sets aside his or her own frame of reference and attempts, without prejudice or preconceived ideas, to *hear* and *understand* the client and to *convey* such understanding to the client verbally and non-verbally. The latter is most important because it is of no benefit to the client if the facilitator understands him or her, but the client is *unaware* of it and cannot see or hear that he or she is being understood. The facilitator should therefore consciously endeavour to demonstrate to the client that he or she is being understood.

It is important to note that the understanding referred to here is not just of the content given by the client while talking to the facilitator, but more importantly, of the person who is being talked to. What does the content shared by the client tell the facilitator about the person who is talking? The question remains whether such understanding is possible. It is, in fact, contrary to proposition 2 of this particular theory. Briefly, proposition 2 states that each person's perception of the world is his or her own reality – a personal, subjective view. As a unique person, the facilitator also has his or her own frame of reference, which differs from that of the client (and of other people).

Activity

Mention a few of your ideas on how to overcome this dilemma.

1 How is it possible to enter another person's life world?
2 What happens to one's own views and perceptions?
3 Is it necessary to deny or distance oneself from one's own perceptions, or to adopt the views of the client?
4 How will you experience such perceptions?
5 Is there another solution?

Rogers (1987: 29) agrees that this is a difficult task. Note what he says in the quotation above: '... in so far as he is able ...' This implies that the facilitator is not able to fully enter into the client's life world. Egan (1994: 107, 115–116) makes provision for the problematic nature of total immersion in a client's life world by distinguishing between *accurate* and *inaccurate empathy*. Inaccurate empathy means that the facilitator has understood the client incorrectly, or not entirely correctly. In such a case, the facilitator must allow himself or herself to be corrected by the client. Bear in mind that the client knows best how he or she perceives his or her life world, and that it makes no sense to argue with the client about his or her experiences. It is the facilitator's task to become familiar with the client's view and to explore together with the client. (This does not mean, however, that the facilitator should adopt the client's perspective. Each retains the right to his or her own ideas, but the facilitating process revolves around the client, and therefore his or her ideas, experiences, and perceptions provide the material with which to work.)

In terms of proposition 3 of the person-centred theory, a client should be seen in *totality*. This means that we need to work with everything that the client provides. (In this section we are dealing with empathy, and the meaning of 'work' in this context is to communicate with empathic understanding.)

According to proposition 7, a person's *behaviour* can be understood only from within the individual's own frame of reference. Therefore the client's behaviour (in and away from your presence) should be understood and such understanding should be communicated to the client.

Behaviour, however, relates to *needs*. In terms of proposition 5, behaviour is aimed at satisfying needs, and needs are therefore also material for empathy.

Needs depend on the person's experiential world (proposition 1), as he or she perceives it (proposition 2). The client's *experiences and perceptions* should therefore also be treated with empathy. Emotions in turn accompany behaviour, and empathy is therefore also applicable to *emotions*.

A part of the total perceptual experiential field is gradually distinguished as the 'self', and, therefore, the *self* also becomes a subject of empathy. The self refers to the way in which the client experiences himself or herself, who he or she is. This may differ from the way in which the facilitator or even family members see the client, but during interviews it is the client's experience of himself or herself that is relevant. When a mother has shared her perception of, for example, her son with you in an interview, that represents *her* frame of reference, and *not* that of the child. When talking to the child, you should not listen with prejudice, attempting to ascertain whether his ideas are the same as those of the mother or thinking that the child is simply lying to you. Give the child the opportunity to share his story, his experiences with you, and try to understand how he experiences himself and to convey your understanding to him in his own language.

Values are attached to experience and form part of the self, and empathy therefore also applies to *values*. In this respect, empathy involves understanding of the distinction between values attached to own experiences and those adopted from others, as experienced by the individual himself or herself (proposition 10).

Empathy is therefore a complex skill requiring a great deal of concentration, verbal and non-verbal communication skills, as well as mental skills (as opposed to the common misconception that it consists of passive, uninvolved listening!). One may well ask, 'Why go to all that trouble? What good does it actually do the client?' To answer the question, we need to turn to the theory once more (it is theory that guides our professional opinions and actions). We can start with proposition 17, which provides the facilitator with some indication of the most useful behaviour in enabling the client to grow. When the client experiences *no threat* to the self, he or she can start allowing into his or her consciousness those experiences that have been painful and have therefore not been symbolized or have been distorted. The client can then face these experiences and start assimilating them. How does the facilitator create a situation in which the client experiences no threat? Proposition 16 provides an indication of those things that the client does find threatening and that should be avoided, namely any experience that threatens the symbolized self (proposition 8). Such experiences will cause the person to protect the self and to deny such experience access to the consciousness. If the facilitator therefore says something that is contrary to the client's frame of reference, the client will protect himself or herself against the facilitator (in the past, this was called 'resistance': the client resisted those actions of the facilitator that were contrary to the self). The facilitator should show the client that he or she poses no threat, but understands and accepts the client.

If the client is fully understood and accepted (and *knows* this), he or she can start restructuring the self in order to cope with those experiences (perceptions, needs, behaviour, emotions, and values) that are in conflict with the self. Once again, the facilitator cannot decide *how* this should be done, or whether the client will accept such experiences or not.

Example 13.1

A young man had grown up in a home where premarital sex was not acceptable. He and his girlfriend have long had a close and intense relationship, although they were still struggling financially. He was not sure that he himself believed that premarital sex is wrong. Depending on your own values, you may have some or other preferred solution to this problem, but that is your business, just as the young man needs to develop his *own* solution, his own values that will fit with his self! This is in fact the objective of the person-centred theory, and empathy is one of the most important aids at the disposal of the facilitator to realize this objective.

13.2 Empathy and the individual

Activity

Make a list of all the facets of the client as a human being that are relevant to empathy.

The following are a number of hints on how to *actively* demonstrate understanding, in other words empathy:
- Use keywords that have a particular meaning for the client, without repeating verbatim everything he or she says. Automatically repeating everything the client says may convey disinterest, lack of involvement, and disrespect to the client and is of as little value as when the client speaks to a parrot.

- Try to feel an affinity with the intensity of the client's experiential world. For instance, if clients become angry, you should try to convey your understanding of their feelings with the same animation. Speaking softly may calm clients down, but it will not encourage them to share the full extent of their anger with you. If you demonstrate to your clients, however, that you truly understand the depth of their experience, they will feel a sense of acceptance and this will encourage them to elaborate on their experiences. Remember, the facilitator's task in this instance is not to change the client, but to accept and understand the client.
- *Avoid* the following question and statement: 'How do you feel?'; 'I know how you feel.' In both instances the client will be quite justified in saying to himself or herself or to you, 'In that case, please tell me how I feel!' Furthermore, the question as to the client's feelings is indicative of inadequate observation by the facilitator.
- Be tentative when feeling your way into the life world of the client. It is no easy task to enter another person's frame of reference, and we should therefore respond in such a way that the client has the opportunity to correct us. Nevertheless, a somewhat inaccurate, tentative response is better than questions or clichés.
- Avoid confrontation and arguments with the client. These serve only as an indication that the facilitator is approaching the client from his or her own frame of reference. The argument might be seen as a threat to the client and, as discussed under proposition 16, this will probably lead to the client's being defensive in protecting the symbolized self. Facilitators can ask themselves what they are experiencing that is creating the need for argument with the client.
- An accurate empathic response may encourage the client to delve deeper. If you are aware of this, such movement will not catch you unawares. It is very important to keep following the thread and intensity of the conversation. The client may find it stressful to delve deeper, and that is *exactly* when he or she will most need your understanding and acceptance.

Various stumbling blocks to effective empathy are described in the literature. Some of these, which are not very obvious, are discussed below:
- *Sympathy:* There is a difference between empathy and sympathy. Sympathy stems from the facilitator's own experiential world, rather than from that of the client. Although their intentions may be good, sympathetic facilitators will be burdening their clients with their feelings, with which the clients then have to cope, rather than facilitators being there for their clients, irrespective of their own needs.

- *Advice, approval, and disapproval:* These aspects also imply ideas arising from the facilitator's frame of reference, rather than from that of the client. Facilitators may believe that their solutions will please their clients (good intentions), but should rather consider:
  - the client's self-determination (proposition 4)
  - that the client has his or her own values, and needs to develop a value system (propositions 10 and 19)
  - that we wish to enable the client to generate his or her own way forward, determined by the client's own perceptions, experiences, needs, self, and values.

It is not always easy to refrain from giving advice. Clients often ask for advice because they do not have solutions of their own (which is, after all, why they consulted a facilitator). It is therefore what they need, and simply to refuse will be insensitive and contrary to the client's frame of reference, which is something that we wish to avoid. What should we do? The propositions of the theory may provide the answer: Proposition 5 states that behaviour (the client's action of seeking help, and his or her verbal and non-verbal communication, which also constitute behaviour) indicates a particular need, accompanied by emotions (proposition 6). What could the emotions be in this instance? (Bear in mind that we are surmising and that the emotions will vary from one client to the next.) If we assume that the client is experiencing anxiety and uncertainty, we may respond as follows: 'You are asking me what to do and you sound uncertain' and/or 'It appears as if you have lost confidence in yourself/your own decisions.' This shows your clients that you understand them and provides them with the opportunity to elaborate on themselves and their experiences or fears.

Activity

Record a few of your own responses that a facilitator could use with a client who does not know whether or not to change jobs.

Example 13.2

The following are five interviews conducted with clients by different facilitators. As you will notice, each facilitator's response has its own unique style, but the *principle* of empathy as basic point of departure is maintained throughout. More accurately, an attempt is made to maintain empathy, and even these experienced facilitators do not always succeed. In some of the interviews this is indicated, in others not. You could try to identify the less empathic responses yourself.

There are two reasons for presenting this variety of interviews:

- to provide a *practical* demonstration of the concept of empathy (it is, after all, not just a theoretical notion without any practical value)
- to demonstrate that each facilitator, as a unique person, has their own style of intervention (the theory serves only as a guideline to be implemented by each facilitator according to their own professional self).

Interview 1

Source: Rogers (1987: 151–155)

The case of a young female client may demonstrate movement in the locus of evaluation. A portion of the second interview may indicate how certain standards and values came to be introjected and the effect these had upon her behaviour. It seems fairly clear that during her earlier life these values provided satisfactory guides to action, but that a sense of discrepancy has arisen, which is profoundly dissatisfying. She no longer wishes to abide by these values, but has nothing to use in their place.

S102: It seems – I don't know – It probably goes all the way back into my childhood. I've – for some reason I've – my mother told me that I was the pet of my father. Although I never realized it – I mean, they never treated me as a pet at all. And other people always seemed to think I was sort of a privileged one in the family. But I never had any reason to think so. And as far as I can see looking back on it now, it's just that the family let the other kids get away with more than they usually did me. And it seems for some reason to have held me to a more rigid standard than they did the other children.

C103: You're not so sure you were a pet in any sense, but more that the family situation seemed to hold you to pretty high standards.

S103: M-hm. That's just what has occurred to me; and that the other people could sorta make mistakes, or do things as children that were naughty, or 'that was just a boyish prank,' or 'that was just what you might expect,' but Alice wasn't supposed to do those things.

C104: M-hm. With somebody else it would just be just – oh, be a little naughtiness; but as far as you were concerned, it shouldn't be done.

S104: That's really the idea I've had. I think the whole business of my standards, or my values, is one that I need to think about rather carefully, since I've been doubting for a long time whether I even have any sincere ones.

C105: M-hm. Not sure whether you really have any deep values which you are sure of.

S105: M-hm. M-hm.

C106: You've been doubting that for some time.

S106: Well, I've experienced that before. Though one thing, when I make decisions I don't have – I don't think – It seems that some people have – have quite steady values that they can weigh things against when they want to make a decision. Well, I don't, and I haven't had, and I guess I'm an opportunist (*laughing*). I do what seems to be the best thing to do at the moment, and let it go at that.

C107: You have no certain measuring rods that you can use.

Interview 2 and 3

Source: Rogers (1987: 246–251)

Most of the time, there is no way of knowing just how the child is reacting to the therapist's acceptance of his or her silence, but an occasional case is revealing. Here is an example from a play contact with a nine-year-old boy who has spent the entire hour painting in silence. Near the end, he asks the therapist about the time.

DICK: How much time do I have left?

THERAPIST: Seven minutes, Dick.

DICK: I might as well go rock awhile. *(He goes and sits in the rocking-chair. He closes his eyes and quietly rocks.)* How much time do I have left now?

THERAPIST: Five more minutes, Dick.

DICK (SIGHS VERY DEEPLY): Ah, five more minutes all to myself.

THERAPIST (VERY SOFTLY): Five more minutes all your own, Dick?

DICK: Yes! *(Said with much feeling. He rocks silently for the rest of the hour. His eyes are shut, in apparent enjoyment of peace.)*

THERAPIST: It feels good just to sit and rock?

DICK:	*(nods)*
THERAPIST:	That's all the time we have for today, Dick.
DICK:	OK. *(He gets up immediately and goes to the door with the therapist. They say good-bye, and he goes out. A minute later, he knocks at the door.)* I thought I'd get you some clean water.
THERAPIST:	You want to help me, Dick?
DICK:	Yes, I do. *(He gets the water. The therapist thanks him and he leaves, skipping down the hall. This is the first time that he has ever made any effort to clean up after his painting.)*

A contrasting case

Although the therapy process need not involve a great deal of verbalization on the child's part, an occasional case presents a striking contrast to 'the silent case'. An example is that of eleven-year-old Henry, which may indicate a child's capacity for sophisticated insights.

Henry was referred for therapy because of his 'nervousness'. He had an assortment of tics, including rapid and continuous blinking of the eyelids, twitching of the lips, mouth and jaw grimaces, shoulder-tossing, feet-kicking, and gasping for breath. He suffered from constipation, wept easily, stuttered, was a social isolate, and was failing in his schoolwork. In short, there seemed to be no area of his life which afforded him satisfaction. During his first therapy hour, he told of often running all the way home from school in order to escape the men waiting in alleys to kill him. He reported his life at home to be an endless round of quarrels, reprimands, hypodermic injections of sedatives, suppositories, and nightmares. His father, a physician, threatened him with shock therapy if his 'shaking' did not cease. It seems that a psychiatrist had told Henry's parents that he shook in order to gain attention, and they were determined to end his 'nastiness'.

In the face of his many problems, Henry felt quite overwhelmed. His own words provide a vivid account of his psychological state during this first therapy hour. The excerpt is from the last half of the hour, and is reproduced from his therapist's notes.

HENRY: One time, my mother said she'd take me to Baltimore. So I got up early, 7 o'clock, and I went into the living-room. It was empty. I should have gotten up at 6 o'clock. She took Michael (older brother) instead.

THERAPIST: They left you when you'd hoped to go?

HENRY: *(Nods. He weeps again.)* Up until I was 6 years old, I had a nurse, Miss Palmer. She protected me from everybody, but now, now she's gone, and – *(interrupts his story with tears)*

THERAPIST: You're all alone without anybody to protect you now?

HENRY: Yes. They say Miss Palmer spoiled me, but I don't think so.

THERAPIST: You miss her?

HENRY: Yes, I do. I have a cousin, Jean. Well, I happened to fall in love with her. Michael says, 'Jean doesn't care for you a bit.' He says Jean likes him better.

THERAPIST: He doesn't want you to be happy?

HENRY: No. He doesn't. He does everything he can to make me miserable. My father always says Michael is right. If I try to stand up for my rights, my father gives me a hypo.

THERAPIST: Things seem to be going pretty badly at home.

HENRY: Yes, oh yes! *(He weeps again. He goes on to relate other incidents. Then, he becomes very insistent upon knowing how therapy can help. Earlier in the hour, the therapist had said that she was there to talk things over with him.)*

HENRY: What good will it do to tell you about it; I don't understand.

THERAPIST: You mean, talking won't help?

HENRY: Yes. What good will it do?

THERAPIST: Sometimes people feel better about things after talking them over. *(The therapists falls into the trap of answering an emotional question as if it were a mere request for information. It leads to difficulties.)*

HENRY: Yes, but what good does it do to feel better about things if they still go on?

THERAPIST: Sometimes boys and girls can understand the way they really feel about things, and it helps them to know what they really want to do about their situations. *(The therapist is still trying to 'sell' the therapy session to the child.)*

HENRY: Yes, but after I tell you about it, what if it's still going on?

THERAPIST: I know you feel pretty hopeless, Henry. I can't change your parents. All I can do is to help you think through your own problems. *(Pause.)* It's hard for you to see it now, I know, but sometimes it helps.

HENRY: Well ... *(Goes on to relate several more incidents.)* I still don't understand. What good will it do to talk about it if they still keep on the same way?

THERAPIST: You mean, what can you do if they don't change?

HENRY: Yes.

THERAPIST: I don't really know. But I hope that's something we can work out together, here, when you come to see me.

HENRY: Suppose it lasts 10 or 15 years and they keep on?

THERAPIST: You just wonder how long you can bear it? *(This should have been the response earlier in the session.)*

HENRY: Yes, oh yes. *(He weeps several minutes.)*

THERAPIST: It all looks pretty black.

This first contact has been presented in some detail in order to indicate Henry's feeling of hopelessness about altering his situation. It is interesting to note that although he stated his inability to see any use in it, he made eager use of the therapist's presence. Despite his stuttering and gasping for breath, he spoke very rapidly, and was astonished when the hour was up. He did not even see the paints and other materials until the third therapy hour. Then he painted a boy in jail, behind heavy black bars – a perfect projection of his feelings. Like many adult clients, Henry began therapy with a view of his problems as existing outside himself, in the actions of other people. Hence, he avidly desired the punishment of his 'villains'. The tenth therapy hour brought some interesting changes, as may be seen in this excerpt.

HENRY: Michael and I had a fight. I wanted the window shut, I felt cold. He yelled, 'Who shut the window?' I said, 'I did!' So he said I was a brat, and he opened it. So then I shut it again. He got up out of bed and opened it and then he hit me. So I threw a shoe at him, and it broke the lamp. He started to cry. He's such a baby, honestly! So then my father came in and he hit me. He always takes Michael's side. I told him, 'Dad, Michael's your favourite.' He says he has no favourites, and that I'm just a little snot. He was lying, though.

THERAPIST: You feel he's pretty unfair to you, is that it?

HENRY: And sometimes I get so mad!

THERAPIST: You really get sore at him.

HENRY: I hate him!

THERAPIST: You despise him.

HENRY: Yes. I'd love to pay him back, too.

THERAPIST: You'd like some revenge?

HENRY: Yes. If only he weren't here.

THERAPIST: You'd like to be rid of him?

HENRY: I'd like to kill him.

THERAPIST: You want him dead?

HENRY: Uh-hm. That would be the end of my problems.

THERAPIST: With him dead, things would be OK with you?

HENRY: That's right. (*Pause.*) But would that end my problems? Supposing he were dead. I'd still be the same, I mean my shaking and all. Now if he'd have got killed earlier, that might have done me some good, but now it's too late for that. I am what I am already, and that's my problem. He's just a fool.

THERAPIST: So that, all in all, you've decided to let him live?

HENRY: Yes. It wouldn't do any good to kill him, I'd still have my same problems, and I'd still have to figure them out. He's supposed to be a grown man, but honestly, he acts just like a baby.

Interview 4

Source: Martin (1983: 126–131)

OBSERVING BOB LEE: Multi-Cultural Counselling and Consulting Centre, San Diego, California

This therapy session was conducted as a demonstration in front of a group of other therapists and counsellors at a workshop on therapy. The session itself interestingly illustrates therapy.

CLIENT: My nervousness is mostly related to the group, I think. Sometimes I have a ... a hesitancy to volunteer because I ... I always want to jump into things all the time. And sometimes I talk too much, and it ... uh ... don't let other people have a chance. That's why I've been waiting (Mm-hm) ...

THERAPIST: It's like there's some kind of ... uh ... enthusiasm or excitement to kind of get in there and get involved, but it's also a conflicting thing because part of you says, 'Hey, let's let some other people have the ... have some time.'

CLIENT: I have been told a lot, even as a facilitator, I step in too much ... and, um, ... I want ... I'm trying very hard not to do that ... I'm getting better at it, but I'm hesitant. Also, something that's coming up – that I realized when I was sitting there was ... the problem that I have ... I can almost start crying about it right away because ... but I don't want to do that.

THERAPIST: Maybe right now you're doing some of that ... like you're coming on a little too fast for your own self ... and you're saying, 'I want to step back a little from this and ...'

CLIENT: Well, it's something that I ... I've dealt with many therapists and I've gone through it a lot *(voice breaks)* and, uh, being in a therapeutic setting with people who are doing it, I start to think about my problem. Whereas, you know, normally I can go through the day and not think about it (Mm-hm) and, uh, being around so many people who I know are good counsellors, part of me wants to talk to 'em about it, and ... and part of me says, 'I'm sick of talking about it.' (Mm-hm) It's, uh, well, I want to tell you what it is, so you won't just be responding to this vague problem and it ... the label for it was originally called 'anorexia nervosa'. And I don't know if you know what this is. (Mm-hm) ... I think the label upsets me ...

THERAPIST: It's like you're having to live with some label ...

CLIENT: *(crying)* Sort of ... I don't think other people label me that any more, but it ... on the outside it looks like it's gone, but it's not ... on the inside of me it's always still there (Mm-hm) and, uh, I feel like it's ... You know what that is, don't you? (Mm-hm) I don't know if we should ...

THERAPIST: Do you want to say more about that? Maybe we ... it would be better if you just said something about it ...

CLIENT: Well, uh ... it's something that happens to you that you don't realize is happening to you in the beginning and, um, it started with me a long time ago when I was in college *(voice breaking)*, and I just ... went on a diet, like a lot of other people go on diets, but I ... just, for some reason I couldn't stop doing it ... I ... It was almost like I had to have complete control ... but anyway, I didn't realize what I was doing, and I had some doctor, my doctor, you know, say to me, gave me this book to read about it, and I said, 'Naw, that's not me,' and eventually I realized it was me, but I still couldn't stop it ... and now, even though I've gained the weight back, I'm terrified by the idea every day ... It's, um, it seems like there was another person inside of me, always talking to me (Mm-hm), and I want to get rid of it so bad ... and I've talked to so many people, and I wasn't going to talk to anybody here because I've decided I can only get rid of it myself ... but I guess every little discussion about it makes it get a little better, so ... I volunteered ...

THERAPIST: Like there's still something compelling in you to tell somebody else about it, and hopefully this time maybe ...

CLIENT: Somebody else who might ... who might be able to help me understand it a little better because I could go around and talk about it sometimes. Sometimes I can talk about it very ... like, therapist. And I've been asked to work with people who've had it, and ... and, and I can't do it because what happens is I get jealous of the patient ... *(crying)* That's hard for me to admit. (Mm-hm)

THERAPIST: It's like that's something you don't like about yourself that you do that ...

CLIENT: That I get jealous?

THERAPIST: Jealous of the patient.

CLIENT: Yeah, I think, it's crazy ... but on the other hand, if I see someone who's really thin or working with someone, and I think, 'How come I can't do that?' ... and I used to have so much control, and I used to be able to not eat, and I used to be able to turn down certain things and stuff, and now I don't have that any more, and I get jealous of the, and I ... feel a little crazy ... now I can go around and have a normal life and no one would guess, there's a former anorexic walking the street, but it's ... it's still there, it causes a lot of problems in relationships ...

THERAPIST: Like you can disguise that from most of the world most of the time pretty effectively, but inside you know that it's still there ...

CLIENT: I can't seem to exactly turn it off, my, uh, my behaviours are changed – I'll sit down at the table and eat, but almost the entire time, I'm ... someone's talking to me, ... it's like 'You shouldn't eat that, you should eat that, this has that many calories, you can't eat the whole day if you eat that,' and I just want it, just 'Shut up' ... I guess ...

THERAPIST: 'Shut up, leave me alone,' those voices just keep hounding you.

Interview 5

BACKGROUND: A black woman is experiencing financial difficulties because the father of her eldest child is not paying maintenance. She is at present living with another man. The client said she had to report the father of her eldest child for not paying maintenance, but she feared him because he used witchcraft.

FACILITATOR: So you are uncertain whether to apply for maintenance, because you are afraid of losing your child through witchcraft.

CLIENT: Yes, his family is very much into witchcraft. I am also afraid of losing my present boyfriend, if he does not like the idea of asking X for maintenance. The problem is, he does not like talking about it. He just says it is my business.

FACILITATOR: This seems to hurt and confuse you?

CLIENT: We fight if X comes around and I can't ask him for money for X's child. I want him to be happy.

FACILITATOR: You want to hurt nobody, not your first or your present boyfriend.

CLIENT: I just want to keep the peace, it worries me, but I just keep quiet because I am used to being hurt.

FACILITATOR: You feel unhappy a lot, and unable to change anything about it.

CLIENT: *(crying)* I do not understand my position and I just walk around, to avoid thinking. I prefer to be alone.

FACILITATOR: You seem confused, alone and hurt. Also unable to believe that anyone can help you.

CLIENT: I have never enjoyed myself, except when I was working and could look after my child.

FACILITATOR: You liked it when you were independent and could look after your child, who is very important to you.

CLIENT: Yes, I cannot even ask my parents for help.

FACILITATOR: You find it difficult to ask for help, your parents, first boyfriend, your present boyfriend ... you trust only yourself?

CLIENT: Yes, but now I am confused and don't know which way to turn.

FACILITATOR: Coming to ask me for help must have been difficult for you, as you prefer to be independent. I am a bit confused, because, on the one hand, you prefer to be alone and independent, but on the other hand you seem afraid of hurting both your previous and present boyfriends?

CLIENT: I don't know ... what do I want from them? Why do I want to protect them and from what? Is it only the witchcraft, or something else?

FACILITATOR: You seem confused at this point. These are some issues which are important to you.

CLIENT: Yes, I have to go and think about them, as I usually do.

Activity

A. Brief extracts from conversations, together with different responses, have been set out below. Select the response that you consider to be the most empathic.
Source: Johnson (1981: 148–151)

1   Siphiwe: 'I never seem to have enough time to do the things I enjoy. Just as I'm ready to go enjoy a nice game of golf or tennis, my brother reminds me of some

writing I need to do, or my wife saddles me with household chores. It's getting harder and harder to have the fun out of life that I expect to have. It's depressing!'

a Wanting to have fun is OK, but don't you think you should do some work too? I certainly wouldn't play golf if I thought that later I would regret not having worked. Life does have responsibilities.

b It's upsetting that your work and household responsibilities are increasing to the extent that you don't have time for the fun and recreation you want.

c Maybe your leisure activities are just a way of getting out of the unpleasant jobs you should do.

d I'm curious. How much time do you spend on your favourite sports?

e You're in a busy time of your life right now. I bet you will have more leisure time as you get older.

2 Frank: 'I never have any luck with cars. Every car I've ever bought has been a bad buy. Not only have I paid handsomely for the cars, but just when they are out of warranty, something major goes wrong. The car I have now needs a new engine. What's wrong with me? Why should I have all the bad luck?'

a You're wondering if it is your fault somehow that every car you own breaks down and has to have costly repairs. All the money you have to pay for car repairs depresses and angers you.

b Your anger about the poor quality of the cars you have owned is being turned against yourself and experienced as depression. Aren't the companies that made the cars to blame?

c What kind of cars do you buy? How many cars have you owned?

d Everyone has bad luck sometimes. I'm sure the next car you own will be more reliable. It's really not your fault the cars have turned out to be bad buys. No one can tell how much repair a car will need when they first buy it.

3 Puleng: 'I am so discouraged! Everything is going wrong in my life. It seems that everything I do is doomed to failure. I might as well not even try.'

a You feel discouraged and ready to give up because of failure.

b Your whole life is a mess and you feel suicidal.

c You are feeling discouraged because things aren't working out for you, is that right?

d You are feeling a little unhappy right now.

4 Tom: 'For instance, yesterday at work I messed up my job, and the boss made me stay until I got it right. She was really cross with me. I felt awful.'

a Your boss was in a bad mood.

b You messed up at work, and the boss made you stay late, and you felt awful.

c   You were depressed because your boss was angry at you and saw you as not doing your job correctly.

d   You're going to get fired because you can't do your job correctly.

5   Fatima: 'Because I had to stay late at work, I was late for my most important class. We had an exam and I know I failed it. I didn't even have time to finish the test. And I have to pass this class to graduate!'

a   You are failing because you messed up at work.

b   You think you did badly on a test.

c   Staying late at work made you late for an important exam, which you didn't finish.

d   You are worried about whether you will graduate after having done badly on an important exam in a required class.

B. The following are excerpts from conversations. Formulate your own empathic responses.

1   A woman (50 years old) is in the process of getting divorced: 'My husband and I have decided to get divorced *(she is speaking softly and slowly)*. I truly dread all the legal implications – *(pauses)* – actually I dread the entire business. I do not know what to expect *(sighs)*. I am middle-aged and don't think I'll get married again. I simply do not know what to expect.'

2   A married woman with two teenage daughters: 'Why does my husband always blame me for his problems with the children? I am always caught in the middle. He always complains to me about them. They complain about him. *(Looks the facilitator in the eye.)* I feel like moving out and leaving them on their own!'

3   A girl (17) in a reformatory: *(She is very quiet and does not respond to the facilitator's greeting; then shakes her head and looks around.)* 'I don't know what I am doing here. You are the third, or maybe the fourth, person to whom they have sent me. It is simply a waste of time! Why do they keep sending me here? Let's end this here and now.'

4   A girl in high school: 'My classmates do not like me and now I do not like them either! Why are they so mean? They tease me ... well, actually my clothes. But my parents cannot afford to buy me the uniform. Well, they do not have to like me, but they should stop teasing me!'

5   Woman (40) talking to a facilitator after being raped: 'It was very difficult for me to come here. A friend said I should call the police. But then I will become yet another story in the newspaper, like the ones you read every day! They will ask me all kinds of questions. Oh no! I would rather just forget about it all. I do not want to relive it over and over again!'

6   A factory worker explains: 'My work is fine. I earn good money, which my family and I enjoy very much. My wife and I both come from poor families and we have a much better life than when we were children. But the work I do is always the same, day after day. I may not be the smartest chap in the world, but I do believe that I have much more to offer than what the machines at work demand of me.'

7   A widow (50), discussing her son (17): 'He knows he can try his luck with me. If he stops talking to me, or becomes moody for a couple of days, I go out of my mind! He gets everything he wants and I know that I am the only one to blame. But I love him very much. After all, he lives with me and he is the man in the house. He is planning to go to the local university, which means that he will still be at home for quite a while.'

8   The mother says: 'My daughter of 15 no longer listens to me and she goes out with friends of whom I do not approve.'

9   A woman comes to consult you: 'I am having problems with my husband. He works overtime a great deal these days and spends very little time at home.'

10 Man (38 years old): 'I am so angry I could explode! My employer gave me a talking to, my car is giving problems, and when I got home the children's toys were lying around in my way!'

13.3 Empathy in the group

Greenberg in Farber et al. (1996: 257) stated that 'growth in a (group) does not occur in any environment, but only in an empathic environment of human dialogue ...'.

13.3.1 Working definition of empathy

According to Rogers in Farber et al. (1996: 296) an empathic facilitator tries:
*   'to assume the internal reference of the client
*   to perceive the world as the client sees it
*   to perceive the client himself as he is seen by himself
*   to lay aside all perceptions from the external frame of reference
*   to communicate something of this ... understanding to the client ... so that the client can
    – explore their inner and outer reality, and
    – explore the world in which that reality was forged'.

13.3.2 The main approaches to empathy in group work

There are two main approaches to empathy in group work:

- The first approach assumes that people can act empathetically only if they have experienced the situation themselves. When group facilitators follow this approach, they have to depend largely on the support of the group members because no facilitator can have shared all the experiences of group members. The group facilitator has to enable the group members who have had the same experiences to show empathy for one another and also to help the other group members to participate in the showing of empathy. The correct use of the communication process by the facilitator is therefore of utmost importance.

- In the other approach, authors or group facilitators such as Corey (1990) maintain that it would be wrong to assume that group facilitators will be able to act with empathy only if they have already experienced the situation. The professional's knowledge and skills will enable them to enter into the inner life of the members by means of the group process. Group facilitators, however, must also be careful that, due to their professional knowledge, they do not become directive and try to force the communication process. The incorrect use of knowledge and skills can therefore also be detrimental to empathy, communication, and group process.

13.3.3 The role of the facilitator in empathy

Empathy in groups implies that facilitators:

- will view the members' experiences through their eyes
- put themselves in the shoes of the group members, in other words understand the members' needs, feelings, thoughts, behaviour, self, and values
- are able to provide accurate feedback on the experiences of the members, although such feedback must not be an exact repetition of the words used by the members (Garvin 1987: 92)
- pay attention to the verbal and non-verbal communication of the group members
- react verbally and non-verbally to the communication of the members. This is done by relating to the group what a member has said, and by showing the members or group that they understand what they are saying or are trying to understand what they are saying.
- communicate within the group process

- behave non-defensively
- act in a non-judgemental fashion
- do not prescribe to the group
- listen to the group with an open mind. This means that facilitators should also be receptive to new ideas. According to Vanderschot (in Lietser et al. 1990: 269), an open mind means that the 'leader is an "empty box" which must be filled by members'.

Example 13.3

It was the last session and the facilitator observed anger in the members. The members said they were cross because the facilitator was going to leave them. The facilitator reflected their feelings and shared that she was also a little cross with herself.

Activity

In a group of teenagers in a children's home, Rina started crying unexpectedly during one of the sessions. Lucy reacted by saying, 'Stop it, the children's home hurts us just as much as it hurts you.'

Give an empathic response to:

1 Rina
2 Lucy
3 the group as a whole.

13.4 Empathy in the community

For the facilitator communicating with individuals and groups in the community, using empathy as described in this chapter is important. From a person-centred perspective, empathy is seen as a 'way of being', it becomes part of you in your everyday life. Empathy is also about not knowing and not assuming and about the acknowledgment of differences. If you move around in the community talking to groups and individuals, the facilitator will have the intention of listening and understanding non-judgementally, then feeding back his or her understanding.

To truly understand what the individuals and groups within the community wish to say, the facilitator needs an appreciation for people. A facilitator who puts people first, respects them, and can appreciate their abilities, skills, and knowledge is one who can show empathy. The people in the community will soon sense whether the facilitator is really trying to understand them and whether he or she can demonstrate his or her understanding of the community.

Here is another quote from an old lady talking about an empathic social work student:

> '*She admired the plans that we made to stretch our budgets and how we survive. Somehow we realized that we had some dignity ... We started to enjoy the company that emerged out of the visits of Matjila. She shared what she became aware of, while talking and listening to us. We experienced that she cared about our nearly desperate situation. She also shared her admiration for our coping skills ...*' *(Louw 2002: 45)*

As this quotation illustrates, empathy may be shown when communicating with the individuals and groups in the community as follows:
- Empathy is applicable to any conversation with individuals and groups within the community.
- The facilitator, by allowing the community to teach him or her, learns from them, listens to them, and thus demonstrates his or her empathic way of being within the community.
- Empathy is sometimes seen as a reflection of feelings. It is much more than that. It is an effort to understand and respect the person's feelings, ideas, perspectives, needs, actions, self, meanings, and values. This does not mean that we bombard the client with questions, but rather encourage the client to tell his or her story. Questions and probes that can be used are as follows:
  - 'Tell me more about ...'
  - 'I am not clear ...'
  - 'Can you please help me out ...?'
  - 'How come ...?'
  - 'Would you please explain that to me ...'
  - 'What do you mean by that ...?'
  - 'Help me to understand correctly ...'
  - 'Please elaborate ...'

Example 13.4

When facilitators are working in communities and they are unfamiliar with the customs and the meanings attached to the customs by the community, such customs may be interpreted from the facilitator's frame of reference. For instance, when some black people receive a gift, the recipient may clap his or her hands and then cup them to receive the article. A white person may interpret this as subservience to the person giving the gift, but this is certainly not the case. In another case, within a white community, it is customary for a man to get up when greeting another person, but in the Shona and Venda communities, it is more acceptable to remain sitting when greeting a person.

Example 13.5

When the facilitator has entered a community, and members of the community indicate that they are wealthy or poor, the facilitator can find out from the community what their perception of wealthy or poor is. The facilitator has his or her own idea of what wealth is, and if the facilitator assumes that he or she knows what this means to the community, the facilitator will probably misunderstand the community. In certain communities, wealth is related to the number of cattle and sheep that a person owns. Wealth is also sometimes related to the number of children a person has. In other communities, money is the norm for wealth, whereas in others, possessions may be the norm.

In connection with the concept of wealth, Davis (1994: 20) gave the following example. In a village in Mauritania, a group of researchers discovered what it means to 'breathe': 'We have three levels of wealth,' the villagers explained. 'Those who have nothing, those who have a little and those who can breathe.' There were only two people 'breathing' in this community of 140 people. Wealth is measured by the number of goats someone owns – a rich person has three.

In another example given by Wenresti et al. (1995: 269–270), in the Philippines wealth is ranked in the following categories:

May sarang (better off)
- have enough money to support their family
- have something to depend on
- can afford to send their children to school until college
- have capital, *sari-sari* store, pump boat, stable job and regular salaries.

Tunga Tunga (middle)
- can send their children to high school only
- have something to support their family
- have small capital and boat.

Pigado (poor)
- no permanent job or source of income
- sometimes cannot eat three times a day
- if they get sick they will suffer hunger
- no capital nor boat
- borrowers of money from other people.

In summary, basic empathy entails taking a not-knowing and not-assuming position and making sure to listen, understand, give feedback, and have a non-judgemental attitude so that people can feel safe enough to share and explore further, which will lead to advanced empathy.

Putting thinking and values into practice: Dealing with unsymbolized experiences

Introduction

In every encounter, irrespective of at which stage of your work with the client it occurs (in other words, whether it is the first or the eighth interview), the basic skills required are to observe and hear clients, in order to understand them and to communicate this understanding to them. The only thing that changes is the *kind* of understanding. Initially, by using the basic skills, one shows understanding of the client's symbolized self. Then the advanced communication skills are implemented to share one's understanding of those experiences that threaten the self, and are therefore not symbolized or are symbolized in a distorted way.

If work is being done with a client's unsymbolized or distorted experiences, the facilitator usually also uses basic empathy because exploration of these experiences could be very painful. The facilitator should be careful to communicate his or her understanding of the pain to the client (rather than ignoring or trying to minimize it). If the deeper response fits, the facilitator could become excited and try to go on too quickly with this issue. This can and must be done, but not necessarily immediately, or without recognizing the associated experiences. If you do not show empathy here, the client might become fearful, feel threatened and anxious, begin to defend again (proposition 16) and perhaps lose confidence in you.

If you realize that a client is feeling threatened, you should immediately show that you understand this and allow the client to move at his or her own pace. In this way you demonstrate that you do not expect anything from the client for which he or she is not ready. Note that this must be *demonstrated* to the client, even if it is only by your choice of words. You could say, for instance: 'It seems as though this issue hurts you very much/is painful/makes you anxious/makes you feel like hiding/running away,' or something of this kind.

In summary, some essential principles for the use of all the advanced skills follow:

1 They deal with the client's *un*symbolized experiences.
2 Only experiences that *threaten the self of the client* are denied conscious symbolization or distorted.
3 To be able to use these skills, therefore, one needs to understand how the self is perceived by the client, and
4 How (by which of the client's experiences) this self is being threatened.
5 Only by enabling the client to understand which experiences are threatening the self, can the self be reconstructed.
6 All of these experiences are understood from the client's frame of reference.

CHAPTER 14

Advanced empathy

14.1 Introduction

Advanced empathy involves the ability 'to see clearly what clients only half see or hint at. This deeper kind of empathy involves '"sensing" meanings of which the client is scarcely aware' (Rogers 1980: 142). It therefore concerns the client's *unsymbolized experiences* as discussed under propositions 11 and 13. It is very important for facilitators not to use their own frames of reference, but rather to build up the skill of understanding clients fully (regarding both their symbolized and unsymbolized experiences and how the latter threaten the self). In a certain sense, facilitators understand clients in ways in which clients do not consciously understand themselves and, in this way, enable clients to understand themselves more fully.

This deeper understanding serves no purpose, however, if clients do not hear it and therefore it must be communicated to them in some way. Martin (1983: 3) refers not only to empathy, but also to what he calls 'evocative empathy', which is 'communicated understanding of the other person's intended message'. Each word in this definition is important. It is not enough to *understand* what clients are saying, facilitators must also *hear* what they *intend*. In other words, they must understand the intended or implied message. In addition, facilitators need to react to the message by communicating this understanding to clients.

14.2 Advanced empathy and the individual

14.2.1 Identification and communication of implied messages

In Section 14.1 we mentioned Martin's guidelines for the facilitator in connection with the implicit message. This means that the facilitator has to be able to hear *more* than just what the client is saying directly.

There is also usually more than one intended message encoded in the explicit message (which usually only has one meaning). The client might, for instance, only convey his or her rage and frustration to the facilitator, while his or her pain and heartache are conveyed implicitly. Clients might convey explicitly what they want changed, but what they want *not* to change or to retain will be implicit in the message, or vice versa. The facilitator must therefore search for the 'other' or deeper messages that have been conveyed previously, or that manifest in other forms such as non-verbal behaviour (e.g. the tone of voice or facial expression).

In everyday life, we regularly listen to people's implied messages. For example, if someone says that he is tall, the implicit message is that he is not short; if we say that someone is thin, it implies that she is not fat; if someone says she is tired, it implies that she does not have a great deal of energy; if someone says he is worried about his child, it implies that he is concerned about the child and that he cares about what is happening to the child. It also says something about the father's self in relation to this child.

The implied message could be related to various aspects of the self, such as the perceptions, needs, behaviour, emotions, the self, and the values of the individual (see Section A).

Example 14.1

A mother comes to ask for your advice: 'I would like to know what to do with my daughter who suddenly wants to do exactly as she pleases, without asking me. I feel I have lost all control over her'. What could the implied message be in a case like this? It could mean that she is uncertain about what to do, as she might be worried about her daughter and their relationship, as well as her 'self' as a mother, which developed in interaction with her daughter. In previous interactions with her daughter, she saw her 'self' as a present, responsible, and involved mother. Her behaviour would fit with this self. Now that this self is being threatened by the changes, she no longer knows how to behave. A new self needs to develop, and until she has symbolized a new self for herself (not you), she might feel helpless and confused. The use of the words 'no longer' makes it sound as though the relationship has changed recently and she might be afraid of losing her daughter, which may threaten her self-structure as a mother.

Your understanding of the implied message can be conveyed to the client in any way that fits with your self, and that of the client. You could say, for instance 'You are afraid of doing something that would estrange your daughter', or 'Your relationship with your daughter is very important to you and you do not want to spoil it', or 'You feel as though you no longer know this child of yours and this confuses you', or 'What has always worked in the past in your relationship with your daughter no longer works, and now you do not know what to do'. The message could be conveyed in one of these ways, or in a combination of them. What is particularly important is that you should see whether it links with the client's frame of reference and enables her to move deeper. If it does not succeed, your intuition was wrong and she will correct you. She might say something like: 'No, this child of mine has always been difficult and I'm getting tired of struggling with her disobedient behaviour.' In a case like this, the facilitator could first fall back on basic empathy, by saying something like: 'You are angry and discouraged and you are in the mood to give up.' The fact that she has come to you for advice indicates, however, that something is preventing her from just giving up and you could therefore add: 'But something is preventing you from simply giving up.' This could enable the mother to explore her own experiences further. The 'sudden' change in the mother/daughter relationship may relate to life-span changes, like adolescence.

If we want to link with the client's frame of reference, we cannot ignore her request for advice. It could help the client more if we listen intently and enable her to symbolize her fears. If the facilitator does give advice, he or she confirms the client's fear that she is not good enough or reliable enough to take decisions and in this way her self-confidence is undermined still further. By enabling the mother to discover for herself what her fears are, and to find behaviour that would be appropriate to any change in her self-structure, she is also enabled to handle herself in a way that suits her.

In a family where sexual molestation occurs, the mother could say something like: 'There are things in our family which we don't like, but we are still a close family.' The facilitator can hear that the closeness of the family (proposition 4) is very important to her and say something like: 'It is so important for you to maintain the family that you are prepared to endure a great deal of pain for it,' or 'You would sacrifice many other things for the sake of your close family,' or 'You are afraid that speaking about the things that are painful will be detrimental to the closeness of your family.'

The examples of distorted values that were given under proposition 10 are also relevant here: The mother's choice of words: 'I *must* punish my child regularly' suggests that someone says she must. The facilitator could say something such as: 'It sounds as though someone is sitting on your shoulder and telling you what to do or what kind of mother to be,' or 'The fact that you feel compelled to apply strict discipline makes it sound to me as though it is not entirely your own choice.'

Activity

Below are a few extracts from conversations. Identify the implied message(s) and formulate responses to convey to the clients.

1 A girl says: 'Perhaps it would be better if I didn't speak about these things.'
2 A couple feels that their new baby, whom they love very much, takes up a great deal of time.
3 A child obtained 80 per cent in a test and his parents say: 'It was probably just a fluke.'
4 A mother is discussing one of her children who has been referred to a doctor and she is angry with the school because she does not think that it is necessary.
5 The parents are upset because their daughter, who has just turned sixteen, suddenly wants to start wearing jeans.

14.2.2 Identification of themes

When clients share their inner world of experience with us, they may talk as if these experiences are separate from each other. But, as we perceive people as a whole, and as the self is central in their experiences, these experiences are usually connected to each other, and the self, in some way. There is often a main theme to their statements. This means that the sentences share the same or similar meanings (although this might not be obvious at first glance, and that is why we need to listen with a 'third ear'). We can ask *ourselves* what the shared experiences have in common. (We cannot ask the client, because we are dealing with unsymbolized experiences, and this means the client is unaware of them.)

These themes are, therefore, not necessarily explicit or obvious in the (sometimes sensational) story of the client, but implicit. Although themes come to the fore repeatedly, only a good listener can hear them.

Egan (1994: 183) reminds us to:

- 'Make sure the themes you discover are based on the client's experience and are not just the artefacts of some psychological theory. Advanced empathy works because clients recognize themselves in what you say.'
- Clients themselves are often unaware of the fact that certain themes are inherent in their story. If these themes are pointed out to clients, it could help them to create new symbolizations and restructure their self.

- The *way* in which these themes are picked up and conveyed to the clients must give evidence of the facilitator's communication skill and must also be meaningful to the client.

The guidelines that were mentioned with regard to tentativeness are also applicable here (see Chapter 13). The facilitator's identification of themes is still hypothetical until the themes have been confirmed by the client. The themes must therefore be conveyed tentatively to the client for him or her to confirm.

Activity

1 Indicate the themes for the groups below:
   a) Afrikaans, English, isiZulu, Setswana, Sesotho, Spanish, German
   b) men, women, children
   c) pears, peaches, apples
   d) parents, brothers, sisters
   e) shoes, earrings, twins
   f) foetus, baby, toddler, teenager, adult
   g) respect, individualization, confidentiality
   h) Freud, Rogers, Skinner
   i) love, hate, aggression, frustration
   j) isolation, alone, lonely, exile
   k) warm, snug, togetherness, closeness
2 Can you think of similar groups of words?

Example 14.2

The client, a young woman, revealed during an interview that she was removed from her parents by the 'welfare' when she was a young child. She was put into foster care twice and each time she was removed after a few months by the 'welfare' and placed somewhere else, until she landed up in a children's home. She was not there long when she had to move again, because she was too old for it. She was in a place of safety for two months, and from there she was moved to various families for weekends and holidays. Each time she felt like an outsider and she still missed her own family. The welfare informed her, however, that they did not know who her own family were.

Various themes can be deduced from this story, such as the many changes and the lack of stability in her life. This is related to the lack of permanent, close relationships (including her relationship with the 'welfare'). The facilitator could therefore hypothesize that it would be difficult for her to develop a close relationship of trust and he or she could explore this theme with regard to his or her relationship with the client, by way of immediacy (which is discussed below).

Example 14.3

The client, a girl in an institution, related during one conversation how angry she was with her parents because they did not take care of her properly. Later she sounded nostalgic about her family and said that if she could speak to her parents now, she would tell them how much she missed them. During a later conversation she spoke about an argument that she had with one of the hostel parents. She is still angry with the hostel parent, but although she wonders what the hostel parent thinks now, she does not see her way clear to speaking to the person. The theme here could be that she does not feel free to discuss negative feelings with the people concerned for fear of losing their love.

Example 14.4

A couple lost their son in a car accident caused by someone who was driving under the influence of alcohol. The husband's reaction to the death of his son was to prosecute the person who was driving the motorcar, and to become so involved in the court case that his wife felt he no longer cared what happened to them as a family. He was never at home and they never had time to speak to each other. The wife's reaction to the death of her son was depression, to such an extent that she sometimes did not get out of bed, did not take care of the house and never went out to mix with people. This irritated the husband a great deal and he felt that she was just thinking of herself and feeling sorry for herself. The couple's experience of the situation was therefore that each one felt that the other no longer cared for him or her and was occupied purely with his or her own thing. After the facilitator had listened carefully to all the factual details of the story, she could identify the theme: both of them were actually grieving in their own ways and assimilating their son's death. By asking for help, the couple also indicated that they needed each other very much. By listening carefully, the facilitator was able to identify this theme and to help the couple hear that their negative frame of reference with regard to each other could conceal a *positive* one by linking their behaviour to grieving and not to a lack of interest.

14.2.3 Avoid negativity and blaming

The skill in and meaningfulness of identifying themes is based on pointing out the theme without blaming anyone or making a particular value judgement about anyone's behaviour. The way in which the theme is conveyed to the client is therefore of the greatest importance. The facilitator can, for instance, begin as follows: 'Correct me if I have misheard, but what I hear throughout is your need for closeness.' The facilitator could then continue by indicating which phrase suggested or implied this. If this is significant to the client, he or she will answer in the affirmative and expand on the subject. It is important, for instance, for the facilitator not to respond that the client has a need for closeness, but that her husband maintains a distance. Such a statement implies a reproach against the husband. If the theme of closeness is identified, the client will make this connection.

Reproaching or blaming a person may be experienced as a threat to the self, against which the client has to defend himself or herself.

Activity

1   What would you say is the direct result of identifying the particular theme in example 14.4?
2   How do you think that the clients might react in example 14.4 above to the new formulation of their situation ('don't care' was changed by the facilitator to 'grieving')?

Example 14.5

Mr A is 40 years old and is unmarried. He was convicted for theft at work (his first offence). He is very worried because his mother, who is 65, will be left alone. He has supported her from the time he left school because she suffers from a chronic illness and cannot work.

Mr A did not pass his matriculation examination and also did not repeat the examination. He maintains that it was just as well that he did not go back because his father died during that year, and he had to support his mother. He took a poorly paid job at a supermarket. Six months after he left school, he had to report for military duty. It was very traumatic for him to leave his mother alone at that stage.

After he had done his military service he started working for the financial institution where the theft occurred later. Although he could have taken professional examinations at the institution, he never did so. After about 20 years' service, his salary was still very modest.

Mr A's social life is very limited. He does not have a motorcar or a driver's licence. He made an unsuccessful attempt to obtain a driver's licence at one stage. He has never tried again since then.

As a child Mr A was hospitalized for a long period because of a bone disease. His mother visited him regularly in hospital, although she was unable to drive and it was very difficult for her to get there.

As a teenager Mr A did not go out with his peers since he did not wish to leave his mother alone. His father used to abuse alcohol and he was very worried about his mother. Because of this state of affairs he does not have many friends.

Activity

1 Which theme(s) could you identify in this example?
2 How could you identify the particular theme(s) in a non-threatening way and convey them to the client? You can give more than one formulation. (Remember that this is merely hypothetical since they cannot be confirmed with the client.)

14.2.4 Helping clients to make connections – connecting islands

A client's statements in one interview or spread over various interviews could look like separate entities to the facilitator and the client. Yet, if one thinks of proposition 3, namely that the individual should be seen as a whole, the facilitator could wonder about the connections between seemingly separate statements.

This skill, which we could call *connecting islands*, is related to the identification of themes. The various stories that the client tells usually have a pervasive theme (as illustrated previously) and are therefore connected to each other. Facilitators who are able to see these connections can give feedback about them to the client. Egan (1994) uses the metaphor of connecting islands to illustrate clearly that the facilitator should not see the islands (statements, stories, experiences, problems, contexts) as separate entities, but should try to determine which of the things that occur on island A are also found on islands B, C, and D. This connection between islands could be horizontal, such as between the various contexts in which people live from day to day: their work, their home, and their circle of friends. There could also be vertical islands, such as similar behaviour that is found among people in various generations. Particular patterns of behaviour, beliefs, values, and experiences that are observed among different generations may be factors that eventually play a very important role in the perceptions or processes of the current family. For example, in certain families we often find very strong female figures in every generation, alcohol dependence, absent fathers, or the idea that achievement is a very important prerequisite for acceptance (see Carter and McGoldrick 1989).

As Egan (1990: 219) correctly points out, clients often speak about these islands as though they have nothing to do with each other. Even if the contents differ, the process that occurs may be the same, as in the case of the husband and wife who are both occupied in a completely different way with their own process of grieving.

The facilitator enables the client to build a bridge between these islands. According to Egan (1990: 219), this bridge is built with empathy and is therefore part of advanced empathy, not merely an interpretation by the facilitator. The identification or connecting of islands (as in the case of identifying themes) is hypothetical and is not correct if it does not have significance for the client. If the client does not accept it, other connections should be sought and 'therefore it is extremely important to check advanced empathic statements with the client' (Egan 1990: 219). This checking of the meaning that the empathic statement has for the client can be done by making the statement tentative (as Martin (1983) illustrates), for instance:

*   'I do not know whether I am correct, but ...'
*   'Correct me if I heard the wrong thing ...'
*   'I might be completely wrong, but what I hear is the following ...'
*   'I will give you my explanation of the situation, but you must tell me if you disagree with it.'

The following comic riddles demonstrate how new symbolization can occur if seemingly separate entities are connected (*You*, 23 March 1994):

*   Which trees grow fingers? Palm trees
*   What do you call a painting of a bad-tempered woman? The Mona (*moaner*) Lisa
*   Heard of the ship transporting red paint that crashed on a brown rock? The crew were marooned.

Example 14.6

In your work with families you can ask yourself what connects the stories told by different members of a family.

The family in this example consists of four children, three sisters (F, 28 years old; M, 24 years old; and S, 22 years old) and one son (B, 20 years old). The parents both died two years previously.

When the facilitator spoke to F, some of her statements were: 'I worry about my brother and sister', 'I have to take care of my siblings', 'I have a family of my own, but my brother and sisters take a lot of my energy', and 'I feel torn between the interests of the different people in my life'.

In an interview with M, the following was mentioned: 'I have to provide for my sister and brother', 'I have to see to it that my sister and brother are taken care of', 'I am afraid for my sister and brother's future', and 'I am not sure that my siblings can take care of themselves'.

In an interview with S, the following was said: 'My sisters would like me to get a job, but I am not sure,' 'Left to my own devices, I would be able to decide what to do,' and 'I don't know whether I can leave the family home.'

In an interview with the brother, the following was said: 'I am the only son of the family,' 'Since my father is dead, I must be the head of the house,' 'I must look after the family home; I cannot do what my sisters ask of me.'

We can connect the islands of each person's statements (vertically – understanding the person as a whole, proposition 3). It can be said that all the statements made by F regarding her own perception of herself and her siblings, point to her need to be responsible for them. She feels older and in charge of them like a (substitute) mother or the head of the family.

The same can be said of M and, in a different way, of B, who believes he should be the head of the family because he is now the only male member.

But looking at S, one gets the overall impression that she no longer needs parental supervision yet she is not sure whether she is ready to leave home.

Connecting the family members horizontally could be portrayed as follows:

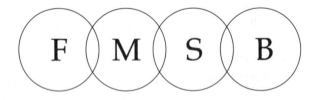

It seems that three of the children perceive themselves in parental (responsible) roles. This implies that they see a family with small (dependent) children. But the experience of the members of themselves as parental figures does not fit with this portrayal of the family self or identity. Even S, who does not feel like a parent, seems to need less parenting and more independence. They are all connected in their differing perceptions of what kind of family they are, what they need from the family, and what they have to give to this family.

Activity

1 Formulate responses to each family member, and to the family as a whole.
2 Connect the following statements by various family members, and formulate appropriate responses to each one, and the family:
Mother: 'Don't you (facilitator) agree with me that we should ...?'
Father: 'I am sure that you (facilitator) can see that my plans for the family are valid.'
Child: 'If you (facilitator) could only see the family from my point of view.'
3 A woman makes the following statements during different interviews:
'I am not sure whether my mother really understands me.'
'I have spoken to my uncle about my life, but he doesn't seem to be able to help me.'
'I have prayed to God about this matter, but my prayers have not been answered.'
What is the connecting 'bridge' and how would you communicate it to her?
4 Which islands that occur in you own family could you connect in ways that you have not thought of before?

14.2.5 Exploring distortions

The examples discussed under proposition 11 of Rogers' theory relate specifically to those experiences that are denied or distorted because they threaten the self-structure for some or other reason. They are therefore part of the client's defences and should be handled cautiously:

> 'The therapist perceives the client's self as the client has known it, and accepts it (basic empathy); he perceives the contradictory aspects which have been denied to awareness and accepts those too as being part of the client; and both of these acceptances have in them the same warmth and respect.' (Rogers 1987: 41).

In this warm, safe climate, clients can explore these inner discrepancies or contradictory experiences of self, and find some way of reorganizing the self.
Please note: These discrepancies refer to inner conflicts of clients' experiences, and not to differences between what the facilitator thinks or expects of the client and the clients' own experiences.
One way in which the facilitator can 'hear' that the client cannot symbolize something is to listen to the *contradictions* or discrepancies between different experiences or statements. An example of this occurs when what clients say verbally differs from their non-verbal behaviour.

Example 14.7

A client says he is feeling well, but he is frowning. The facilitator could say something like: 'I heard you saying that you are well but from looking at you, unless I am mistaken, the expression on your face says something else?'

Example 14.8

The client says that he and his mother have always had a good relationship, but every time he mentions her, he frowns or clenches his fists. In a case like this, the facilitator might wonder whether he is not sending two different messages. The example could also be extended to a value conflict (proposition 10): If the client has taken over the value that to be a good son one must have a good relationship with one's mother, he will not feel free to symbolize any negative experiences about her. The facilitator could therefore begin by first maintaining the symbolized self: 'It is very important to you to have a good relationship with your mother', or 'You see yourself as a good son, who loves his mother' and then the facilitator could add: 'You are afraid that it will be destroyed', or '... and it might therefore be difficult to allow yourself to be angry at her, sometimes?'

Example 14.9

The client says at some stage of the conversation: 'I do not like being told what to do.' Later he says again: 'I am afraid that people will reject me if I do ...' The first statement could mean that he needs to do his own thing, to be independent. The second statement, however, indicates a need for other people's approval. The question is, therefore, whether the client is aware of the discrepancy and further, can these two seemingly conflicting experiences be integrated into one self?

The statements that clients make over a period of time should also naturally be related to each other. Refer also to the advanced empathy skill, the linking of islands.

It is usually easier and more tentative to end such a response to the client with a question. If the client denies the discrepancy, the facilitator should *not* insist that it is correct. The principles that were discussed in Chapter 13 on accurate empathy are also applicable here. Clients know what they are experiencing and what they are ready for. Even if your observation is correct, it could be that the client is not ready yet to examine the question. The facilitator must therefore fall back on basic empathy and listen and observe further, to see exactly what the client is experiencing and when he or she is ready to delve more deeply.

Exploring the discrepancy does not necessarily imply that one part of the discrepancy needs to be changed. It is therefore not a veiled form of criticism, but rather an effort to enable clients to symbolize themselves more fully. There could, for example, be a conflict between two needs: a mother needs to be alone sometimes, but also to be a good mother who spends a great deal of time with her husband and children. If she is not aware of the two needs, they could disrupt and immobilize her. If she is aware of the fact that both needs are important to her, she could accommodate both in some way in her self-structure and/or behaviour. The facilitator cannot predict or determine what she will do with her new symbolization.

Activity

How would you react in the situations below?

1　The wife says that it is very important to her to be a good wife to her husband, but at the same time she seems rather cross.
2　A woman says that she feels that her eldest child is becoming big and independent, but then she says that he is the only son and man in the house.

Exploring discrepancies between information received according to someone else's frame of reference and the symbolized self of the client.

It can happen that the facilitator has to deal with a client who has received some news about the self that does not fit with the symbolized self. This could pertain to medical information (like diagnoses of illness), or to some other event in the client's life. The one who imparts the information can become very frustrated if the client refuses to accept the given information. The person-centred facilitator can, in terms of the theory, understand the threat the information might have for the client and by exploring the 'what and how' of the threat, enable the client to also explore the nature of this threat.

Example 14.10

A mother of four children who is the only breadwinner and who has been very strong, healthy, and independent all her life, is admitted to hospital with a kidney problem. After many tests, the doctors inform her (from their frame of reference) that she is a chronic patient who will have to come in for dialysis three times a week. They try to convince her that she will always remain sick. They cannot understand that she refuses treatment and are amazed when she discharges herself from hospital. Taking into account the earlier discussion of the self, how do you think this woman has always experienced herself? Do you agree that this self is now threatened? In addition to the fact that her self-structure is threatened, the children who are waiting for her at home, and who need her, also stand in the way of her symbolizing the information about her illness.

Example 14.11

A girl is in a place of safety and is waiting to hear to which children's home she will be sent. She arrives early for the appointment with the social worker.

H: (social worker): You are early. I wonder whether it means that you are anxious?

M: Yes, I can't wait to hear where I am going. Isn't there anyone we can contact?

H: You would like to know as soon as possible. *(She phones the Department, which informs her that M is going to X. She tells M. The girl's face falls and she looks worried.)*

H: It seems that you feel that this is not good news?

M: I have heard a great deal about the place and very little of it is good. They say that it is a bad school which is full of gangs.

H: You are uncertain – not just about the transfer, but also about your safety?

M: *(with tears in her eyes)*: I will miss P and S *(her friends)*. They cried when I told them I was being transferred.

H: You feel unhappy because you have to leave your friends behind. You will miss them a great deal and you are also worried about them; that they will miss you.

M: *(sighs)*: Yes, but still I am glad that I will be nearer to my mother, because she does not have the money to come and visit me here. I don't know why I am confused, because I knew from the beginning that I would not stay here forever.

H: Are you surprised that you allowed yourself to become attached to the place and its people?

M: Yes – as I said before, it isn't easy for me to start relationships with people. And now look at me.

Silence

M: I wonder if I will also be able to make friends with the others at the new place?

H: I am not quite sure what I'm hearing ... hope or uncertainty?

M: I don't know exactly. I will have to think about it and then we can talk again before I go.

In this case, the information received was only a part of the overall process between a facilitator and the girl. The facilitator also heard her fears, not only the symbolized ones, but also the unsymbolized or implied ones, and was not afraid to explore the girl's feelings openly. In this way they could move together to new symbolization and experiences.

14.2.6 Difference between implementing the basic and advanced skills

At the beginning of this chapter, we discussed the difference between basic and advanced skills at a theoretical level. However, they also entail different actions or skills (implementation). This difference is not always easy to identify, as both are types of empathy, from the client's frame of reference, and deal with clients' experiences. It is the kind of experience that differs as well as what the facilitator does with clients' experiences. As we have now discussed all the different types of advanced skills, we can look at how the implementation of the advanced and basic skills differs.

Example 14.12

The father of a 16-year-old boy says to the facilitator: 'My son does not listen to me any more. He comes and goes as he pleases, without asking or even telling me where he is going. I really don't know what to do.'

If the facilitator responds with something like: 'You seem concerned (or worried or frustrated) about the way your son is behaving' or 'the change in your relationship with your son is really upsetting you', this demonstrates basic empathy.

Please note: substituting one feeling word for another does not change basic empathy to advanced empathy, because you are still dealing with the same experience, in the same way!

However, if you move (advance) to the implied message, the implied threat to the self of the father in interaction with his son, this becomes advanced empathy. One can ask oneself why the father is so upset about the son's behaviour? How does this behaviour affect the father as a person?

Please note: it is the father's experiences we are dealing with here, not those of the son. Only the son can know his own experiential world and he is not in the room to share it with us. The father is, and we need to understand his experiential world, as influenced by his perception of the son, their relationship and himself. We need to take care not to become a 'ghost' voice, that is, not to speak for, or about, a person who is not physically present in the room.

The facilitator could respond with something like: 'You feel that your son does not respect you as his father, like he used to do. And now you could be wondering whether you are still his beloved and needed father figure.' Or you could say: 'Being a caring and responsible father appears to have been a big part of who you are, and now you seem to wonder how to deal with the possibility that you might not be needed quite as much as before.'

This example shows that the advanced response moves beyond the obvious experiences shared by the father, to how these experiences affect him as a person, his self (identity) as a father.

Another way of highlighting the difference between the basic and advanced skill is by exploring the difference between summarizing and connecting islands and developing a theme.

Example 14.13

A man, 29 years old, who has lost the use of his legs in an accident, says: 'My girlfriend does not visit me here any more. My family say that she is seeing someone else. I also don't know whether I can still go back to my old job. I wonder whether I will still be able to earn enough money to support my brothers and sisters. I am so frustrated at not being able to sort this out for myself.'

If, in your response, you just list all the things that have happened to him since the accident, you would be summarizing, that is, demonstrating basic empathy. However, seeing a connection between these things and how they affect the self (of the client as a person), and developing a theme from that connection, would be advanced empathy.

The theme can be identified by looking at what all the experiences he mentioned have in common. In this example, the theme seems to be one of loss: not just of his mobility, but also of the relationships he had before, for instance with his girlfriend and his family. The self that developed in interaction with his siblings, was that of a strong provider, and he fears that this self will now be lost to him. He also fears the possible loss of his independent self.

For your response to show advanced empathy, it needs to include something of this deeper understanding. You could say something like: 'You have lost so much through the accident. It seems as if you fear that you can no longer be the same, strong, independent person who not only does things for himself, but also takes care of others.'

These examples illustrate that the advanced skills are used to express a much deeper understanding of the client, about himself and what is threatening him as a person. It goes beyond what he has expressed directly, to what is only implied about what is really bothering him, (threatening the self) but of which he is not consciously aware.

If it is accurate, he might confirm it, if he feels safe and is ready to symbolize the experience. On the other hand, we might be wrong, and he can then correct us, by exploring what does fit with him. It could open up a new path of exploration. As long as we remain tentative in our responses, and allow clients to guide us, it is not so much the accuracy of our responses that matters, but our genuine attempts at really understanding the client in depth and demonstrating this to him.

Here it is again important to remember what Rogers said about not being passive, but rather, to actively attempt to share our deeper understanding with clients.

14.3 Advanced empathy in groups

This subsection is built on the theory and skill discussed in the previous subsection. Therefore, reading the examples mentioned and doing the activities of the previous subsection are prerequisites for you to understand this subsection.

The difference between empathy and advanced empathy is that in empathy you communicate to the group what they have said. In advanced empathy, on the other hand, the facilitator helps the group to communicate more clearly what they imply, hint, leave out, or state unclearly. For example, what are Lucy and Rina really saying to the facilitator and group members in the activity in Chapter 13? Are they unhappy with the children's home and if they are, what are they really unhappy about?

The facilitator can use advanced empathy skills to enable the members to create new perspectives, by making the implied explicit, identifying new themes, and connecting certain ideas expressed by the group members (Egan 1990: 216).

Example 14.14

Example 3 in the introduction to Section C shows how advanced empathy was used to enable the young people to improve their situation. After picking up that they were bored with the way they were spending their free time, the facilitator enabled them to explore how dissatisfied they were with their present situation and how they could choose to improve their situation.

Although dissatisfied, the members believed that they couldn't change their present situation. They, however, expressed the need for a camp and the desire to form a club. By enabling the members to recognize their abilities, the facilitator enabled them to plan a camp and to form a club which they then did, successfully.

Activity

Identify the skills of advanced empathy the facilitator used to enable the members to improve their situation in the above example. Motivate your answer.

14.4 Advanced empathy with communities

Basic empathy is one of the first skills in the helping process because, as Martin (1983: 3) puts it, 'for any other things to work, you must first make your client (community) feel deeply understood'. The same applies to communities. Their members must feel heard and understood.

Advanced empathy in community work means that facilitators try to hear the implied messages (the real needs) and themes in a community, connect the islands, and connect the themes. Freire (1972) refers to these themes as generative themes. Sometimes messages about needs are so clear that it is impossible to miss them, but these messages can also be 'hidden' or given in the form of solutions.

Ideally, in participatory work, unsymbolized experiences can be discovered by the groups in the community themselves. When collecting information, talking to the rest of the community, or drawing maps of the community, the groups have to look back, reflect, and evaluate what they have found, and so discover their own generative themes, connections, and implied messages (unsymbolized experiences).

Feedback to the rest of the community will be planned and decided on by the group or team. During the process of symbolizing needs, themes and issues, the facilitators' empathic 'way of being' or attitude is of the utmost importance.

Example 14.15

The example cited here is from a 'participatory rural appraisal' (PRA) – also called participatory learning and action (PLA) – exercise done in a rural community.

Three facilitators moved into a rural community. Firstly two groups of people took them through the community, showing them what the community looked like:

their houses, what they had planted, their cattle, etc. After that, they started drawing a map of the community on the ground. Cormack (1993: 16–18) continues:

> Soon a few men were busy, and a crowd of about 60 people had gathered. Some of these gave suggestions to the 'artists', who responded with dialogue or argument. Gradually point by painful point, the group moved toward a general agreement. Moment by moment they added to the expanding, increasingly detailed map. In the meantime several children took a keen interest too. But some of the men had an attitude of 'This is men's stuff, get scarce!' They shooed the children away. One of the facilitators called the boys to the side and asked them to draw their own map. Three or four boys were soon busily drawing, while a much larger group of boys watched and gave suggestions. In the meantime the men's map grew and grew. They added rivers, mountains, the school, two churches, and a skull of an animal to indicate livestock losses. Eventually they covered a sizeable area – about 15 metres by 10 metres. When everything was done, we asked them to explain everything on the map to the facilitators. The map became a powerful means for the people to get a 'big picture' of their area, as well as a strong way of showing the power of a joint community effort. When the map explanation was done the crowd applauded enthusiastically – a strong affirmation of their joint effort, and success at that effort.
>
> When the boys completed their map, it contained several items not included on the men's map. The boys described these to the crowd. The differences and similarities on the two maps were discussed with the people and it was also clear that they drew the maps from their frames of reference. For example, the men focused much more on the economic material things like roads, crops, cattle, and gardens, while the boys focused on the river where they play, the men plowing with oxen and women carrying firewood, etc.
>
> The women also joined in their own mapping and sharing with the rest of the group.
>
> After a while some men came over to watch – fascinating! When some men tried to comment or correct the women, the women told them to stop interfering. Everybody, men, women, and boys, felt their input was significant.

The result of this effort according to Cormack (1993) is that the facilitator hands over the (drawing) stick to the people to tell their stories, see their similarities but also differences, identify themes and strengths and also find their own possible answers.

All these discussions probably brought a deeper understanding within the people of their community and themselves without the facilitator actually communicating it directly to them.

Example 14.16

The following example also illustrates very well how to work on an advanced level with a community. Du Plessis (2002: 84–86) (as previously mentioned) worked in a remote rural community. After the community shared their stories and identified the themes of unemployment, crime, lack of education, lack of vision, etc. she worked with the different interest groups to explore these issues in greater depth. One of these was a group of unemployed people from the coloured community.

The unemployed people described unemployment as a monster. They described their situation as one in which they were having a 'rough time', and said that 'it hurts', 'we and our children are hungry', 'we steal, then we land in jail but not our children', 'the children cannot concentrate at school', 'we drink,' 'we get ill', 'we die'. They were now talking not on a needs level but on a much deeper, painful level, where the real unsymbolized issues existed. They further experienced themselves as failures, without any dignity; unable to sleep, and prone to fighting.

It takes advanced, deeper understanding from the facilitator to facilitate the people's exploration of these painful, unsymbolized experiences. They also start taking control (proposition 14). We will continue with the example under 'Creating new perspectives'.

14.4.1 Creating new perspectives

The aim of this skill is to remobilize and reactivate the individual, group, or community and create new hope. We try to create alternative stories and change stories of despair to stories of hope. The people in the communities often have negative perceptions of themselves and their situations. ('We are poor, the government does not provide, we have no resources, we have no power, our women are powerless.') They feel trapped and unable to get out of their dilemma. The aim of creating new perspectives is to facilitate the process of generating new or different perspectives (symbolizations) by the community themselves.

The main points to bear in mind when creating new perspectives (symbolizations) are the following:

- The new perspectives (symbolizations), in the end, must be more meaningful to the community than the existing perspectives.
- The perspectives grow from dialogue, critical awareness (conscientization) and discussions between the facilitator and the community, so they are authentic. This is not just the facilitator's idea of how to keep the community 'happy'.
- The new perspectives (symbolizations) may have a mobilizing effect. People may develop a new perspective on themselves, their community, and what behaviour will fit with these new perspectives, and thus, find ways of actualizing this community's self. They restructure themselves and develop new stories.

The PRA/PLA as illustrated in the example above shows how this exercise can also create a new perspective or perception within the community about themselves. The facilitator comes to value the community's own skills and communicates this to them. As a result, the community starts seeing itself in a new light. They start to value resources and skills that they never valued before, and their human dignity is also respected.

In the rural community described in example 14.16 (Du Plessis (2002: 87–88), the unemployed started to think of how they could overpower the *monster* of unemployment. (This would not have occurred in one session; it is a process.) They started to think about ideas for working together and generating income. After researching the feasibility of many ideas they decided on three projects that could be feasible in this particular community, namely printing, coffin manufacturing, and rusk-baking businesses.

Enabling the community to become aware of their own implied message (such as concern for the safety of their children, or the pain, hurt, and powerlessness they've experienced) instead of the expressed solutions (for example needing a crèche as in example 8.5 or needing a job) is advanced empathy and brings about a deeper understanding of themselves as a community.

Advanced empathy is a continuous action throughout the helping process. For example, if a community makes certain decisions and takes certain actions and they fail, the facilitator can take them through a process of reflecting on what happened, why it happened, why they made the decision at that time, and what they learned from it, so that they can 'embrace error' (Korten 1984) and move on. Paolo Freire's facilitation of the process of conscientization can also be seen as advanced empathy that creates new perspectives on their world.

CHAPTER 15

Immediacy

15.1 Introduction

If one looks at the concept 'immediacy', it brings to mind a sense of closeness. This is because it relates to the *relationship* between the facilitator and the client, in the here and now, that is, immediately. In other words, it relates to what is happening now, between us and how it affects the professional relationship we are trying to build. It is a skill used to understand and enhance this relationship and to deal with any possible stumbling blocks that might damage this relationship.

To build up trust is not always easy and clients might be cautious in trusting you initially, but also later in the relationship, when you are getting close to the painful experiences that they have hidden from themselves. It is important to have empathy with this caution, and not to expect trust at any time, but always to work on building it. Immediacy is one skill that can be used to do just that.

Please note that immediacy is used to develop the relationship, not to destroy it. This means that we cannot blame clients for our feelings or experiences. It is not an opening to confront clients or to give clients 'a piece of our minds'. The latter actions imply behaviour from our own frame of reference, whereas immediacy, like all the person-centred skills, is from the client's frame of reference. Also, to judge or criticize clients at any time will only threaten them, and they will then feel that they have to defend themselves against you, which will destroy the relationship you have been trying so hard to establish.

This is not always easy to do, as we might sometimes feel threatened by what clients say or do, and be tempted to defend ourselves against them, or to blame them for our experiences. Here it is important to keep in mind that we, as human beings, are also self-determined. That is, we determine who we are, as facilitators, what our experiences are, and which of these experiences threaten our self. So, if you feel any kind of emotion in interaction with the client, you need to understand yourself, and be able to access what is happening inside yourself and take responsibility, not only for what you are experiencing, but also for dealing with it. We cannot expect our clients to help us to deal with our own experiences. They are there to deal with their own experiences, not yours. Also, as we are unique people, we need to find ways of dealing with our experiences that fit with our self as facilitators.

Some facilitators believe that to be congruent means to be honest with clients. I believe it means being honest with yourself. If you honestly want to be an effective facilitator, then it seems counterproductive to impose your own experiences (feelings, needs, values, expectations), from your own frame of reference, on clients, just to make yourself feel better. There are some exceptions, like setting certain limits for the therapeutic relationship, regarding for instance sexual and aggressive behaviour. It is, however, still important to accept and understand such behaviour in clients. It can also be useful to provide a number of other outlets for the need for aggressive behaviour, like boxing gloves, a punch bag, hitting pillows, or other breakable non-injurious toys. (This can be used with both adults and children.) Providing other means of expressing anger has a threefold purpose:

1 It prevents breakages in the therapy room and injury to both facilitator and clients, thereby also preventing the breakdown of the safe therapeutic relationship.

2 It provides ways for clients to find new behaviour that fits with the self (proposition 12).

3 It communicates acceptance of the client's experiences and needs, while simultaneously providing a safe way of expressing them.

Example 15.1

Cl: I think emotionally I'm dying for sexual intercourse but I don't do anything about it ... The thing I want is to have sexual intercourse with you. I don't dare ask because I am afraid that you'd be non-directive.

H: You have this awful tension, and want so much to have relations with me.

Cl: Can't we do something about it? This tension is awful! Can you give me a direct answer? I think it might help both of us.

H: *(Gently)*: The answer would be no. I see that *you desperately* want this, but I could not do that.

Cl: *(Pause. Sigh of relief)* I think that helps. It's only when I am upset that I feel like this. You have strength, and that gives me strength.

'As in setting any limit in the therapeutic experience, this is something that is purely the responsibility of the therapist, and he (sic) takes that responsibility. Therapists should not attempt to evaluate (judge) the client's experience by a statement such as "that really would not help you". He simply takes responsibility for his own behaviour, at the same time indicating understanding and acceptance of the client's experiences.' (Rogers 1987: 211)

15.2 Immediacy with the individual

15.2.1 Guidelines for the implementation of immediacy

(a) Self-based statements

Self-based statements involve comments that the facilitator makes on what the client is relating, or comments on certain processes that the facilitator identifies, which include the facilitator and their relationship, for example:

- The client asks the facilitator: 'How well are you qualified?' The facilitator responds by saying: 'I hear that you want to make sure that I am qualified enough to really be of assistance to you, otherwise you might find it hard to trust me.'
- The client asks the facilitator: 'Do you have children?' The facilitator can respond by saying: 'You seem worried about whether I will really be able to understand your concerns regarding you and your children, unless I myself have children?'

The following deductions can be made from the two examples:

- The facilitator includes himself or herself in the response. The personal questions are related to the client's needs and concerns about the facilitator and their professional relationship. These concerns are usually implied, that is why immediacy is an advanced skill.
- Furthermore, these concerns are treated with respect and understood as part of the relationship-building process. It would not be useful to become defensive, and to try to convince the client of your ability to be of assistance. Rather, demonstrate this ability by the use of immediacy.
- The commentary must be *sincere*, otherwise the client will not accept it. If the remarks have significance for the client, this kind of immediacy could give them a different perspective on the process happening between them and the facilitator; something they have not seen for themselves (about themselves, you and your relationship).

Immediacy can also lead to further exploration since the facilitator and clients become aware of, and explore, any issue hampering the process.

(b) Dealing with stumbling blocks in the professional relationship
This skill can also be used when the facilitator experiences that there is some kind of a stumbling block that hampers the therapeutic relationship and there is no progress in the deepening of the relationship. This immediacy enables the facilitator to gain momentum in the interview again by addressing the issue at hand, for example: 'It seems to me as if what is happening between us at the moment does not fit with your expectations of where we are to go.' Immediacy requires exceptional maturity from the facilitator to expose the facilitator-client-relationship (and therefore himself or herself) to 'discussion'.

To promote this kind of immediacy, avoid any phraseology that might make clients feel that they are being blamed for any experience, such as: 'You are busy ...'. This might sound as though the facilitator is blaming, and thus threatening, the client, and denying the client's own perception of the situation.

(c) The hypothetical (or tentative) nature of immediacy
As in the case of all the skills that have been discussed thus far, immediacy is also treated hypothetically. Because the facilitator could misunderstand the relationship or the interaction (as seen from his or her frame of reference), the immediacy is suggested hypothetically to the client. If the hypothetical response is significant to the client, it will create a certain momentum/heightened intensity in the interview and the relationship. If the facilitator's hypothesis is incorrect, the client will usually correct the facilitator by bringing up another issue.

Anchin and Kiesler (1982: 17) refer to the *usefulness* of the hypothetical explanation that the facilitator gives to the client. If what the facilitator conveys to the client has *meaning* and is *useful*, the client will accept it and expand on it.

Example 15.2

A male client asks you how old you are. The implied message could be that the client wonders whether you are old enough or experienced enough to help him. He wonders whether he can entrust himself to you with confidence. To argue about this, or to try to convince the client, is meaningless. Rather prove your maturity by not being threatened and by demonstrating your professionalism in your behaviour. You could rather say something like 'I hear you saying that you wonder whether I am the right person to help you', or 'I wonder whether you find it difficult to trust a young person with your experiences'.

Example 15.3

A female client says, 'Do you think I am doing the right thing now?' If we listen to the implied message again, the client is not only unsure about herself, but she also trusts you more than herself to do the right thing. The facilitator could therefore say something like: 'It seems to me that you are not very sure of your decision, and you would feel better if I confirmed it', or 'It is important to you to do the right thing and you would feel safer if I supported you'. At another level, the facilitator could wonder whether the client might not feel that her humbleness is a prerequisite for the relationship between them. In a case like this the facilitator could ask something like: 'Is it important to you in our relationship that I should affirm your decision?' or 'I wonder whether you might feel that you would affront me if you did not ask for my approval?'

Example 15.4

The members of a group are all quiet and no one actually wants to speak to the facilitator. The facilitator could say something like: 'This silence between us makes me wonder if you find it difficult to speak to me or trust an outsider?'

Example 15.5

The client indicates that he or she did not choose to come, but was told to do so by someone else. The facilitator could then say: 'It sounds to me as though you feel that it is not necessary for you to be here', or 'I hear that you are actually angry about having to be here and having to speak to me, because you feel that you do not really need it'.

Activity

Formulate immediacy responses to the following statements by various clients:

1 The client sits down in your office with a very angry expression on his face, folds his hands over his chest, and stares in front of him without saying a word.
2 The client has shared different ideas (stories) with you and you are not sure which of these is the most important to her.
3 The members of the family laugh and giggle from the moment they walk into your office.
4 The client, a hard-working businessman, says: 'I am very tired today', and sighs heavily.
5 The couple look at each other and then the wife asks: 'Are you married and do you have children?'

15.3 Immediacy with groups

As stated by Egan (1990: 227), immediacy is 'a complex skill'. This is so because immediacy demands competence in a variety of skills of which empathy, self-awareness, and advanced empathy are the most important.

Immediacy is an important skill for group work because it gives the facilitator the opportunity to:
- establish whether his or her style fits the group
- develop relationships with the group and individual group members
- enable the group to understand themselves and one another better, and
- develop open and mutual communication in the group.

Egan (1990: 229) adds that immediacy can also be used when:
- the group is bogged down: 'Perhaps we must stop for a while and summarize what is happening in the group', or 'I wonder whether we as the group should stop to explore or discuss what is happening in the group'.
- there is tension in the group: 'It looks to me as if we are angry with one another.'
- members don't trust one another: 'I notice that you are afraid to talk. Perhaps we need to discuss the issue of trust first.'
- members are waiting for the facilitator
- there is a struggle between certain members. This is experienced by other members as painful. In this situation, the facilitator may focus on the non-verbal behaviour of the other members, for example, 'I notice that certain members are not at ease when Nonceba and Matlakala disagree with one another'.

When facilitators believe in the abilities of the group members, the group is given the opportunity to see whether they can't resolve the situations mentioned above on their own. This is done in a safe climate.

Sections C and D discuss skills you can use to improve communication with individuals, groups, and communities. Rogers warns us not to practise these skills in a recipe-like way. The situation and the people (members in the case of a group) will decide which patterns we must follow. Rogers uses all these skills but particularly:
- silence
- empathic guesses, e.g. 'I guess some part of you feels "here I am hit with another blow"'
- personal statements, e.g. 'I care and am not just sitting here like a lump'
- reflective responses, e.g. 'It really hurts, doesn't it?'

15.4 Immediacy with communities

Immediacy as discussed in this section can be applied when working with communities. For us it is about the facilitator's symbolized congruency with the people in the community. Congruency and immediacy form the basis for an open, trusting, respectful relationship in which people can grow.

Immediacy refers to congruency, openness, and transparency between the facilitator and all the people in the community. Facilitators cannot be selective. They need to deal with all the people in a similar manner (although they may like certain people more than others). If facilitators treat people differently or become part of subgroups they will get into difficulties.

Immediacy is also more than a skill but an attitude. Empathy is a 'way of being'. It is a skill and way to open up issues between people, including the facilitator and the community in order to be able to move forward and is, therefore, an advanced skill.

Example 15.6

In a semi-rural area an informal settlement developed. A teacher became involved with a group of women from the community who started a crèche for the stimulation of the children in the community. In her report she wrote the following:

> *In the first few weeks the facilitator was constantly met with the words: 'the mealie meal (chicken/rice/sugar) is finished'. This led to a lot of stress and the feeling that the food was not well managed. The cook felt that she was mistrusted. Some of the parents even accused the cook of using the gas and food for her own family. After a number of intense community meetings the group decided on measures to prevent these misunderstanding and this mistrust from developing further. They would keep the food locked up, rationing the food, changing the menu from two full meals per day to one at midday, changing to a meal that was more easy to prepare; and using more fresh and cheap vegetables.*
> *(Adapted from Ox & O' Neill 2002: 72)*

Opening up issues among the members that were creating stress in the community allowed them to take more ownership (proposition 14), be more involved, and become more effective, and clarified the relationship of the facilitator in the community.

Some special considerations

Introduction

We have often been asked whether the person-centred approach can or will work under all circumstances. Although one can never give any guarantees, we have found the approach to be useful, but not without difficulty, in most situations. We would like to share some of our ideas and practical experiences with you. Again, we would appreciate any comments, experiences, examples, and criticism for and against the approach.

In the next chapters, we will try to demonstrate how the thinking, attitudes, and communication skills (on a basic as well as an advanced level) discussed in the previous chapters can be operationalized in specific circumstances. These circumstances are:

- cross-cultural encounters between people
- conflict situations between people
- the self of the facilitator.

CHAPTER 16

Cross-cultural communication

16.1 Introduction

It is not the objective of this discussion to provide information about different cultures, but only to put down some person-centred ideas (guided by the propositions) for facilitators who communicate with individuals, groups, or communities with cultural experiences different from their own.

During our person-centred journey, we have developed an awareness of the uniqueness of the experiences of all people and their values. The value of uniqueness/individualization is relevant in respect of each client with whom the facilitator communicates, but it is of particular importance with people from other cultures. Instead of viewing cross-cultural communication as an obstacle, we should rather try to learn about and develop appreciation for the person's culture and make it an enriching experience for all people involved.

Working cross-culturally from a person-centred perspective implies that:

- any person is considered as being from another 'culture' with his or her own frame of reference
- there is no recipe or method available to use – it is a person-centred *process*
- the facilitator respects, values, and appreciates the client and his or her own culture, resourcefulness, and skills and allows the client to show the way to respectfully crossing the border into his or her frame of reference and world
- it is a learning process for both the facilitator and the persons involved in the process of finding common ground and understanding
- to assume is to stereotype. Admitting to not knowing is to discover/ construct, learn, and appreciate.

Working cross-culturally also implies that we as facilitators have to symbolize our own prejudices and biases toward people from other cultures. Catherine Bateson (1994: 17), an anthropologist, described how she dealt with own experiences in a community (in the Philippines) that was very different from hers (USA).

> 'A death occurred down the street where the houses were poorer and more rural in style. The family I had been living with would be going to the paglalamay or 'wake' and they urged me to come. I did my best to prepare for my part, asking a series of questions about what would be happening, and got instructions on how to give an abuloy, a 'contribution' of less than a dollar, to the young woman whose mother had died. We went together to the house, staying until late in the night.'

She said that when she came back she wrote two kinds of notes:

> 'One narrative describes the body laid out in its coffin, surrounded by lamps. The relatives had gathered, and neighbours were coming and going, expressing condolences, and offering money and then standing and gossiping. Boys and girls were playing word games and flirting at the door, and gambling tables and barbeques were set up outside, with general merriment continuing through the warm night, noisily audible in the room where the body was laid out. The other kind of notes concerned my own feelings: My reluctance even to go to this house, intruding on the grief of others; my embarrassment over the act of giving the abuloy.'

She wrote how different these practices were from what she is used to.

In writing in this way Bateson tried to symbolize her own experiences and tried to get to an understanding of the practices and beliefs of the culture she was involved in. From a person-centred perspective, the facilitation of change or development takes place through dialogue. This transformation or change occurs when there is symbolization of the unsymbolized experiences, change in the thoughts, perceptions, values, and behaviour that have formed the prevailing vision of reality (Natiello 1990: 283). We as facilitators cannot change people's behaviour, but we believe that through facilitating the participatory development of new or different frames of reference (personal realities) about themselves and their situations, people will become empowered and have a vision of how to change or better their own situation.

If we listen, ask, explore, and learn, the people will show us the appropriate way to collaborate with them in their endeavours to grow and develop.

16.2 A person-centred perspective on culture

We can describe culture as being person-centred, existing in the minds of people, in their feelings, meanings, values, and behaviour. Culture is individual, distinguishes us from others, and shifts the focus from the problem to the person and also determines our understanding of others' behaviour (refer to propositions 1, 2, and 6). Furthermore, culture is also seen as always in flux; it is forever changing and adapting to new information (proposition 1). However, more important is the fact that no two people share exactly the same cultural world. Although people may come from the same ethnic group, you may still have different perspectives (proposition 2) and experiences of the culture.

Authors such as Le Croy (1992) and Egan (1994) take this approach (particularly proposition 2) so seriously that they see working cross-culturally not only as working with people from other cultures. Le Croy (1992: 215), for example, mentions differences such as gender, sexual orientation, and socio-economic, cultural, and racial differences. These may influence each person. According to Egan (1994: 52), every person can be seen as coming from a different cultural background: 'Any two-way conversation – even one between two identical twins is, in a very real sense, a cross-cultural event, because each person is a different individual with differences in terms of personal assumptions, beliefs, values, norms, and patterns of behaviour.'

This implies that the facilitator should be sensitive towards each person, sharing perspectives with each person, group, or community. Apart from individual culture, every group and community also has its own 'culture' or frame of reference that is part of their decisions and behaviour (propositions 2 and 7).

16.3 Working cross-culturally

16.3.1 Cross-cultural communication and the facilitator

If facilitators feel relatively good about themselves and their own value systems, they might be in a position to be more open and not be threatened by the different value systems of the people from other cultures (or even the same culture). They can be more accepting and open to listening to the person/group/community in front of them, without having the need to change (or confront) their value system.

The theory (thinking/perception), values, and skills (action) used when working cross-culturally are exactly the same as with people from your own cultural group. Empathy is empathy – a 'way of being', regardless of the people we are in contact with. We simply might have to adapt the phrasing or way of expressing our empathy.

Cross-cultural work sometimes offers the advantage that facilitators are aware that they do not know what meanings clients attach to particular situations. Facilitators then explore these meanings with their clients. When facilitators and clients come from the same culture, facilitators are inclined to presume that they know which meanings the people attach to the situation and therefore do not necessarily always explore them. Facilitators make assumptions that have not been validated by their clients. For example, if I talk to an Afrikaans-speaking farmer living in Namibia, he might indicate that the nearest town is close to his farm. In my mind, I think of 10–20 km as close, but he may refer to 100 km as close. Distance in the context of Namibia is different from distance in Gauteng, the Karoo, the Netherlands, or the USA.

As is required in working with people in the same culture, cross-cultural work requires that facilitators determine what prejudices or stereotyping they have in respect of other cultures and why they differ from them or feel threatened by them. Okun (1992: 245) points out that facilitators are often not even aware of their prejudices or discomfort. Subtle forms of racism occur:

> ... when helpers apply different strategies with clients from different ethnic groups, or when they modify the helping process in any way based on unsubstantiated attitudes and assumptions about race rather than on the nature of the helpee's problems (or person). Some helpers have been heard to say that responsive listening is not effective with black helpees, that directive, behavioral techniques are more effective; however, responsive listening has been found to be equally effective in developing helping relationships with all helpees ...

Empathy can, despite some facilitators' beliefs, also be used in African cultural groups. It may be a question of phrasing things differently or using other ways of communicating, such as metaphors and stories, as the following examples illustrate.

Example 16.1

This example is from a context where an Afrikaans-speaking facilitator worked with a Setswana-speaking family. The following is an excerpt from the interview with the family. The facilitator paid attention to the mother's strong emotions about her husband who was, according to the mother, not much interested in her and the children.

MOTHER: 'He doesn't know what standard they are in.'
FACILITATOR: 'That hurts you a lot.'
MOTHER: (crying) 'It is too much.'
FACILITATOR: 'You feel that you take all the responsibility alone.'
MOTHER: 'Yes!'

Both the mother and the facilitator were able to speak English and could therefore communicate easily. You will immediately ask, but what about clients who are less fluent in English and do not have the known affective words in their language? Wildervanck (1989: 76) found the following: 'According to the students they found it difficult to translate the messages containing a verbal skill into their own black languages, saying that individual words of affect did not feature in these languages.' For the younger people (client and helper/facilitator) who could understand English, this was no problem, but as soon as the particular black language had to be used, especially in a more traditional situation, they experienced difficulties. To overcome the problem, the lecturer and the students went in search, among other things, for certain metaphors that could be employed as empathy. They found the following examples (Wildervanck 1989: 94–95).

Example 16.2

Mrs L from a rural village came to the facilitator: 'My husband drinks home-brew all weekend. He has spent all the money ... Now we have no money for food and I have five children to take care of. He has also chased me out of the house.' The students decided that the best empathic response would be to say: 'You have grabbed the clay cooking pot by its hot side.'

The metaphor may be explained in that the inhabitants of the rural villages usually cook their food in clay pots on open fires on the ground. The pots are usually placed at the perimeter of the fire, and consequently the one side of the pot always becomes much hotter than the other. If you take the pot by its hot side, you will burn your hands, indicating problems and frustration.

Example 16.3

Iqhina liphum' embizeni (isiZulu)
Direct translation: The steenbok jumps out of the cooking pot.
This saying means that the person missed a wonderful opportunity, for example in the situation where a person failed to secure a job that he or she was convinced he or she would get.

Example 16.4

U bva mikandoni
Direct translation: To come from the breast milk. It means to take after one's mother.
A father may complain about having the same problems with his daughter as with his wife. The helper may use this response to convey her or his understanding about his view of the problem.

16.3.2 Crossing borders

When working cross-culturally, the facilitator, the person, the group, or the community has to (dialogically) cross certain borders. By crossing borders we do not mean either invading the physical territory or the personal space of others, but rather going beyond our own mental and social borders and reaching out to others' worlds in a gentle and non-threatening way (proposition 16). Borders are not seen as obstacles, but a learning experience.

Lifschitz et al. (1992: 140) state that every therapeutic (or relationship) endeavour can be conceptualized as a journey across cultural borders, and hence is multicultural – although some journeys involve more borders than others. These borders might be more prominent when dealing with somebody from another culture, but they also exist when you enter a relationship with a person from your own culture, but with his or her own experiences and frame of reference (propositions 2 and 7).

The following are possible borders:
- language, phrasing, and non-verbal behaviour
- frame of reference (including meaning, values, problems/solutions, humour, etc.)
- traditions, customs (e.g. appropriate clothing, age and gender).

(a) The language border

The language border might be a difficult one, specifically if the facilitator and the client cannot share a common language. In such a situation the facilitator usually has to use a translator or interpreter. An interpreter or translator can be very useful in:

- rephrasing what the facilitator says in a manner that is understandable for the person
- acting as a guide for the facilitator to act in accordance with, or show respect for, the client's culture.

However, we have to take some issues about the translator into consideration:

- Translators translate according to their own personal frame of reference.
- Translators may add their own experiences, interpretations, prejudices, and comments.
- Confidentiality may be violated.

Difficulty in using language and even using a translator can actually be an asset in the sense that it puts facilitators in a position to:

- use very clear and simple language
- check continuously with clients whether they understand them correctly and thus work from their frame of reference
- be creative in the use of alternative communication media like play, mime, etc.

If applied with great care and sensitivity, this way of working can be empowering for clients when they have to explain and guide facilitators through their culture or frame of reference.

(b) The frame of reference border

Ayee (1993: 16) states that:

> *If the world view of two people engaged in dialogue differs very greatly, communication is often difficult or can be hampered. The different presuppositions, beliefs, understandings and concepts in the minds of the participants distorts the presentation and reception of the communication ... However, it is possible for people holding totally divergent world views to engage in meaningful communication. This can be achieved if both people consciously attempt to understand each other's frame of reference and subject all stereotyped ideas and perceptions to careful scrutiny during the dialogic encounter.*

Example 16.5

Okun (1992: 35) provides the following example of how a facilitator did not try to understand the perception of a particular person:

A job placement counsellor describes a night shift technical job to a Russian immigrant, a 34-year-old woman named Anya. The client listens politely, and through an interpreter, explains why she can't consider night work.

ANYA: 'I no work night. My mother needs me. I must take care my mother.'

COUNSELLOR: 'You're feeling responsible for your mother and as much as you need a job you're not sure how you can do this. It must be difficult for you, being in a new country with strange ways and needing to find a job but still meet your family obligations.'

ANYA: 'I need work, yes, I need money. I need to be a good daughter.'

COUNSELLOR: 'I admire your sense of loyalty, Anya. But I am concerned about how we're going to be able to find a job for you. It's been over a month since you first came in and this is the first time a job for which you are qualified has come up. You must realize this. I don't know if or when another opportunity will arise.'

ANYA: 'I need work ... I need take care of mother ... I need make life.'

The counsellor is, to some extent, sensitive towards the dilemma in which Anya finds herself, but according to Okun, his reasoning is from his frame of reference, in that to his mind employment should be the priority for Anya. For him he would not be helping her by 'coercing' her into accepting the job because this will simply aggravate her dilemma. She may accept the job and then not arrive on the second day or ever again, and she will then be seen as lazy or workshy without taking into account the dilemma in which she finds herself. It would be more useful if the counsellor, instead of pressuring her to take the job, were to explore her confusion as well as show respect for her loyalty towards her mother and the expectation that she take care of her mother.

It might be crucial for the facilitator to cross the border by learning about the person's frame of reference and trying to understand his or her behaviour from his or her viewpoint and respecting it. The person, group, or community is the expert on their own frame of reference. Let them guide us.

Example 16.6

A facilitator working at the cancer association had a client who had a mastectomy. The client believed that this was a spell from her husband preventing her from being desirable to other men. She also found that some of the women with cervical cancer were viewed by their own communities as being punished for being unfaithful to their husbands.

(c) Traditions and customs border
Respecting the client's customs and ways of communicating can refer to aspects such as making or avoiding eye contact; who should sit, stand, or walk first; how a man should act towards a woman and a woman towards a man, and adults and children towards each other, in the particular culture.

Example 16.7
A story is told of a man who visited a family. In his culture, the man takes the tea tray from the woman when she enters the room and holds it for the guests to help themselves. When the mother of the family entered the room with the tray, he jumped up politely to take it from her, upon which she berated him with 'Sit, you glutton, you will get yours!' because their custom is for the women to serve the guests.

Le Croy (1992: 215) regards the attitude of the facilitator as the most important factor in cross-cultural work. This links again with the credo of James Yen who said, 'Go to the people, learn from the people'. Facilitators should move into a community/group/family and let them guide them through their customs and ways of communication, and learn from them appreciatively and respectfully.

Activity

McGoldrick (1982: 27) proposes the following important activities that may be used during training in cross-cultural work:
1 Discuss your own experience/feelings of stereotyping, for example as a Jewish person, a Greek person, an Afrikaner, a woman, an African person, a Xhosa person, a Zulu person, a German, an American, etc.
2 Explain which person in your family (or context) has had the greatest influence on your ethnic/cultural identity.
3 If your family were to consult a facilitator, which type of approach would they prefer and what would they find acceptable? For instance, what should the facilitator do and not do? Compare your own ideas about this question with the ideas of your own family.

CHAPTER 17

People in conflict

17.1 Introduction

It is often asked whether the person-centred theory is applicable in conflict situations, especially if it is then expected of the facilitator to act as judge or to solve the conflict. It might be useful to keep in mind that from this theoretical perspective, the facilitator is expected to be non-judgemental and to believe people are capable of resolving their own issues.

Activity

How could the different perspectives implied by the questions below affect the helper's approach?
1 How does the facilitator view and deal with conflict situations?
2 How does the facilitator deal with the people in conflict situations?

In this book, our approach is and remains *people-centred*, no matter what the issue at hand may be. That means that we concentrate on the identity (self) of the people and their experiences, whatever these may be.

As the propositions can direct our ideas about the people in such a situation, we will start by looking at some of the propositions and their relevance to people in conflict, as well as the communication skills, to demonstrate ways of thinking about and communicating with people in conflict. (Contrary to Section A, the propositions will be applied here in numerical order, not according to themes.)

In a conflict situation, it is often difficult to hear, accept, and communicate your understanding to all the parties concerned without taking sides. This is often motivated by the facilitator's own experience and perception of the situation, that is, we want to take the side of the one whose experiences or views coincide with our own; or we want to take the side of the 'underdog', the one we perceive to be getting the worst in the situation. No matter what our motivation might be, we have to be aware of it (be congruent with ourselves) and find some way of dealing with it that is not detrimental to the people concerned.

One way of avoiding taking sides is to remember that all parties are people, with needs, emotions, a sense of self, and values, and they are all acting in a way that makes sense and seems necessary to *them*. We do not have to agree with them, but we have to understand their behaviour and its motivations, so that we can communicate this understanding to them.

17.2 Propositions 1 and 2 in the conflict situation

No matter who the parties concerned in the conflict are, *all* of them are unique, and experience and perceive the world in their own (changing) way. This experience (of the conflict situation, themselves and each other) is their reality.

Facilitators can only understand the world of each one if they *listen* to them all with careful attention and acceptance. In order for all the parties concerned to be aware that the facilitator understands their perceptions (of themselves, each other, and the conflict situation), the facilitator has to communicate this understanding to them in some observable way, through *empathy* (both basic and advanced).

Example 17.1

An elderly lady and her grown-up son were in conflict about her future. The son insisted that she leave the home where she had been living for the past fifteen years and that she move into a home for the elderly. She maintained that she was quite capable of managing on her own and deciding for herself what to do. He became angry at what he saw as her 'stubborn' refusal to see sense, and she at what she called his 'interfering' in her life and trying to treat her as a child:

SON: 'Mother, you cannot go on living here alone! It is dangerous for you and I cannot stay with you to see that you are safe.'

FACILITATOR: 'It seems as if you are very worried about your mother and you feel responsible for her safety.'

SON: 'Yes. I am the eldest child of the family and since my dad died, I am now the head of the house.'

MOTHER:	'I am still the master of my own fate. I may be old, but I am not a child to be told what to do. I cannot just leave this house.'
FACILITATOR:	'You fear that because you are getting older, people will no longer treat you with respect. Respect for your wishes and ability to decide for yourself.'
MOTHER:	'Yes. I have my reasons for staying, but as I am old, nobody seems to want to listen to what they are or to take them seriously.'
FACILITATOR:	'There are very strong reasons keeping you here, but you are afraid that if you voice them, you will be laughed at.'
MOTHER:	'Yes.' *(Starts crying)*
SON:	'Mother, I do love you and I do care about what happens to you.'
FACILITATOR:	'You want your mother to know that she and her future are very important to you.'
MOTHER:	'Yes, but what about the present?'
SON:	'I see only that you are living in dangerous conditions now.'
FACILITATOR:	'It seems as if you two have different priorities that you care about. You, Mr Z, care about the safety of your mother's future, but you, Mrs Z, have something else that is important to you here and now, but that you have difficulty discussing.'
SON:	'Mother, is it something I can help with?'
MOTHER:	'There you go again, trying to help me as if I can't help myself.'
FACILITATOR:	'Mrs Z, you feel that you can take care of this matter on your own, but yet something keeps you back?'

Silence

MOTHER:	'I can only tell you that it concerns your dead father. I still feel his presence in this house and I have to talk this matter over with him. I can't just go and leave him here. That is all I am prepared to say now.'

It turned out later that the lady talked regularly with the husband and feared reprisals from his spirit if she just left. She then consulted a traditional healer, who helped her with a ritual that would enable her to make peace with her dead husband. This was the tradition in her culture, of which the son, of a different generation and not with the same beliefs, was unaware.

17.3 Proposition 3 in the conflict situation

This proposition helps us to keep in mind that we are concerned with the whole world of the people in conflict, not just the content of the issue at hand.

It is also useful in reminding us that we are dealing with the whole *person*, which places the propositions that follow below in a meaningful context.

The facilitator's responses are then directed at all that the people bring and imply, and not just to the conflict situation itself. As we will see under propositions 11 and 13, there might be extraneous aspects, not directly related to the conflict as defined consciously, which have some bearing on the situation. This would necessitate the use of basic as well as advanced communicating skills, with all the parties concerned.

17.4 Proposition 4 in the conflict situation

Is the issue/conflict related in any way to the maintenance/protection or defence of the organism/person(s)? What are they afraid of losing?

For each person, the conflict could be a way of 'fighting' to maintain or actualize the self. If the facilitator understands this, and communicates his or her understanding to the clients involved, they might come to understand themselves and each other a bit better.

17.5 Proposition 5 in the conflict situation

What need is motivating the behaviour of the people in conflict? It could be related to the above need, that is, to maintain or protect the self. Or it could be some other felt need. It could be an unsymbolized need, as we will see under propositions 11 and 13. Whatever the case may be, the facilitator needs to fully understand the symbolized as well as unsymbolized needs, and at some stage to communicate this understanding to the parties concerned.

17.6 Proposition 6 in the conflict situation

Emotion accompanies the behaviour. Thus, if the emotion is intense, the need is very important to the person(s). We need to hear that which is important and how important it is to the client.

If there is intense anger, then the need motivating the behaviour is probably very important to the person (whether they know it or not, i.e. whether it is symbolized or not). Here it is important to understand and fit with the intensity of the expressed emotion (and thus the seriousness of the felt need and behaviour to meet the need). In conflict situations, facilitators themselves may feel threatened by the emotion, especially if it consists of anger. Facilitators might then experience a need to calm the situation, motivating them to behave in a way that will 'pour oil on the troubled waters'. However, if clients do not see that facilitators fully understand the depth of their feelings, they might shout even louder in order to be 'heard', that is, to be understood. Facilitators need a lot of courage to stay with the emotion, to understand it fully, and to show this understanding to the clients.

Example 17.2

The clients are shouting at each other.

FACILITATOR: (*In a loud voice*) 'You two are really extremely angry with each other. You feel like shouting the house down' or 'Your anger is so strong, that you can hardly contain it' or 'This is a very serious matter to you and it feels like no one hears just how important it really is!' or 'You really want the other one to listen to you, to understand what you are feeling, but no matter what you do, the message just does not seem to come across.'

This kind of comment can be directed at both parties at once, if both are very angry. This can be relevant also to group members and clients from a community who are fighting about some or other issue.

17.7 Proposition 7 and people in conflict

This proposition reminds us that it is very important to understand *all* the parties involved in the conflict, from their own frame of reference, not that of any other person involved, including the facilitator. This implies that each person should be given the opportunity to express their experiences, no matter how threatening these experiences may be to the facilitator.

Conflict implies behaviour, that is, people disagreeing or fighting about something. This behaviour needs to be understood from the clients' frame of reference, and as mentioned under proposition 5, in terms of the needs motivating this behaviour. This could be difficult for facilitators, as we might believe one person is right and the other(s) wrong, but keep in mind that our professional value system precludes any form of judgement, and instead, urges us to enable the people in the conflict to find their own value system and way forward, that fits with their 'selves'.

Activity

In the examples described in this chapter, please check whether the facilitator was able to demonstrate understanding and acceptance, to each person involved in the conflict.

17.8 Proposition 8 in the conflict situation

In order for facilitators to understand what aspect of the self is being maintained (proposition 4), they need to gain some understanding of the self as experienced by the client concerned. Here the facilitator has to be careful not to see one person through the perceptions of another person. For instance, if the wife talks about the husband and who he is, that facilitator has to bear in mind that her experience of who he is is her reality and it tells us about how she views the world (and her husband), but it does not tell us how the husband sees himself. The same would apply if the husband told the facilitator about his wife.

Example 17.3

WIFE: 'My husband is never at home these days. He has turned into a real workaholic, so that I don't see him any more.'

FACILITATOR *(To wife, not husband)*: 'You really miss your husband. It seems to you as if you are fighting a losing battle with his work, for his attention' *(Basic empathy, with wife's experience, emphasizing her need for his attention).*

HUSBAND: 'But I work so hard because I have to provide well for you, as my family.'

FACILITATOR *(To husband)*: 'It is important for you to be a good provider, to look after your family's material needs' *(Basic empathy with husband's experiential world, his need and self, as a good provider).*

WIFE: 'We also need you at home. It feels as though I am not married any more.'

FACILITATOR: 'You don't feel like a wife any more' *(Advanced empathy with self of wife, her need to be a wife).*

HUSBAND: 'I don't know which way to turn. I have to be a good provider, but that doesn't seem to be enough for you.'

FACILITATOR: 'It seems to you as if you are not giving enough to your family. No matter how hard you work, and how much money you provide, something else is expected of you, which you just can't provide' *(Basic empathy with dilemma of husband, of feeling unable to give what is required of him).*

WIFE: 'But money is not the issue here! We need your attention, your companionship.'

HUSBAND: 'But I have to work so hard, to give you a good home, all the things that you want. I am tired after such a hard day's work.'

FACILITATOR: 'There seems to be some misunderstanding between the two of you ... Mrs C, you seem to be asking for quality time with Mr C, and Mr C, you seem to feel that if you give this time to your family, you will fail at providing what you think they really need from you, that is, money.' *(Advanced empathy, connecting their statements to create a theme, of how time is spent.)*

WIFE: 'How did the money become such a big issue in our home?'

HUSBAND: 'But you and the kids keep on asking me for this, that and the other! I feel that I just can't keep up.'

FACILITATOR *(To husband)*: 'And you would feel like a failure as a provider if you did not give them everything that they ask?' *(Advanced empathy with his fear of being a failed provider).*

WIFE: 'I never realized how seriously you take this providing bit in our relationship. We don't always mean to have whatever we were talking about, at that time. Sometimes it is nice to dream. Also, it would not hurt the kids to wait, save or work for what they want.'

HUSBAND: 'But I would really like to give you whatever you want!'

WIFE: 'You spoil me. I realize that. But what I really want is to spend some time with you. For us to have some fun together.'

FACILITATOR: 'Mrs C, you need time spent on doing things together as a family, while you, Mr C, feel your time is better spent on providing for the material things for your family. Mrs C, you want to provide a nice family togetherness, and you, Mr C, want to provide nice items for the family. For both of you, the family is important and you want to provide what you think it needs and what is best for them. You just have different ideas about what this 'best' consists of' *(Advanced empathy, connecting their needs and their ideas about the self of the family as a whole).*

The couple now have a better understanding of themselves, their needs and fears. But as they were also listening to the facilitator's responses to one another, it enabled them to understand each other a bit better. In this example, the emphasis has now shifted from what they don't do or give each other and the family, to what they do and want for the family. How each one can provide what is required, without feeling like a failure, can more easily be negotiated now.

The same applies to conflict situations in groups or in a community. If one group member, or a member of a community, talks about another person, be it another group member, another leader or member of that community, he or she is revealing only his or her own perceptions and experiences, not what the other person is 'really' like.

Example 17.4

Group member A is angry at group member B, because B told other people in the group about something A shared with B. Now A says that B is a big mouth. If the facilitator looks at what A is saying about herself, it seems as if A values confidentiality, trusted B to keep a secret, and now feels disappointed. B might respond that he did not think that telling other people in the group about what was shared violated the confidentiality of A's trust, as he also trusts the group. It seems as if A and B have different perceptions of confidentiality, of the group, of trust, of friendship, and of how to be a friend.

Example 17.5

One member of a community might describe another as domineering and bossy, wanting to take over the arrangements for every meeting. The person under discussion might regard herself as assertive, as taking initiative and inspiring or leading her fellows in the project. Maybe both have the need to be active, to be recognized as important and valued members of the community. How they behave in order to fulfil this need might be different, however, as their sense of self is different and behaviour mostly fits with the sense of self (see proposition 12). Maybe one expects the other to behave in a certain way, which is not in accordance with the other's experience of the self.

17.9 Propositions 9 and 10 in the conflict situation

The conflict could be around values taken over from others, or an expectation that someone should take over a value from another. For instance, parents may expect their daughter to believe in the same values as they do, while the daughter has developed other values in interaction with her peers. The parents could then say something like: 'We did not raise you in this way' or 'Your friends have a bad influence on you'. The child may respond: 'You are trying to tell me what to do' or 'You are just not giving my friends a chance' or 'My friends understand me better than you do'. The facilitator can hear that the way the parents feel they raised their child (values they hold) is important to them and they might fear that they have failed as parents (parental self) if the child does not hold the same values. They might also experience an emotion like fear of rejection by the child (whether it be of their values or of themselves as parents, or both, if the identity of their selves as parents incorporates the values they hold). The child may be torn between the values experienced in interaction with the parents and those experienced in interaction with the peer group. She may have symbolized that to be accepted by the peer group, she has to take over their values, whether she experiences them directly or not. Whether the values of the friends are directly experienced or not, the child seems to value (and need?) their friendship and acceptance. The intensity of the need will accompany the behaviour as expressed by the conflict (proposition 6).

If one relates this idea to a group, one could use as an example a group member who has developed the value of swift and decisive actions to resolve problems. Another group member has developed the value of intense and thorough consideration of all the pros and cons of any proposal before taking action. These two might get into conflict about what is to be done when. Although both might have the best interest of the group in mind, their ideas about what is 'best' might differ.

17.10 Proposition 11 in the conflict situation

The experiences of the people concerned may not be consciously symbolized. So although they may say that X is what the conflict is about, there might be other, unconscious experiences involved, which further complicate the conflict situation and until these experiences are symbolized, the conflict might not be resolved.

This might manifest in a situation where the same issue is mentioned in arguments over and over again. Such repetition can be an indication that the discussion of the symbolized experiences is just not enough and there is thus a feeling of dissatisfaction with what is happening, but without really knowing why there is this dissatisfaction.

This unawareness could also relate to propositions 4 and 8, that is, where there is a struggle to maintain the self, but the specific experiences defining the self and/or the need for maintaining it are not symbolized.

Example 17.6

The wife may say she is a homemaker and has to stay at home and raise the children, like her own mother did. The husband concurs, as that is also what he experienced while growing up. Their symbolized view of a parent self is therefore that the mother stays at home while the father works. Yet when he gets home, he might complain about the amount of money she is spending, while she says he does not understand her needs and that she is tired of sitting at home all day, just to be blamed for their financial situation in the evening. The husband's unsymbolized need may be for an extra income to alleviate the financial burden, but that would threaten the symbolized self as discussed above (and if the value of a wife staying at home was taken over from his parents, he might fear that he was betraying them, thus his self as a good child to his parents might also be threatened). The mother might feel disillusioned and/or bored with staying at home all the time, but to admit this would threaten her self, and depending on whether the value and self as homemaker was experienced directly or taken over from her parents, the same conflict regarding her parents might subconsciously be present as for her husband.

So facilitators should ask themselves what the conflict is about on a deeper, maybe even subconscious level, for all the people concerned.

The symbolized self can be understood and maintained by communicating it through basic empathy. The unsymbolized selves, however, can be communicated by using the advanced skills.

17.11 Proposition 12 in the conflict situation

Behaviour usually fits with the self of the person, so the facilitator should ask:
- Who do the people involved experience themselves to be?
- In what way does the behaviour fit with their sense of self?

17.12 Proposition 13 in the conflict situation

Sometimes behaviour is motivated by unsymbolized experiences (see proposition 11). Are there any such experiences involved here? Is the conflict perhaps about denial of a behaviour that somebody is accused of, but denies strongly, because it does not fit with the symbolized self? See also propositions 14 and 16 in this regard.

Example 17.7

The nurse and doctor at an Aids clinic were trying to get a male patient to admit that he had Aids, as they had just told him that his blood tests had shown this to be so. He denied that it could be possible. Another member of staff was consulted and acted as facilitator. While listening to the patient, she heard him state repeatedly that he was a good husband and that he had not slept with anyone but his wife. She indicated to him that this issue of fidelity seemed important to him, more so than whether he had Aids or not. He was very upset and after a while he could verbalize that he was afraid that it might be said of him that he had slept with a widow before the required period of mourning had ended, which is absolutely forbidden in his culture. If people were to think this, then he would be cast out of the community. He was afraid that having Aids would be attributed to such a transgression. The patient was not immediately aware of this perception and how much he feared the community's reaction (as he perceived it); neither were the doctor and the nurse, as he was not immediately able to tell them about it. They were also not aware that such a perception around Aids existed. As the people involved in the conflict became more aware of each other's ideas, they were better able to understand and communicate with each other.

17.13 Proposition 14 in the conflict situation

Any experience inconsistent with the self can create tension. This could refer to the issue around which the conflict revolves, or, if the experience about which the conflict is centred is not symbolized, then that experience, as well as the conflict, could create tension.

Besides these aspects, it could be that the behaviour of the conflict itself (like fighting or disagreeing) does not fit with the self. (See proposition 13.) This would mean that the conflict behaviour, and the experience that one is unable to control this (fighting) behaviour, can add to the total stress of the situation.

Activity

What responses, in terms of basic and advanced empathy, could you have made to the people concerned in the situations below?

1 A woman says something like: 'I really don't know why I fight with my husband (child/mother-in-law). It is just not like me to do this, but I can't seem to help myself. It's driving me crazy.'

2 Group members can say (to each other and/or the facilitator) that they just don't know why they are always arguing in this way because it does not happen in other situations. They feel like avoiding the sessions.

3 A community that is divided into different sectors is known for its high crime rate. They held a session in which crime and what could be done about it was discussed by members of all the sectors of the community. Each group representing the different sectors maintained that crime was not so bad in their own sector and that they could therefore not do anything about it.

17.14 Proposition 15 in the conflict situation

When people can symbolize the experience that threatens the self, they can change (restructure) the self to accommodate these experiences.

Example 17.8
A woman whose symbolized self was that of a soft and yielding person might come to realize that there are some things she considers worth standing up for, and thus fighting for, if necessary. This does not mean that she is less feminine (as she fears), but that she is a feminine person who occasionally takes a firm stand. She found new behaviour to fit this new self, that is, after conflict with the teacher of her child, during which she had shouted at the teacher, she said: 'I am sorry my vehemence surprised and hurt you. I know I do not usually come on so strongly, but I realize now that when my child is punished, I just see red. I now realize you did what you thought was best, but I really do wonder whether, between us, we can find a different way of punishing G that is less humiliating for him.'

17.15 Proposition 16 in the conflict situation

When the symbolized self is threatened, the person(s) will defend that self strongly. So is it possible that the self of the people concerned is threatened in some way? How?

In a group, members could be fighting to protect their individual selves, but also the self or identity of the group as they perceive it. For instance, after one member suggests that they do something, others might respond that is not what they are here for, or what they have been doing up till now.

17.16 Proposition 17 in the conflict situation

In a conflict situation, it is very important to create a context/environment in which the participants feel unthreatened by the facilitator.

The conflict is most probably an indication that a certain measure of threat already exists, either in their own experiential world, or as perceived by the other participants in the conflict situation.

The facilitator needs to express understanding of this threat and enable participants to explore the origins of it, without either minimizing or contributing to it (the threat).

That is why the use of communication skills as discussed in Sections C and D is so important, with regard to all the participants, as stressed in the introduction. If one participant in the conflict feels threatened by the facilitator, he or she will not only feel threatened as a person, but might even blame the other participants for involving the facilitator, and withdraw from the session, more angry and hurt than before. Resolving the conflict might then become more difficult for everybody concerned.

17.17 Propositions 18 and 19 in the conflict situation

If the people involved in a conflict situation become more aware of who they are (self), their own experiences and values, and give themselves permission to be and explore the whole range of their own experiences, they will probably feel less threatened by the other people in the conflict situation and their views.

They will be able to accept themselves and not be threatened by unsymbolized experiences, be these their own experiences, or those of the others involved, as perceived by themselves. By accepting who they are, they might allow others to be themselves, without feeling the need to change the other. People might say something like: 'I understand now where you are coming from. I do not agree with you and I don't feel the same way. I think we can agree to disagree.'

Group/community members can use this kind of understanding as a basis for negotiation: 'We have come to realize that there are different needs in this group, and now all that remains is to find ways to meet all the different needs, without offending anyone.'

CHAPTER 18

The self of the facilitator

If we use the person-centred theory as the basis for our argument, then the propositions of the theory apply to the facilitator as well. After all, the facilitator is also a person, with unique experiences and perceptions that have to be dealt with in some way.

Can we evaluate ourselves in terms of this theory and see whether we are congruent with it? Be warned that such an exercise might be experienced as very threatening by some facilitators.

Here we can already do an exercise by asking ourselves what we make of the concept of *congruence*.

- Do we use it to evaluate (and thus judge) our clients?
- Are we aware that it pertains to us?
- Are we true to ourselves and what we believe in?
- Do we maybe see our work as an opportunity to give clients 'a piece of our mind'?
- Are we aware of (most of) our own experiences, so that our behaviour towards our clients is not motivated by unsymbolized experiences? (See propositions 1, 5, 11, 13, and 15.)
- How do we perceive people in general and our clients in particular? For instance, do we perceive people as self-determined with our whole being? (See propositions 2, 3, and 4.)
- If we have some reservations in this regard, do we know what they are, why we have them, and how they affect our interaction with our clients?
- What are our needs for helping others? Our needs motivate our behaviour during the helping process, and if we are not aware of them, they might influence our behaviour without us having control of it. (See propositions 5, 13, and 14.)

- For instance, do we need to be needed? If so, what implication does that have for the way in which we behave towards our clients so as to have this need met?
- Do we need to be in control of ourselves and/or other people, and how does this motivate our behaviour?
- How do we experience our 'selves'?
- Can we make a distinction between our professional and our other selves (like mother/father, child or wife/husband)?
- Are there differences in the way we interact with our children, our spouses, our parents, and our clients? If this is the case, can we still see ourselves as being congruent?
- How has our professional self developed? Did we act as facilitators in interaction with our parents and/or friends while growing up?
- Did our experience or sense of who we are professionally develop in interaction with the people who were part of our training? This includes our first clients because this would have been an important experience, and if a negative value was taken over from it, similar situations might still (even unconsciously) threaten our professional self today.
- What are our values regarding people in general, and clients and facilitators in particular?
- Are these values of our own experience, or have they been taken over from others, like lecturers, supervisors, colleagues, or important political and religious figures in our lives (past and present)?
- Do the clients' statements or behaviour threaten our self in some way, so that we feel a need to defend or explain ourselves? (See also proposition 16.)
- Are we aware of any experiences that threaten us, and how we deal with them? Do we, for instance, blame them on the client?
- What can we do with experiences with which we are uncomfortable, without really knowing why? Are we even allowed to have such experiences?
- Do we expect ourselves to always feel good about ourselves and our clients? If yes, what happens if we do not feel this way?
- Can we accept and deal with most of our experiences, even troublesome ones? If not, what do we do with these experiences?
- Can we accept that other people are different from us, without wanting to change them or ourselves? If so, what implication does this have for our role as facilitators?

Any feedback about the content of this book will be appreciated. Please forward your comments to the authors care of the publishers at: Oxford University Press (Southern Africa), PO Box 12119, N1 City, 7463, or by e-mail to oxford.za@oup.com.

Bibliography

Agere, S.T. 1981. The promotion of self-reliance and self-help organisation in community development in Zimbabwe: A conceptual framework. *Community Development Journal.* 17(3): 208–215.

Anchin, J.C. & Kiesler, D.J. 1982. *Handbook of interpersonal psychotherapy.* New York: Pergamon.

Ayee, E.S.A. 1993. A participatory communication approach to rural community development. (Unpublished thesis). Potchefstroom: PU for CHE.

Balgopal, P.R. & Vassil, T.V. 1983. *Groups in social work: An ecological perspective.* New York: Macmillan.

Barret-Lennard, G.T. 1988. Listening. *Person Centered Review.* 4 (November): 410–425.

Bateson, M.C. 1994. *Peripheral visions. Learning along the way.* New York: Harper Collins.

Bawden, R. 1991. Towards action research systems. In O. Zuber-Skerrit (Ed.) *Action research for change and development.* Sydney: Avebury.

Blakely, E.J. 1979. *Community development research: Concepts, issues and strategies.* New York: Human Science Press.

Boy, A.V. & Pine, G.J. 1983; 1990. *A person-centered foundation for counselling and psychotherapy.* Springfield, IL: Thomas.

Bradshaw, B. 1993. Management by objectives versus community. *Together.* (July–September).

Brill, V.I. 1990. *Working with people: The helping process.* (4th edition). New York: Longman.

Bruwer, E. 1995. *Beggars can be choosers.* Pretoria: University of Pretoria.

Burkey, S. 1993. *People First: A guide to self reliant, participatory rural development.* London: Zed Books.

Carter, B. & McGoldrick, M. 1989. *The changing family life cycle.* (2nd edition). Boston: Allyn & Bacon.

Chambers, R. 1983. *Rural development: Putting the last first.* London: Longman.

Chambers, R. 1994. *Challenging the professions: Frontiers for rural development.* London: ITP.

Chambers, R. 1997. *Who's reality counts? Putting the last first.* London: ITP.

Compton, B.R. & Galaway, B. 1984. *Social work processes.* (3rd edition). Homewood, IL: Dorsey.

Corey, G. 1985; 1990. *Theory and practice of group counselling.* Monterey, CA: Brooks/Cole.

Cormack, P. 1993 Letting the people tell. *Together.* (April–June): 16–18.

Cormier, W.H. & Cormier, L.S. 1985. *Interviewing strategies for helpers.* Monterey, CA: Brooks/Cole.

Cornwell, L. 1986. Gemeenskapsontwikkeling: wetenskaplike konsep of metafoor? (Ongepubliseerede MA-verhandeling). Pretoria: Universiteit van Suid-Afrika.

Crocker, D.A. 1991. Toward development ethics. *World Development.* 19(5): 457–483.

Cruikshank, J. 1994. The consequences of our actions: A value issue in community development. *Community Development Journal.* 29(1): 75–89.

Davis, R. 1994. Getting inside: PRA as a first step. *Together.* (July–September): 19–20.

Davison, C., Frankle, S. & Smith, G.W. 1992. The limits of life style: reassessing 'fatalism' to the popular culture of illness prevention. *Social Science Medicine.* 34(6): 675–685.

DeVito, J.A. 1991. *Human communication: The basic course.* (5th edition). New York: Harper Collins.

Douglas, T. 1976. *Groupwork practice.* London: Tavistock.

Dunham, A. 1970. *The new community organisation.* Ithaca, IL: Peacock.

Du Plessis, M.J.M. 2000. 'Die ontwerp van 'n gemeenskapsontwikkelingsmodel: 'n Maatskaplike werk persektief'. (Ongepubliseerde D Phil). UOVS.

Du Plessis, R. 2002. The narrative approach and community development: A practical illustration. *Africanus. Journal of Development Studies.* Vol 32(2): 76–92.

Edward, A.D. & Jones, D.G. 1976. *Community and community development.* The Hague: Mouton.

Egan, G. 1990. *The skilled helper: A systematic approach to effective helping.* (4th edition). Monterey, CA: Brooks/Cole.

Egan, G. 1994. *The skilled helper: A problem management approach to helping.* (5th edition). Monterey, CA: Brooks/Cole.

Egan, G. 2000. *The skilled helper: A problem management approach to helping.* (6th edition). Monterey, CA:Brooks/Cole.

Farber, B.A., Brink, D.C. & Raskin, P.M. 1996. *The psychotherapy of Carl Rogers – Cases and commentary.* New York: The Guilford Press.

Feuerstein, M.T. 1986. *Partners in evaluation: Evaluating development and community programmes with participants.* London: Macmillan.

Flood, M. & Lawrence, A. 1987. *The community action handbook.* (2nd edition). Sydney: Ncoss.

Freire, P. 1972. *Pedagogy of the oppressed.* New York: Seabury.

Freire, P. 1994. *Paolo Freire: On higher education: A dialogue at the National University of Mexico.* Albany: State University of New York.

Freire, P. 1998.*Pedagogy of freedom: Ethics, democracy and civic courage.* London: Rowman & Littlefield.

Friedman, J. 1984. Planning as social learning. In D. Korten and R. Klaus *People-centered development.* 273–279. West Hartford, CT: Kumarian.

Garvin, C.D. 1987. *Contemporary group work.* Englewood Cliffs, NJ: Prentice-Hall.

Germain, C.B. 1980. Social work identity, competence and autonomy: The social work perspective. *Social Work in Health Care.* 6 (1).

Gilliland, B.E., James, R.K. & Bowman, J.T. 1989. *Theories and strategies in counseling and psychotherapy.* New Jersey: Prentice Hall.

Glassman, U. & Kates, L. 1990. *Groupwork: A humanistic approach.* London: Sage.

Gooddal, G. 1984. Political development and social welfare: A conservative perspective. In D. Korten and R. Klaus *People-centered development.* West Hartford, CT: Kumarian Press.

Hancock, M.R. 1997. *Principles of social work practice: A generic approach.* New York: Haworth.

Hanson, N.R. 1961. *Patterns of discovery.* London: Cambridge University Press.

Harman, W.W. 1988. Development for what? Emerging trends of promise and concern. In J. Burbridge (Ed.) *Approaches that work in rural development.* Munich: Sauer.

Henderson, P. & Thomas, D.N. 1989. *Skills in neighbourhood work.* London: Allen & Unwin.

Hepworth, D.H. & Larsen, J.A. 1990. *Direct social work practice: Theory and skills.* Belmont, CA: Wadsworth.

Hersey, J. 1988. 'Jimmy Yen: Crusader for mankind.' *Reader's Digest.* April: 151–192.

Hope, A. & Timmel, S. 1984. *Community worker's handbook.* Books 1, 2 & 3. Parktown: The Grail.

Hope, A. & Timmel, S. 1995. *Training for transformation.* Book 1, 2 & 3. Gweru: Mambo.

Hugo, E.A.K., Schoeman, J.H. & Engelbrecht, J.F. 1982. *Gemeenskapswerk.* Pretoria: Heer.

Jackson, A.O. 1979. Die rol van die etnoloog in gemeenskapsontwikkeling. Lesing gelewer vir die vakkundiges van die Departement Plurale Betrekkinge.

Johnson, D.W. & Johnson, F.P. 1975. *Joining together: Group theory and group skills.* London: Prentice-Hall.

Johnson, D.W. 1981. *Reaching out: Interpersonal effectiveness and self-actualization.* Englewood Cliffs, NJ: Prentice-Hall.

Kadushin, A. 1990. *The social work interview.* (3rd edition). New York: Columbia University Press.

King, C. 1965. *Working with people in community action.* New York: Association Press.

Kishindo, P. 1993. The case of non-formal vocation education for out-of-school youths in rural Malawi. *Development Southern Africa.* 10(3): 393–400.

Konopka, G. 1972. *Social groupwork: A helping process.* Englewood Cliffs, NJ: Prentice Hall.

Korten, D. 1984. *Community organising and rural development: A learning process approach.* West Hartford, CT: Kumarian Press.

Kotze, D.A. & Swanepoel, H. 1983. *Guidelines for practical community development.* Silverton: Promedia.

Kotze, P.M.J. 1989. Wanvoeding: 'n Kontekstuele benadering. (Ongepubliseerde MA-verhandeling). Pretoria: Universiteit van Suid-Afrika.

Le Croy, C.W. 1992. *Case studies in social work practice.* Belmont, CA: Wadsworth.

Lietser, G., Rambouts, J. & Van Balen, R. 1990. *Client centered and experiential psychotherapy in the nineties.* Leuven: Leuven University Press.

Lifschitz, S., Kjoadi, D. & Van Niekerk, S.M.F. 1992. Three views of a psycho-therapy service in Mamelodi. In J. Mason, J. Rubenstein & S. Shuda (Eds.) *From diversity to healing*. Johannesburg: South African Institute for Marital and Family Therapy.

Louw, H. 2002. 'Process is power in small grassroots participatory development efforts'. *Africanus. Journal of Development Studies*. 32(2): 44–58.

Martin, D.G. 1983. *Counselling and therapy skills*. Monterey, CA: Brooks/Cole.

Mavalela, H. & Schenck, R. 2002. The story of 'Phela O Phedise' income generating project. *The social work practitioner/researcher*. 14(1): 48–66.

McGoldrick, M., Pearce, J.K & Giordano, J. (Eds.) 1982. *Ethnicity in family therapy*. New York: Guilford.

Mda, Z. 1993. *When people play people: Development communication through theatre*. London: Zed Books.

Meador, B.D. & Rogers, C.R. 1973. 'Client-centred therapy'. In R.J. Corsini (Ed.) *Current psychotherapies*. Illinois: F.E. Peacock.

Menike, K. 1993. People's empowerment from the people's perspective. *Development in Practice*. 3(3):176–183.

Meyers, B.L. 1994. From Lystra to Louga. *Together*. (July–September): 3–5.

Middleman, R.R. & Wood, G.G. 1990. *Skills for direct practice in social work*. New York: Columbia University Press.

Mitchel, W. 1987. Social work with communities. In B.W. McKendrick. *Introduction to social work in South Africa*. Pinetown: Owen Burgess.

Natiello, P. 1990. The person centered approach, collaborative power and cultural transformation. *Person Centered Review*. 15(3): 268–286.

Ngubane, H. 1977. *Body and mind in Zulu medicine*. London: Academic.

Odendal, F.F., Schoonees, P.C., Swanepoel, C.J., Du Toit, S.J. & Booysen, C.M. 1987. *HAT Verklarende woordeboek van die Afrikaanse taal*. Johannesburg: Perskor.

Okpala, D.C.I. 1992. Planning and development in Africa. *Third World Planning Review*. 14(1): iii–vii.

Okun, B. 1992. *Effective helping: Interviewing and counseling techniques*. (4th edition). Monterey, CA: Brooks/Cole.

Ox, E. & O' Neill, M. 2002. Establishing of a crèche in the Popo Molefe informal settlement using a people-centred participatory approach. *Africanus. Journal of Development Studies*. 32(2) 59–75.

Parkash, M.S. & Esteva, G. 1998. *Escaping education: Living as learning within grassroots cultures*. New York: Lang.

Parnes, S. 1981. *The magic of your mind*. New York: Creative Education Foundation.

Pierce, D. 1989. *Social work and society: An introduction*. New York: Longman.

Pitt, B. & Michel, M. 1992. *Making workshops work*. Cape Town: Erip.

Pradervand, P. 1990. *Listening to Africa: Developing Africa from the grassroots*. New York: Praeger.

Rahim, S.A. 1994. Participatory development communication. In S. White (Ed.) *Participatory communication*. New Delhi: Sage

Rahman, M.A. 1993. *People's self-development: Perspectives on participatory action research.* (2nd edition). London: Zed Books.

Reid, K.E. 1991. *Social work practice with groups: A clinical perspective.* Monterey, CA: Brooks/Cole.

Rennie, D.L. 1998. *Person-centred counseling – an experiential approach.* London: Sage.

Rogers, C.R. 1951. *Client-centered therapy.* Boston: Houghton Mifflin.

Rogers, C.R. 1974. *Encounter groups.* Middlesex: Penguin.

Rogers, C.R. 1977. *Carl Rogers on personal power: Inner strength and its revolutionary impact.* London: Constable.

Rogers, C.R. 1980. *A way of being.* Boston: Houghton Mifflin.

Rogers, C.R. 1987. *Client centered therapy: Its current practice implications and theory.* London: Constable.

Rogers, C.R. 1989. Do we need a 'reality'? In H.C. Kirschenbaum & V.L. Henderson (Eds.) *The Carl Rogers Reader.* London: Constable.

Rogers, C.R. 1990. Client-centred therapy. In M. Kirschenbaum & V.L. Henderson (Eds.) *Carl Rogers dialogues.* London: Constable.

Rogers, C.R. & Freiberg, H.J. 1983. *Freedom to learn.* (3rd edition). New York: Merrill.

Rubin, H.J. & Rubin, I. 1986. *Community organizing and development.* Columbus, OH: Merrill.

Schwartz, W. & Zalba, S.R. 1971. *The practice of group work.* New York: Columbia University Press.

Shrivastava, O. 1989. Participatory training – some philosophical and methodological dimensions. *Adult Education and Development.* 32:3–21.

Shulman, E.D. 1982. *Intervention in human services.* (3rd edition). St Louis: Mosby.

Shulman, L. 1979. *The skills of helping: Individuals and groups.* Ithaca, IL: Peacock.

Swanepoel, H. 1992. *Community development: Putting plans into action.* Johannesburg: Juta.

Swanepoel, H. & De Beer, F. 1994. *Guide for trainee community development workers.* Johannesburg: Southern.

Sykes, J.B. 1982. *The Oxford dictionary of current English.* Oxford: Clarendon Press.

Thomas, P.N. 1994. Participatory development communication: Philosophical premises. In S. White (Ed.) *Participatory comunication.* New Delhi: Sage.

Tubbs, S.L. & Moss, S. 1991. *Human communication.* (5th edition). New York: McGraw Hill.

Van der Kolk, C.J. 1985. *Introduction to group counselling and psychotherapy.* London: Thomas.

Van Niekerk, A.J. 1992. *Saam in Afrika.* Kaapstad: Tafelberg.

Wenresti, G.G., Vincent, C.E. & Nestor, C.B. 1995. Rapid rural appraisal and participatory research in the Philippines. *Community Development Journal.* 30(3): 265–275.

Weyers, M.L. 1987. Die plek en rol van skakelwerk in gemeenskapswerk: 'n Maatskaplike werkondersoek. (Ongepubliseerde DPhil-proefskrif). Pretoria: Universiteit van Pretoria.

Wildervanck, J. 1989. Toward an ecology of communication and its implications for social work interviewing. (Unpublished MA dissertation). Pretoria: University of South Africa.

Wood, J.K. 1995. The person-centered approach: Toward an understanding of its implications. *The Person-Centered Approach Journal*. 2(2).

Wood, J.K. & Jatoba, E. 1994. The person-centered approach's greatest weakness: Not using its strength. *The Person-Centered Journal*. 1(3): 96–104.

Yaccino, T. & Yaccino, D. 1994. Insiders and outsiders: Are we asking the right questions? *Together*. (July–September):14–16.

You 23 March 1994, p. 187. Cape Town: Naspers.

Zeig, J.K. 1987. *The evolution of psychotherapy*. New York: Brunner/Mazel.

Index